THE RISE OF THE ROGUE EXECUTIVE

THE RISE OF THE ROGUE EXECUTIVE

HOW GOOD COMPANIES GO BAD AND HOW TO STOP THE DESTRUCTION

Leonard R. Sayles

Cynthia J. Smith

An Imprint of PEARSON EDUCATION
Upper Saddle River, NJ•New York•London•San Francisco•Toronto•Sydney
Tokyo•Singapore•Hong Kong•Cape Town•Madrid
Paris•Milan•Munich•Amsterdam
www.ft-ph.com

Library of Congress Catalog Number: 2005924352

Publisher: Tim Moore
Executive Editor: Jim Boyd
Editorial Assistant: Susie Abraham
Development Editor: Russ Hall
Director of Marketing: John Pierce
International Marketing Manager: Tim Galligan
Cover Designer: Chuti Prasertsith
Managing Editor: Gina Kanouse
Project Editor: Rose Sweazy
Copy Editor: Elise Walter
Indexer: WordWise
Compositor: Jake McFarland
Manufacturing Buyer: Dan Uhrig

© 2006 by Pearson Education, Inc.
Publishing as Prentice Hall
Upper Saddle River, New Jersey 07458

Prentice Hall offers excellent discounts on this book when ordered in quantity for bulk purchases or special sales. For more information, please contact U.S. Corporate and Government Sales, 1-800-382-3419, corpsales@pearsontechgroup.com. For sales outside the U.S., please contact International Sales, 1-317-581-3793, international@pearsontechgroup.com.

Company and product names mentioned herein are the trademarks or registered trademarks of their respective owners.

Printed in the United States of America

First Printing, August 2005

ISBN 0-13-147772-2

Pearson Education LTD.
Pearson Education Australia PTY, Limited.
Pearson Education Singapore, Pte. Ltd.
Pearson Education North Asia, Ltd.
Pearson Education Canada, Ltd.
Pearson Educación de Mexico, S.A. de C.V.
Pearson Education—Japan
Pearson Education Malaysia, Pte. Ltd.

For Professor James Wesley Kuhn, who has been a colleague, supportive friend, and mentor.

To honor his pioneering studies of the corporation and society; inspiring students and colleagues to explore the ethical dilemmas and the neglected interrelationships among economics, sociology, business organization, and public policy.

CONTENTS

CONTENTS

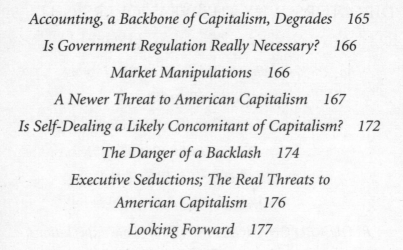

13

SEEKING AND VALUING REAL LEADERSHIP 199

ACKNOWLEDGMENTS

From Leonard Sayles

I frequently sought the counsel of Kathy Ripin, a former executive with one of the banks we mention. Her experience, ideas, and candid criticisms were always helpful. Other values follow from proximity— Ms. Ripin is my spouse. Columbia Professor, James Kuhn, shares with me the same half-century, research-based perspective on the executives and strategy of American corporations. His wise, critical comments on many of the cases we include were invaluable. And he is a much better economist.

Sam Brown is exceptionally knowledgeable about contemporary corporate finance and its more exotic instruments. He is also a fine University of Chicago trained economist and staunch defender of the virtues of free markets. As always, he provided provocative challenges.

Another long-time friend and experienced business writer, Richard Schlesinger, frequently responded to my need for encouragement and support during the more onerous stages of this study.

Fine librarians in Dobbs Ferry and Naples invariably secured books I needed on short notice. America is fortunate in having its widely decentralized public library system.

I had written this before I became aware of how blessed I was to have Rose Sweazy as our Project Editor. Having struggled for 4 years with this ever-changing subject, I wanted the final, final draft to include spring 2005 data as well as some benefits of hindsight. Ms. Sweazy accepted with good grace, better than I deserved, what grew to literally hundreds of those corrections. But, as they say, the omissions and commissions are still all mine.

From Cynthia Smith

The time and candor of friends, colleagues, and professionals who talked over some of the difficult aspects of this book is deeply appreciated. William R. Yeack, Dr. Erika Bourguignon, Dr. L.S. (Al) Rosen, Janice Molloy, Wayne R. Philpott, Greg Koser, and Dr. Amy Zaharlick have all been particularly helpful and supportive in this effort.

An understanding family helps tremendously through the long process of research and writing. Mitch, Sara, and Penelope Rose have been great about the sacrifices, and have been a source of regeneration when energy flagged.

We both appreciate the time, effort, and excellent feedback from our reviewers. Louis Columbus provided some specific feedback that was very helpful in the final stage of completion.

We also both appreciate the support and guidance of Jim Boyd, our executive editor. Jim's experienced, steady hand takes a lot of stress out of this difficult process. His judgment in selecting reviewers and support resources is unfailingly excellent. Russ Hall, our development editor, was also an invaluable resource, and his expert advice greatly improved our work. The entire production team is distinguished by their professionalism, and it has been a pleasure to work with them.

ABOUT THE AUTHORS

Dr. Leonard R. Sayles received his doctorate from MIT in Industrial Economics. He has been a professor at the Columbia University Graduate School of Business for four decades; now Emeritus.

In a series of research projects and books, he helped transform conventional views of business leadership. His widely cited leadership studies won a number of national awards in America, and many were republished in Europe, Latin America, and Asia.

He advised the head of NASA in its formative years and published a major study of its management methods sponsored by the National Academy of Science. He also has been a consultant to major American corporations.

He lives with his wife in Dobbs Ferry, New York, and Naples, Florida.

Dr. Cynthia J. Smith is an anthropologist who has conducted numerous field-based studies of businesses. She is co-author of *Inside Arthur Andersen: Shifting Values, Unexpected Consequences*. This book is an analysis of events deriving out of the Enron collapse that led to the fall of Arthur Andersen. The book traces the decades-long shifts in values of the firm, with emphasis on changes in leadership over time. Dr. Smith was a member of Arthur Andersen's Management Development Group during the 1980s.

During the 1990s, Dr. Smith spent several years collecting field-based data on three Silicon Valley–based, "new economy" companies. She was inside each of these organizations for one to two years, which makes the data distinctive from typical academic studies or journalistic access. These primary research materials are used in our analysis.

Dr. Smith is a lecturer at The Ohio State University.

INTRODUCTION

As in everyday life, we often worry about the wrong things. The predictions that the new millennium would bring catastrophic computer failures proved wildly exaggerated. Instead, the new millennium brought unanticipated, massive failures in our business system. We have learned that the illicit practices that deceived investors, cost so many jobs, and tarnished the reputation of American business had begun at least a decade earlier.

Enron and what followed deserved an explanation. That has been our obsession for four years. Our focus was why and how American business developed vulnerabilities and distortions that were more ingrained and worrisome than the deflation of the infamous stock market bubble. And then, what were feasible changes that would strengthen American business to cope with the tough challenges of globalization? We hope that more honest and broader recognition of the problems will be a constructive force for change in American business.

Following is a brief description of our game plan; a preview of this book. Business has a profound impact on all our lives. Everyone seeking to understand the trials and tribulations of the contemporary business world will find much to reflect upon in the forthcoming chapters. Ours is the "story" behind the "stories," those surprising headlines of the past few years. The analysis and conclusions should be especially helpful to anyone evaluating a company as a possible investor or employee or executive or board member.

Chapter 1, "The Tipping Point: How Good Companies Go Bad and Executives Become Rogues," uses a number of case examples to help the reader understand how so much that has happened to hurt business (and investors and workers) is an "inside job." There are not the traditional "villains," such as government interference or intractable trade unions or even a few criminal types who have wormed their way in. Now, deep-seated problems lie inside the prestigious executive suite and those with whom executives work.

Chapter 2, "American Business at Risk: Picking Up the Pieces and Looking Ahead," discusses American business and how its management had enormous prestige at home and overseas. Here is an overview of the last half century; a kind of rise and fall from grace. Remember our shocks at the depravities of Russian oligarchs? That sense of American superiority is chastened by the embarrassing revelations of corporate misdeeds and executive hubris.

The powerful influence of the stock market and corporate stock prices on decisions made in the executive suite is the focus of Chapter 3, "The Stock Market and Executive Decision Making." Included are the unanticipated consequences of more executive stock ownership. There is a good deal of "tail wagging dog" here. Desired stock price drives the creation of ever more fanciful and sometimes fraudulent financial "engineering."

Many have observed, correctly, that most modern companies could not operate effectively and efficiently without the power of computers. But these powerful technologies tempt and facilitate financial mischief. Chapter 4, "Black Boxes and Big Black Lies," discusses the techniques by which managements can use the power of computers to fool, deceive, and even cheat.

With Enron's demise, the auditing world's gold standard, Arthur Andersen, completely fell apart. Its unprecedented collapse was almost inconceivable and is still not understood by most Americans. Chapter 5, "The Shocking Destruction of Arthur Andersen, Auditing's Gold Standard," is based in part on research by those who worked at Arthur Andersen and provides a vivid picture of how the unthinkable occurred.

The Security and Exchange Commission (SEC) is responsible for the fair operation of our markets for securities, the vehicles by which investors' money get channeled into corporate treasuries. Public auditing, overseen by the SEC, is *the linchpin* of our market system. Chapter 6, "Auditing the Public's Auditors," deals with this crucial oversight mechanism. Continuing discussion of Arthur Andersen, as well as other auditing firms, highlights lingering issues that must be resolved if the public's auditors are to function effectively.

Shareholders are also supposed to be protected by corporate directors. They represent the shareholders, who "elect" them, by having the power to select or fire CEOs and approve compensation and big money executive decisions, such as mergers or acquisitions. Why their abysmal failures have been frequent in financially scandal-ridden companies is the subject of Chapter 7, "Directors: Why the Weak Oversight."

In a huge, dispersed country like the U.S., we depend on the broadcast and print media to provide much of our information about what is happening and what may occur in the future. To be sure, the wealthy have personal advisors and money managers (and some people, hopefully not many, may even have seers). Our research in Chapter 8, "Too Silent Critics: Journalism," suggests that the media failed to provide its audiences with any hints that popular, well-regarded companies were showing signs of financial failure and executive mischief before they crashed and burned.

Business school professors, at least those with tenure, don't have to worry about being punished by writing unpopular, counter-cultural books and articles. Other than their peers, they don't have to please any interest group. Yet business faculty with the expertise to evaluate corporate behavior and corporate financial issues, like the media, did not "get on the case" of wayward corporate executives and their accounting and finance mischief. Regrettably at times, fawning was more in evidence than objective evaluation. The reasons for their failure to predict or study and expose emerging problems are the subject of Chapter 9, "Too Silent Critics: Academe."

Draining the treasuries and shareholder equity in many corporations that failed or became financial cripples were the fees they paid. Most of these companies were the truly happy hunting grounds of investment bankers and consultants. Chapter 10, "Fees Galore," provides an overview of how these services multiply and how big these numbers can get.

"Free enterprise fundamentalists" say not to worry. Executive and board failure to exercise responsible leadership and prevent financial misdeeds are nothing new. Both the incompetent and the dishonest get washed away in the flushing action of the market place. Free markets self-regulate, and the well-run companies win. Chapter 11, "How We Nearly Lost American Capitalism," takes issue with some of these unrealistically optimistic reassurances.

At the heart of many of the corporate misdeeds and their financial crises are the cosseted CEOs, many overpaid and under-responsible. With the arrival of the new century came a new class of culture hero: the mythic executive. Almost single handedly, they were boosting share prices, or so it was believed. Who cared about their overwhelming sense of entitlement and indulgent compensation excesses? Chapter 12, "The Mythic CEO: Why Real Leaders Became an Endangered Species," assesses their leadership shortcomings and the costs of having them appear to displace shareholders as the real owners of the business. CEOs who require extraordinary compensation, who want to "pig out" at the corporate trough, are likely to have little patience to lead in the tough, painstaking task of building a robust business that can maintain sustainable economic growth. Excessive compensation demands from a CEO candidate should have been a clear warning signal to boards.

Chapter 13, "Seeking and Valuing Real Leadership," examines the style and performance of those we call "real leaders," whose focus is on building businesses, not family fortunes. Most of these seek to learn about and take an interest in company operations and underlying constraints on efficiency and growth. They demonstrate personal involvement, not well-guarded isolation, and a sincere belief in personal and corporate integrity. They are less obsessed with short-run stock market evaluations and their public persona than "mythic leaders." Robust, adaptive, high morale organizations that build and sustain shareholder value over time are the result they seek.

Chapter 14, "We Can Do Better," is more than a traditional conclusion, a summing up of preceding themes. We seek to provide a more realistic frame for twenty-first century American management decision making.

It used to be said pridefully that the business of America is business. Strong companies provide jobs, job satisfaction, challenging executive roles, and good investor returns. Our standard of living depends on companies that can be globally competitive and durable. We wanted our research to contribute to those goals. Our strategy has been to identify the underlying "fault lines" that first appeared when Enron unraveled…and the challenge for executive leaders in American business today.

The demands of a global economy, volatile technologies and consumer tastes conflict with some well-embedded executive values and corporate practices. Our studies convince us that survival demands will trump the past practices and self-serving approaches that have hurt business flexibility, competitiveness, and integrity. American business hopefully has had its fill of mythic, iconic leaders and making financial engineering a major corporate strategy.

1

THE TIPPING POINT: HOW GOOD COMPANIES GO BAD AND EXECUTIVES BECOME ROGUES

Through the 1990s, most Americans grew accustomed to good financial news. We enjoyed one of the highest standards of living in the world, a product of the dynamism of our business system. Keen competition combined with the driving force of good management efficiently provided a constant flow of new and better products and services. Our free enterprise, management styles, education, and executives were all being copied—the envy of the world. Americans felt proud of the unusual degree of peace and prosperity free market capitalism had provided.

Pride so easily tips into arrogance and prosperity into greed. With the new millennium came startling revelations of destructive cracks in our much-heralded enterprise systems. In the years following, large numbers of Americans began to lose faith in the integrity of business and its leaders. A small cadre of executives were exploiting their positions to "hog" corporate profits with unconscionable pay packages and breaking the law in the bargain.

Business scandals are just another part of the stream of daily news that is full of scandal. The wars in the Middle East bring stories of prisoner-of-war torture and war profiteering. Our all-American pastime, baseball, is scandalized by revelations of steroid use. America's Catholic Church sex scandal has been in the news off and on for several years.

The media confesses to its own scandals, inflated circulation numbers, made up stories, and shilling for politicians. School administrators and teachers are caught helping students cheat on proficiency tests and fudging their books to make dropout rates appear lower.

Americans are still learning about new and troublesome examples of self-aggrandizing executives and misconduct in American business a full five years after the first publicized revelations that all was not well in corporate America. Even as these stories continue breaking, the financial news suggests that senior executive compensation is still increasing, often providing eight-figure annual earnings.

Headlines Just Keep Coming...

Here is a just a handful of disturbing financial stories reported in the final days of 2004 and early 2005:

- The CEO of America's largest insurance broker, Marsh & McLennan, resigned under pressure. His company is alleged to have engaged in bid rigging and secretly restricting clients' choice of carriers to those paying extra commissions. It is also alleged that the CEO and several other senior executives are involved in unrevealed partnerships that acquired ownership interests in other insurance companies.

- A number of CitiGroup's Japanese-based bankers have been fired after the firm was barred from engaging in private banking in Japan for some unspecified time. The Japanese government accuses Citi of tolerating deceptive marketing practices and providing channels that could be used for money laundering for high-income Japanese.

- The top two executives of Fannie Mae are out. America's largest and formerly highly respected, government-backed corporation supporting the market for residential mortgages was engulfed in scandal. A federal review of its accounting disclosed accounting irregularities that require a $9 billion restatement. Investigations are probing

---

whether accounting manipulations were done for the sake of executives gaining substantial bonuses.

- Time Warner is having to revise its financial statements to reflect AOL's misstatements of revenues.

- American International Group (AIG), one of the largest insurance companies in the world and formerly one of America's most highly regarded public companies, has had to admit that its accounting may have been misleading to investors. It used a variety of complex financial instruments and partially owned off shore reinsurance companies to "smooth earnings" and increase reported reserves.[1] At the same time, serious questions have been raised about some transactions of Warren Buffet's Berkshire Hathaway's subsidiary, General Re. As with AIG, these are alleged to have been conducted to accomplish an accounting effect.

It is no longer just the risky dotcoms and their high-tech brethren who get in trouble. The diversity and prestige of corporations in the news suggest there are some underlying forces affecting a broad swath of business. Americans should be concerned that many executives are still tempted to engage in or encourage actions that show this new, troubled face of free enterprise.

We have sought to step back from the headlines and salacious details. Our studies disclose a number of destructive distortions in the components of our business system that together over the past decade have conspired to produce the distressing headlines about accounting irregularities, fraud, and the tales of exorbitant executive compensation. Understanding what has been going wrong and how it can be checked and reversed requires going behind the bad guy stories to a view of how the parts fit together and play off of each other.

Remember, America in the 1990s was pulsing with the easy profits of a new gold rush. Investors shoved to get in on the ground floor of new industries and new marketing ploys—just before they tanked into a subbasement. As shareholders and employees began experiencing enormous losses, CEO celebrities became villains.

At first, it was easy to assume that the Enron implosion and the uncounted number of dotcom failures were anomalies. They represented an inflammatory mixture of some truly rotten apples combined with wild shareholder exuberance and investment analyst and entrepreneurial excess. The half a decade following proved this view too optimistic. As we tip into the last half of the first decade of a new millennium, we look for signs of real change. (One hopes that the popularity of Donald Trump's television show, *The Apprentice*, is not a reflection of reality or being mistaken for a model to emulate.)

In the extraordinarily tough global economy, America can't afford economic vulnerabilities and weakness. We are no longer the unchallenged market leader in many industries, and competition gets tougher by the day. Manufacturing is fast becoming an endangered species in the U.S., and even our mainstay, financial services, is outsourcing some functions overseas.

We expect that free enterprise capitalism combines the self-regulation of the marketplace with powerful motivations for ambitious entrepreneurs and talented executives. Enormous energy and creativity is released in a free capitalist society. Overpriced or poor quality goods or services, outdated technologies, defective business plans, and ineffectual managements and companies—all get rejected (in time) by market forces.

As in much of life, there are "snakes" in the garden. Embedded in this marvelous, self-managing, self-cleansing motivational engine that generates innovation and growth is the potential for exploitation and cheating. We've known this. The real work has always been in keeping the proportion of such incidents low.

In the past, some American business tycoons sought to "beat the system" by anti-competitive maneuverings in the marketplace. Many presumably free markets became manipulated markets. While business executives universally professed allegiance to free enterprise, it was often expedient for some corporations to engage in collusive price fixing and dividing up the market with like-minded competitors. These market-manipulating executives always professed more loyalty to free enterprise than to free markets. Monopolies provide easier and greater profitability. Our effective anti-trust legislation, when enforced, is a testament to the strength of these lurking temptations and the need for some government intervention.

Today, the Inner Dynamics of Business Are the Culprits

Today's threats to American capitalism are primarily *internal* to the corporation, very different from efforts to monopolize external markets.

Management has been changing, not always for the better. The change started with modest deviations from accepted good accounting practice, pushing the limits, such as not expensing stock options. When no resistance was forthcoming, sophisticated number games and executive self-serving became a ground swell of malfeasance. Modest dithering with the accounting tipped over into flagrant fraud. For example, technically, Enron had been bankrupt for years before its bankruptcy filing in December 2001. As we shall see, many other companies were running on fumes generated by financial engineering.

When chief financial officers privately asked the head of the Security and Exchange Commission (SEC) to make rules harder so it would be easier for them to resist the orders of their CEOs, it became obvious that some things needed to change in the 1990s.[1] They didn't, and Americans paid a heavy price.

Concurrently, executive compensation became obscene, scandalizing Europeans who saw their executives adopting American values. Top management can be earning 1,000 times the average worker's pay versus 50 or 100 times not so long ago, if American trends are followed. More extraordinary and more troubling, executive pay is taking a significant bite out of the net earnings of many companies—10% of the shareholder's stake in one study![2]

It appeared that the system had been rigged to favor the very few on top. They had become the beneficiaries of corporate largess, reflecting what appeared to be soaring profitability or shareholder value. We learned too late that many executive performance measures were hollow successes, highly rewarding to executives and short-lived for employees and investors. For many companies, reported earnings were more myth than reality.

These changes in executive values and decision making have consequences more serious than the loss of investor confidence and portfolio profits. What has emerged threatens the future vitality and global competitiveness of their companies. Chapters to follow look closely at the major players in this flight from excellence. Included, of course, are senior executives, corporate boards, auditors, investment bankers, and the investor community. It is also important to understand why business journalists were so slow to spot corporate deception and executive fraud, and business academics and consultants so slow to spot the failure of theories.

The following is a preview of the major forces that led to the misshaping of executive decision making and many high cost failures—to employees and investors, not executives.

Individualism Run Amok

Americans are justly proud of our individualism. It is a bedrock societal value, and it has contributed to our economic growth and our freedom. But there can be too much of a good thing. Americans are notorious for believing that if a little is good, a lot is better. We often learn lessons the hard way, by tending toward excess. This has happened in the case of our idealization of individualism.

Many profligate executives display a perverted individualism. They are narcissists who have an excessive sense of personal entitlement, demanding egregiously high compensation packages, adorned with every conceivable perquisite. These executives reveal a desire to have it *all* now believing they are worth it, no matter how outrageous "it" is.

Such corporate leaders have become obsessed with personal wealth building and the financial well being of their family and future generations. Exhibitionism is no longer perceived as the poor taste of the *nouveau riche.* It is telling the world that you are a great success and worthy of celebrity status. There is little evidence the trend is abating.

A threatening side effect of skyrocketing executive salaries is the pain caused to the tax-supported public sector. A mid-sized city's Head Start program director paying himself over $800,000 in a three-year period is an example. The tide of rising corporate executive earnings lifted the boats of all types of executives.

Celebrities have deferential subordinates and media attention, which build the sense of entitlement. Entitlement means never having to feel embarrassed by bestowing upon yourself costly New York City pads and GulfStream jets as well as unconscionable monetary rewards. And never having to say you're sorry because there may be no relationship between the size of your executive bonus and real corporate performance.

Two law professors explode the myth that excessively high executive earnings have something to do with exceptional performance.[3] Instead of pay relating to performance, their findings show the weakness or indifference of boards of directors, the subject of Chapter 7, "Directors: Why the Weak Oversight."

Designing lucrative, complex compensation agreements, astute management of option grants, overseeing carefully arranged option execution, and accumulating as much personal wealth as possible, have become major distractions from the business of running a company for some top executives. Energies are siphoned off to exploit "insider trader" advantages. Big option grants and share sales are fine tuned to coordinate with the release to the press of both good and bad corporate news.

A couple of examples suggest the severity of the compensation problem. The CEO of Global Crossing managed to convert options to stock to cash to the tune of three quarters of a billion dollars very shortly before the company imploded. One year, several of Computer Associates' top executives are alleged to have shared a bonus of a billion dollars based on earnings inflated by cooking the books.

Severance payments are perhaps the most obvious indicator of the heights (or depths) of this new age executive greed. Severance had legitimate origins. Shareholders were concerned that attractive acquisition offers would be ignored by executives wishing to retain their high paying positions. Thus, the promise of a kind of insurance. Lose your job and you get some payout.

Pure greed took over when companies started paying for non-service. Severance often now comes without a change in ownership, just departing. Thirty to 50 million dollars and more is not unusual severance, and the infamous examples are over a hundred million. Often, these payments are made after relatively short service and regardless of whether or not performance was considered good or even acceptable. Michael Ovitz, former president of Disney Co., is a prime example. He received $140 million in severance payouts after only a 14-month tenure. Shareholders brought a lawsuit, which is still not resolved seven years later. Meanwhile, Ovitz has control over the money. There are plenty of examples, such as Carly Fiorina, Hewlett-Packard's CEO, who was asked to resign rather than being fired, so she collected her multi-million dollar payout.

Almost forgotten are the traditional expectations of executives: after two or three decades of service and reasonable salaries, a good pension to make for a comfortable retirement. It was taken for granted that executives looked to the future. They made sacrifices today for tomorrow's rewards and the tomorrows were measured in decades.

By way of contrast, a recent report notes that executives who might have earned hundreds of millions during their tenure were also likely to retire with annual pensions of at least a million dollars, and often significantly more.[4]

Diminished Sense of Personal Responsibility

Retaining or improving one's status and its associated remuneration has become the primary goal. Professionals, as well as executives, seem to have lost their sense of responsibility to the company and shareholders and to uphold the standards of their fields or disciplines. Boards of directors, corporate counsels, and auditors often appear caught up in the same "me first" drive as executives. Professionals countenanced incredible departures from "good" corporate practice and accepted standards in order to share some of the largesse. Apparently, their consciences rested easily with the knowledge that "everyone" was doing it. Any latent anxieties were reduced by the knowledge that they were insulated by their company's liability policies.

Investment bankers, at least until recently, seem to have felt no qualms about selling "damaged goods," no concerns that their reputations as trusted bankers would be sullied. The financial news featured the lives and times of senior executives who apparently felt no pangs of conscience when they treated shareholder funds as their personal piggy bank.

Social critics bemoan such examples reflecting a culture that does not encourage personal responsibility and accountability. Social norms, the rules of proper conduct, the distinction between right and wrong have all become ambiguous and less constraining in twenty-first century America.

In part, this may reflect the growing discrepancy between risk and reward. At least until recently, executives who crossed the line in their managerial decision making in order to pump up company earnings, and therefore the value of this year's bonus and stock options, were unlikely to face serious penalties.

Emphasis On the Short, Short Run in Companies

Going up the management hierarchy always meant having a longer time horizon. Economists took for granted that top management would seek to grow the business and to build robust organizations with solid reputations that could weather the inevitable vicissitudes of the real world and gradually grow their earnings and dividends. By definition, top management took a long run view of strategic decision making.

Management strategy and decision making has been transformed in many companies. Very short-run thinking replaced those longer time horizons and tough tradeoffs among goals and "stakeholders." What counts is this quarter's earnings or revenues and how they will compare with this period's earnings' "guidance" previously provided to "The Street." It was only the short-run "bottom line" that was pursued with a vengeance.

CEOs themselves also became short run. This has major consequences for the executive's time horizon. A half-dozen years in the job is becoming typical in contrast to the traditional assumption of service through retirement. Careerist job-hopping is one reason, but also there are the terminations following anemic share price growth.

Investor Impatience

Not many years ago, most shares were held by what we called "investors," whose objective was long-run growth in share price and steady dividends. Of less consequence were traders, who played the market for very short-term profits. Increasingly, the distinction has disappeared. Pension funds seeking better returns and the enormous numbers of new shareholders expecting rapid growth of their share prices have transformed the stock market. Pressure for continuous growth in share price has become focused on quarterly shareholder value that may not even be tied to real income or earnings. "Good" companies must have predictable and regular increases in their bottom line. What should be normal, good and bad surprises, good and bad quarters or even years, came to be viewed as indicators of a very poor investment.

Many CEOs have rebalanced their priorities. They devote substantial attention to their company's share price. Getting or maintaining personal prestige is part of the motivation, perceiving stock price as a measure of executive success. (Of course, as noted, stock prices directly relate to the size of the small fortunes that may be locked up in options.)

Finance and Accounting Assume a Central Role

The role and status of the finance and accounting functions of business have been enhanced in this new stock market. In many companies, the ability to manipulate numbers, income statements, and balance sheets is as, if not more, important than the ability to produce goods and services and being competitive in the marketplace. These corporate specialists, working closely with their outside counterparts—the auditors and the investment bankers—became the Brahmins of the company. Incredibly, in some companies, like Enron, accounting and finance became profit centers.

Naïve observers of business thought that accounting was simply a straightforward system of recording and reporting the "facts." In the same vein, it was taken for granted that the finance specialists helped the company to manage its funds. They sought to help balance inflows of cash (from operations) with expenditures. When necessary, they were knowledgeable on how to use external funding sources, such as banks and capital markets, to supplement those generated by operations.

Imaginative new financial products enabled companies to hide debt and losses, even converting some into profits. A variety of creative techniques became available to "smooth earnings." Skinny profit years could be pumped up, and fat years could be slimmed down. Off-balance sheet special purpose entities and finite reinsurance could be used to hide financially embarrassing liabilities and losses from the average investor and even from many investment analysts and regulators.

Byzantine financial transactions, "financial engineering," having nothing to do with building the business became the vehicle for "cooking the books." Both the profit and loss statement and the balance sheet and their accompanying notes had become less transparent. They had become another form of advertising.

What started as legitimate, modest massaging of the numbers to hit a bonus target or satisfy stock market analysts gradually became bolder and more deceptive. "Creative" new age approaches to accounting and the use of derivatives allowed top management to manipulate the apparent performance of their companies. Reported profitability and corporate financial soundness were often the product of the risk tolerance and creativity of these paired money and numbers managers—finance and accounting.

Some accounting shenanigans were foolish in the extreme: A major software company, Computer Associates, allegedly added the value of new contracts that were signed in the next year to the previous year's income. Of course, the result was that the following year was missing the income from those contracts for year-end financial reporting. So it became necessary to manipulate the contract dates again. The process was repeated year after year—stealing income from a succession of years. In fact, nothing was being gained. The accounting deceptions were eventually uncovered, resulting in a costly prosecution.

Wheeling and Dealing

Mergers and acquisitions can make strategic sense for many companies: obtaining a new technology, filling out a product portfolio, gaining access to a new market, spreading overhead, and getting additional economies of scale, for example. But they can also be a tempting quick and easy way to improve the company's appearance.

Greater size equates with justifying higher top-management compensation. Many of these business combinations also allow a company to show almost immediate increases in revenue or earnings. This kind of revenue or earnings comes more easily and much more quickly than squeezing greater profitability out of "growing the business" and finding ways to increase productivity. Mergers and acquisitions also became another personal revenue stream for executives, who often made millions for themselves upon closing these deals.

Many of the world-class corporate scandals and bankruptcies of recent years were in companies that appeared to demonstrate extraordinary growth but had little operational follow through. Two of the more obvious are Enron and WorldCom. For all its glamour and apparent growth, Enron was never able to run anything that was really profitable, and WorldCom had a reputation for poor performance. WorldCom and Enron, like many companies that had rapidly blown through many acquisitions, had enormous problems integrating them into their business operations.

Neglecting the Heart of the Business

To see how dealing and financial machinations trumped building the business, look closely at how the customer is treated.

The customer base is at the core of every company. Successful companies always seek to protect their reputation in the marketplace. Serving the customer's needs was an obvious component of almost every corporate decision. Loyal customers were a critical part of the company's "crown jewels" to be guarded at almost any cost.

In sharp contrast, it has become acceptable to deceive, even "con," the customer in some major companies. Again, the motivating force is obvious: the focus on short-term financial appearances and executive self-interest. The extremes of short-run thinking and the derogation of the customer may be an explanation of what otherwise is inexplicable.

There are horrific examples in recently exposed corporate transcripts and email of investment banking traders and stock analysts being derisive of their clients and taking pleasure in their deceptions and exploitation.[4] Some of the most obscene are the tapes of Enron trader phone conversations joking about the plight of "grandmas" during the California energy crisis. Investment analysts had no remorse when they recommend stocks to clients at the same time they bad mouthed them to colleagues, saying candidly that the stocks being pushed are dogs and likely to go belly up.

Management encouraged or countenanced self-destructive policies that must have looked good in the very short run but were devastating within a few short years. Surely, most readers of these widely published business stories must have asked themselves, "But how could they? What could management have been thinking?" The two corporate examples cited at the beginning of the chapter: CitiGroup (in Japan) and Marsh & McLennan (with its bid rigging when its major clients sought new insurance) are almost unbelievable examples of mistreating your customers.

What Could Management Have Been Thinking?

Here is an example of executives "shooting themselves in the foot," deception and cheating that comes back to whack the originator:

- Numerous mutual funds destroyed their reputation by allowing a small number of investors to misuse the funds (by overnight trading and buying and selling at "stale" prices). Funds earned very modest extra management fees by granting these special privileges to hedge funds and a few "select" clients. Their corrupt trading and wrongful pricing cost the other 99% of the funds' investors dearly. When the corrupt practices were revealed, some funds lost half of the investors' money. In one case, the value of a fund family to its owners dropped half a billion dollars in a matter of weeks.

In broad segments of American business, disturbing conflicts of interest have been revealed in the last several years. Organizations entrusted with making certain purchases for clients have been shown to have investments in their preferred list of sources. In several well publicized cases, suppliers got on a preferred list by paying kickbacks. Such practices, of course, are familiar ways of doing business in less-developed parts of the world. Most of us presume we are a more advanced capitalist society.

Breaking the Cycle

As we have seen, there have been major changes in the decision calculus of an increasing number of executives. These began with fairly minor shifts in the trade offs and presumptions about what was proper and what was questionable. Over the past decade, the choices of too many executives tipped over into the acceptance of deceit and corruption.

Corporate earnings were fictionalized, relying on deceptive accounting rather than marketplace performance. In some instances, reported earnings have become "designer" products, engineered to meet "The Street's" expectations or bonus hurdle levels. Worse yet, financial shamans have found ways to hide debt and dissemble the company's financial health. Incredibly, companies close to bankruptcy have been made to appear reasonably healthy to the dismay of even sophisticated investors and creditors. At the same time, executive compensation packages have gone over the top and miraculously continue to climb.

The widely observed changes in values and practices eat away and degrade the vitality of American business. In a tough global economy, a show and tell mentality won't "cut it" in the market place. Almost as scary, these trends undercut the reputation of American corporate executives and American capitalism, now dubbed by many foreigners as "predatory capitalism."

There is growing cynicism about top management's commitment to serving shareholders' interests versus their own. More critical books are appearing that question whether business goals are consistent with the values of American society. Americans traditionally espouse belief in fairness, candor, and honesty. Where scandals have been rampant, corporate values have shown themselves to be a shocking departure from these beliefs.

Many business leaders still seem insensitive to the widespread public resentment and cynicism surrounding "greedy executives," a term frequently used whenever the subject of business arises in everyday conversation. Public confidence in the financial system, in free enterprise, and in executive integrity is of incalculable value. If found too lacking, at some point, the political system will exact regulatory penalties.

But American business appears eager to forget and forgive the last five years. There is widespread grousing that the Sarbanes-Oxley Act of 2002 requires cumbersome and costly paperwork, and many suggest that procedures and parts of it need to be repealed. This major piece of federal legislation sought to deal with well-known sources of fraud and deception. It was hastily enacted and may need some refinement, but it addressed some major issues effectively and should not be gutted.

Clearly, many corporations need to be more realistic about the seriousness of corporate misbehavior and learn how to attract, select, and compensate a quite different style of corporate leadership. (Something we shall discuss in Chapter 13.)

Change will not come easily. Contemporary American business culture provides a worrisome foundation for the excesses of executive behavior. Playing accounting games, conflicts of interest, and executive self dealing are now deeply embedded in the structure and values of many businesses, as well as their boards, bankers, and "flexible" auditors.

Change requires that both corporate boards and CEOs understand this and become committed to a new look in the executive suite. How to select executives who can practice a leadership style that builds businesses in contrast to engineered "bottom lines" is a tough challenge. Business itself and shareholders have much to gain by leaders committed to building robust and dynamic organizations and staying within both the spirit and letter of the rules. Fortunately, we have no reason to believe candidates are in short supply.

Private business is a major segment of American life. No fixed wall separates these economic institutions from our social and political life, our civic morale and morality. Regrettably, probably not in our lifetime, will senior corporate executives be perceived with the same respect and status they had before the new century began. America is a dynamic country; social and economic problems do get solved.

2

AMERICAN BUSINESS AT RISK: PICKING UP THE PIECES AND LOOKING AHEAD

Americans surely are distressed by the nonstop series of revelations of executive misbehavior and business deceptions—some trivial, most appalling. Even though corruption and scams have existed throughout our economic history, the current period is unparalleled in scope. In the past, fast buck artists, con men, and exploitative businessmen have come and gone. Michael Milken, Ivan Boesky, Robert Maxwell, and their contemporaries helped produce "a decade of greed"—the 1980s. Little did we know, as we breathed a sigh of relief when Milken and Boesky were locked away in jail, that the "decade of excessive greed and arrogance" was just beginning—the 1990s.

Stock market crashes are not unusual, either. Investors should have learned that stocks are always risky and the business cycle lives on. Optimism about stock prices is contagious. When fueled by the rising share prices and the accompanying exuberance, a self-reinforcing boom cycle is touched off. The market becomes bullish and expands.

The 1990s boom market amassed vast amounts of new capital investment directly from America's middle class. At first, middle-class Americans mostly invested in the market through "safe" mutual funds. Then, they invested more speculatively, even to the point of giving up jobs to become "day traders." Corporations also amassed middle- and working-class capital through investments made by pension fund managers.

Inevitably, the market tops, and the steep decline comes as a painful surprise. Those who go bust usually accept a considerable amount of blame, realizing they were foolishly greedy and got in over their heads. They were the "greater fools" who came in to buy too late. Many promise themselves "never again." Eventually, excitement will return; shares will move up in price in response to a new innovation, and people will be talking about the easy profits to be made.

But recent financial history has a darker scenario. It was not one sick industry (such as the 1980s savings and loan scandals—including the one involving Charles H. Keating, Jr., for instance, which by itself cost U.S. taxpayers some $2.6 billion). Remember ZZZZ Best? A teenager from California, Barry Minkow, was able to list and sell stock in his ZZZZ Best company on Wall Street back in the 1980s with entirely fraudulent claims that would bilk investors out of millions before Barry landed in jail. The kid actually used White Out to change his financials, which he then Xeroxed and filed! That was considered a wildly unusual case.

Surely not all or even the majority of American businesses have become ZZZZ Bests. But as we have seen, a significant number of well known, large companies and the professionals that advise them have engaged in a startlingly broad array of financial misdeeds. All more sophisticated than smeared White Out.

With their huge bundles of options, executives became a new class of specially privileged shareholders who easily could engage in big time insider trading, often breaking trust with "outside" investors. Substantial numbers of these executives have demonstrated greed far exceeding old fashioned self-serving. Executives who may have already earned several hundred million dollars from their companies push for still more generous compensation plans. Some CEOs were treating "their" companies as personal honey pots, dipping into corporate funds for whatever they wanted to take.

Remember that in its heyday, Enron was the seventh largest U.S. company, as well as the favorite of large numbers of mutual funds and investment advisors. Its logo and CEOs, Ken Lay and then Jeffrey Skilling, were American icons. Now everyone knows this was a sham; its attractiveness and prestige were the result of financial smoke and mirrors and legerdemain, not profitability. Close investigation finds that in 2000, 96% of Enron's income and 105% of its reported cash flow were attributable to accounting violations. Additionally, Enron's true debt was hidden from the world by a half; it was reported as $10 billion versus the actual $22 billion. It was a Potemkin village, a high false front on the outside with nothing on the inside.

Most of the knowledgeable experts in America—investment analysts, business journalists, business school professors, auditors, attorneys, boards of directors, credit rating agencies, bankers—missed the call. How was that possible? When this question is delved into, the answer is shocking. They missed the call because they were in on the act.

Auditing firms that are supposed to assure shareholders that management has been honest were duped in some cases but partners in deception in others. Boards of directors were revealed as acting more like facilitators than overseers, more form than function, indifferent to even the more obvious financial shenanigans. Many of their members joined in the money grabbing and engaged in obvious conflicts of interest. Some of America's most prestigious investment banks and law firms contributed to management's cheating of shareholders. Because more Americans own stocks today than during previous market crises, there is much more pain. In the 1929 market crash, it is estimated that less than 10% of households owned stock; today, it is over 50%. Many had pension funds heavily invested in the stock of an employer whose financials had been manipulated. Pensions disappeared and continue to disappear by various means. Large numbers of employees were funding their own pensions with 401(k)s. Those often contained a large percentage of common stock, in many cases, in the same companies in which stock had been inflated by erroneous financial reporting and by dishonest investment analyst recommendations.

Worrisome conflicts of interest appear rampant in companies that manage our savings. Many of those that give financial advice worked both sides of the street. Everyone can recall the investment analysts, who provide research-based advice on future stock market perform- ance of individual companies. Many investors learned too late that investment analyst stock predictions were often biased by the primary interest of their employers—getting more investment banking busi- ness. Good corporate customers got good ratings. Period.

Wealthy CEOs became important clients as individuals. Some selected investment banking advisors for their companies on the basis of whether they received generous personal allotments of "hot" new issues that guaranteed them an overnight profit.

Some companies in the business of managing pensions' funds also got a kind of payola for favoring certain mutual funds. This is not much different from the secret incentives to brokers to push mutual funds managed by their employer as "the very best" for their clients. As embarrassing, many directors on boards of public companies also had business relationships with those companies. It is unlikely that they would endanger these by being too critical of management.

Adding insult to injury, tax abuse and evasion on a vast scale has been uncovered. Another scandal tainted public auditing firms who devised and sold abusive tax shelters by the hundreds. Attorneys, along with auditors, made a fat living selling opinion letters that were intended to shore up these schemes by "certifying" them as being consistent with IRS regulations.

The government's major regulatory agency, the Security and Exchange Commission (SEC), was seriously under-funded during the heyday of these misdeeds. It missed nearly all the fraudulent financial reporting until long after most of the damage was done.

Business groups fought vigorously against any new government regula- tion. One important piece of legislation finally did pass, the Sarbanes- Oxley Act of 2002, but almost immediately, there were efforts to weaken its provisions. The legislation missed many needed reforms. For exam- ple, tax consulting by audit firms had been the source of many account- ing abuses because it created serious conflicts of interests, but it was left untouched. It took a massive tax abuse scandal a year later to get tax consulting added to the list of prohibited services for auditors.

Large numbers of Americans suffered triple jeopardy; millions of jobs disappeared and pensions were lost as a result of major shocks to the business system. Many personal equity investments shrunk to a small fraction of their cost. The checks and balances, like the SEC, boards of directors, public auditors, and even the media, failed their duty to protect the public interest.

Business Rises to the Top

First, some perspective: For decades, America's business acumen and effectiveness has been applauded and copied. (To be sure, there was an earlier period when Japan seemed to do everything better.) The logos of American business giants—IBM, GE, McDonald's, and Coca-Cola to name a few—have worldwide recognition and prestige. Both American management and management training were considered "best in class." In fact, the American MBA has been transplanted around the world. (This might be a worry these days for countries that question American business ethics.)

Free enterprise and free markets make a great combination. Americans take pride in how much of the world came to adopt the U.S. ways of producing and distributing goods and services. American business has a well-deserved reputation for its fast adaptation to changing tastes and the potential of new technologies Although Calvin Coolidge is derided, there was much truth in his famous remark: "The business of America is business."

In the years since World War II, consumers around the world have gotten the word that free enterprise-style capitalism gives the average citizen a good deal. Socialism and its offshoots, promising a better life for the average person, failed to deliver. State socialism and central planning consistently failed to produce the variety of readily available, reasonably priced, up-to-date merchandise. Shoddy merchandise and always short supply were the more likely products. Karl Marx was dead and dead wrong, and the brilliant Scottish economist, Adam Smith, got it right.

Inefficient, state-owned, and mismanaged enterprises all over the world, in capitalist countries as well as failed socialistic or communistic states, are being sold to private companies. "Privatization" has become an everyday word. Even what seemed like hard-core public enterprises are being sold. The British government sold its rail lines; the Hungarians sold part of their phone system; the Dutch privatized its much admired operation of the Skipol Airport in Amsterdam. Recently, the Russians sold part of the government-owned, second-largest oil company, Lukoil, to the American giant ConocoPhillips. Israel has perhaps gone the farthest the fastest by raising a vast amount of quick capital to fuel economic growth. In the U.S., closed, tightly controlled monopolistic markets are also increasingly being opened to ambitious entrepreneurs. Their energy and risk tolerance were supported by increasingly robust capital markets and a legal system that protected private property.

Americans took great and sometimes smug satisfaction in disparaging rapacious Russian oligarchs who were stealing the country blind. U.S. companies depended on efficiency and customer satisfaction to attract customers and capital, not cronyism, kickbacks, and loopholes in an inadequate legal system, questionable accounting, and few protections for shareholders.

The prestige and importance of private business in America was taken for granted. In surveys of community status, senior business executives were often at the top of the heap, having more prestige than most government and military leaders, lawyers (certainly), as well as other professionals.[1] More recent surveys indicate that senior business executives have plunged toward the bottom of the list.

But Then, the Second Big Bang

That prestige and the almost worldwide admiration for American business tumbled in time to greet the millennium. For all Americans, in addition to the image of free enterprise, the shock was consequential. Its reverberations are still being felt.

There were the series of dotcom failures in early 2000, but those were put down to the cyclical nature of the technology sector and greedy investors' susceptibility to hype. There were massive Internet-based company failures. Many were small, often little more than startups. Lawsuits were brought against dotcoms that had misled investors, but the press hardly mentioned them.

By the end of 2001, the average person first learned about what was happening in business and the stock market through the incredible, abrupt bankruptcy of Enron, the Wall Street favorite, a Texas-style force of nature. Then, the other dominoes began to fall. Shortly after came other large company shocks: Tyco, Qwest Communications, Global Crossing, WorldCom, HealthSouth, Adelphia, and Nortel, to name only a few. All had practiced artificial profit inflation and cost deflation and executive self dealing. Accounting seemed to have become a disinformation system.

Many failed company executives, like Enron's, faced criminal charges. A very few have already been jailed; many are awaiting trial or are currently in the dock. Most are also facing a barrage of shareholder suits. Even as more scams were revealed and still more employees lost their jobs, senior executive salaries continue to soar into the stratosphere.

Over 30 years, in 1998 dollars, the average real compensation of the highest paid CEOs went from $1.3 million to $37.5 million. Average U.S. salaries in the same period went up only 10%; real wages are stagnant or down. Yet, the top CEOs are now earning 1,000 times an average worker's pay compared to 39 times at the start of the 30-year period.[2]

Many CEOs are earning hundreds of millions in a single year, counting the value of the total compensation package. To most readers of financial news, this is only part of the scam; shareholders are being exploited. Top management's compensation has become obscene.

Next in line to be exposed were top-of-the-line investment banks: CitiGroup, JPMorgan Chase, Morgan Stanley, and Merrill Lynch, to name a few of the household names. They had profited by the issuance of stocks and bonds that became worthless. Often, their investment analysts, advising stock brokers and their private banking customers, were little more than touts for stocks that they privately admitted were pure junk.

In the new millennium, widely regarded mutual fund families took their fall. To millions of American shareholders, some of the funds were almost the traditional "widow and orphan" investments: no risk, with highly responsible management. A number of fund managers sold out their integrity to quick buck artists, sometimes their own management. They used influence and loopholes to exploit the funds and hurt the average shareholder.

Revelation of bad faith and bad performance also rocked the community of professionals that provide the vital oversight functions for these corporations. In theory, these help assure the shareholder and the government that financial statements and reports are legitimate. Some famous public accounting firms, "white-glove" law firms, and the blue chip executives and professionals who served on corporate boards of directors turned out to be well-paid contributors to these destructive scams. The well-regarded, gold standard of public accounting, Arthur Andersen, did not survive its involvement in the Enron scandals.

Questions have been raised about American corporations paying their fair share of taxes. The total income taxes paid by all U.S. corporations as a percentage of all such taxes has fallen precipitously. "From 1995 to 2000, the 5 years of the Wall Street Bubble when corporate profits soared, more than 60% of American corporations paid no federal income taxes according to a study of the General Accounting Office, the investigative arm of Congress."[3]

An increasing number of examples of wide-scale use of abusive tax shelters by wealthy executives and even some companies has come to light. They are abusive because they have no economic purpose aside from saving taxes. Especially distressing is the case of the partners who founded the hedge fund, Long Term Capital Management. They took huge gambles and lost. The losses were considered potentially destabilizing to financial markets, so the Federal Reserve bailed them out, saving partners' money as well as humiliation. It was later revealed that the partners also sought to avoid paying income taxes by using a questionable tax shelter.[4]

Insurance brokerage company bid rigging came to light in late 2004. Major firms, such as prestigious Marsh & McLennan, were dummying up fake bids that duped corporate customers into thinking they were getting a good deal when there was actually no competitive process at all. Given the fact that employees pay an increasing share of these high insurance premiums, these practices hurt many average Americans. These manipulations are one of the reasons insurance costs have shot up dramatically.

Hardly surprising, Americans have moved from idolizing CEOs and having uncritical admiration for them to cynicism. They have begun to question whether the system is rigged to benefit a favored few at the expense of employees and shareholders. Many Americans believe they deserve an explanation of how so much could go wrong with no notice at such cost.

While Europe has not been totally immune to these kinds of disclosures, respect for American business management and practice has diminished significantly. Not surprisingly, the French use the term *capitalism americane* when they wish to be derisive.

The court hearings, the depositions of participants, and the media coverage all have been like a nasty divorce proceeding. One sees what had really been going on among all the parties behind their cultivated public image. But a more powerful analogy to what the world has learned about some of the inner workings of the American business system has been provided by Roger Lowenstein, an insightful student of the subject:

> (It is) as if an attic trapdoor had been flung open exposing the family's supposedly demented aunt, and all of her cousins, nieces and nephews had seen a ghostly reflection of themselves.[5]

A Temporary "Fall from Grace" or Embedded Threats to Business Effectiveness?

To be sure, all the misdeeds, the cheating, and deceptions still represent seemingly small numbers of individuals and organizations. Unlike previous scandals, the perpetrators are not concentrated in a specific industry or are the product of isolated miscreants. America has in place a number of laws and established watchdog agencies at the federal and state level, like the Security and Exchange Commission, that should prevent oligarch-like behavior. Robber barons were supposed to be part of our history, not our contemporaries scheming in a nearby executive suite. The rogues were in post-Soviet Union Russia, surely not in America with its strong belief in playing by the rules.

Some solace came from presuming that this was just another price we paid for the stock market "bubble" and the now infamous, Greenspan-named, irrational exuberance. But some of the criminal investigations have disclosed that a significant portion of the executive-cooked books began to be composed in the early 1990s and even before.

Most of American business is still healthy, managed with vigor and reasonable integrity. The private business sector is a significant contributor to our well being and economic and political power. But the financial shocks, scandals, revelations of incredible excess, greed, and outright criminal activity can be read as a kind of shot across the bow, early warnings of a number of "cracks" in corporate leadership styles and values that threaten our economic vitality and the cohesiveness of our society.

Those who feel most strongly that free enterprise is self regulating and self cleansing are not worried. They feel sure that government regulation is needless and damaging. New regulations are clumsy and costly. They point to higher audit fees and compliance costs incurred because of the Sarbanes-Oxley Act's requirements. They insist that everything will be fine if what is already on the books is enforced and argue to roll back some of the provisions of the Sarbanes-Oxley Act.

Addressing the problem by making new laws does have inherent limitations. However, this is not a rationale for failing to make new laws in addition to vigorously enforcing existing ones. Their potential for negative consequences must be carefully considered, and adjustments must be made along the way if necessary. Of all the revelations of the past few years, one of the most shocking is that much of what was done was technically within the rules or the result of lax enforcement. Many of the successful prosecutions deal with obstruction of justice (destroying records, lying to investigators) rather than financial offenses.

It could be instructive to think about how early Vietnamese villagers created "the institutional foundation of the village—the procedures and rules that had been developed to manage daily life and to provide the law and order and property rights essential to a stable existence."[6] Villagers committed their customs to writing, leaving a minimum to chance.

As the leader of the village [Cochinchina] stated, "In our village, the inhabitants are decent, but, as manners change with the times, and as it is to be feared that some day future generations may lose sight of the decent sentiments with which the inhabitants are inspired today, we are compelled to establish the following set of regulations...."[7]

What Does the Future Hold; How Embedded Are the Defects?

Americans deserve an explanation of why and how their temporal gods failed them. Too high a price in self-confidence, in personal economic security, has been paid to forgive and forget. The war against state socialism was won; American-free enterprise won, hands down, so we thought.

Now American business faces extraordinary market challenges. We have entered a period of what some have termed predatory capitalism. There is a Hobbesian jungle savage, "take no prisoner" competition for market share.[8] The Asian Tigers are back, fiercer than before, now that China is among them. Competitors, especially for American jobs, seem to spring up overnight.

There are few protected markets, few natural or unnatural monopolies. Inflation has not been providing "free" bottom-line profits. Deregulation and globalization have created something close to Adam Smith's perfect competition.[9] It was competition that prevented excessive profits and redistributed resources from dying industries to those that were growing. Perfect competition was the ideal of a free market as generations of Economics 101 students dutifully learned, but no company, perhaps outside the storied "rag trade," expected to have to live with it.

The barrage and battering of the news detailing executive greed and corporate misdeeds has gone on now for years. Many Americans have grown weary of the bad news, except for the more salacious revelations. Everyone agrees that financial sinning is bad; worse, it has been destructive of the reputation of American business and devastating to many average Americans' financial well being.

It is comforting to believe that the corporate embarrassment that must accompany such negative public relations would be a force for healthy change. After all, the widely circulated photos of handcuffed senior executives taking well-staged "perp walks," the large federal and state corporate fines, increasing numbers of jail sentences, and thousands of shareholder and government law suits…all should certainly help to clarify management thinking.

Unfortunately, the continuing news reports of financial deceptions in major companies suggest this view may be naïve. Transcripts of long-delayed trials and new congressional testimony reveal the real depths of some of the financial deceptions. Executives can be tempted to opt out of seeking to maintain their company's competitive edge in a demanding global economy by wheeling and dealing instead of by "building the better mouse trap." Buying a competitor or negotiating a merger can be a good deal easier, more ego-satisfying, and more rewarding than building a business. An immediate revenue or profit surge is pleasing to shareholders and will surely boost bonuses. No matter what happens, lurking in the background are enormous severance awards. Let someone else worry about the long run.

As always, much depends on the leadership exercised by senior management. During the recent years of corporate wilding, management's view of its leadership role shriveled. Motivation consisted solely of hard-driving people. The executive's job was to set high goals for subordinates and then richly reward those who made it and harshly punish those who failed. As we have learned, this is an open invitation to dissemble and to appear successful at the expense of other parts of the organization.

Americans all have a stake in the willingness of corporate leaders to avoid such seductions. Success in a very unforgiving global economy, where no slip goes unpunished, requires continuous improvements in effectiveness, spawning and coddling new products and services. Most of the skills required to build a business focus on incremental, even modest gains in revenue and profits in contrast to a "big score."

As a byproduct of this narrow view of management, employees lost most of their feelings of identification with the company and with that went their loyalty. Repeated job cuts and outsourcing make job retention an everyday risk, and there is no confidence in the unseen leaders. For all any employee knows, her company is the next to fall.

The most massive failures, such as Enron and WorldCom, were abysmally managed. Like the gang that couldn't shoot straight, they were incapable of effectively implementing any of their clever deals or integrating their acquisitions. American executives have and can do better—much better.

Capitalism and democracy are mutually supportive. The extremes of the failures in our business sector point to deep problems in our democracy. Politicians are responsible for ensuring that sensible regulatory regimes protect the public interest and that lobbying does not unduly favor special interests. When the performance and reputation of American business is put at risk, America is at risk.

3

THE STOCK MARKET AND EXECUTIVE DECISION MAKING

E veryone (well, almost everyone) knows that the stock market is an essential element for a capitalist system. It is the essence of capitalism. One of the first reforms in countries moving away from socialism or state control of business is the introduction of a marketplace for the sale and purchase of shares in their newly privatized companies.

Stock markets facilitate raising money for growing a business, providing long-term capital. Selling stock is usually a better method of raising money, aside from meeting short-term needs, because there are no required interest payments and no dependency on money lenders. Those funds become part of the company's permanent equity capital.

Investors buy stock, or "give" some of their savings to "strangers," because they believe they will get back more than they invested from the future stream of dividends and the price appreciation of the security. It is the stock market that provides an honest auction site where potential buyers or sellers can bid what they consider a good price. The ongoing interaction between buyers and sellers with differing expectations, of course, determines the value of the stock at almost any moment in time. The "going price" is a market price; not an arbitrary determination by an owner or a government official.

That's the simple theory; however, there have been problems with the practice in recent times. We have witnessed a major change in the influence of the stock market on corporate affairs in the past decade. To exaggerate slightly, stock prices have shifted from being an effect to being a cause. Share prices were a reflection of corporate performance; increasingly, at least in some companies, performance is tailored to influence a company's share price. Too many corporate executives have given their company's share price the highest priority in their decision making. This shift in focus has introduced very troublesome distortions in critical executive decisions.

The Public Rushes In

The Depression years and long periods of share price stagnation discouraged the general public from participating in the stock market. Stocks were either for the very wealthy or the little guy wanting some excitement. However, over the past two decades, public participation in the stock market has soared. Rising share prices, enthusiasm generated by new technologies, and glowing media coverage contributed to middle class Americans viewing stocks as a good place to put savings.

At the same time, pension funds realized that earnings on their investments needed bolstering. Even conservative funds shifted more of their balances into equities. Big state pension funds pressured their money managers to increase investment returns. Often, that means shifting away from fixed income securities. Additionally, employees whose company-paid pensions were disappearing were buying their own stock-filled 401(k)s and participating in employee stock purchase programs. Many also converted regular insurance policies into variable annuities—again a shift to equities. About half of American households have stock investments, many in mutual funds.

As stocks began to take off in the 1990s and with growing media attention, investors' expectations soared. Many did not anticipate waiting years to get significant capital appreciation; they expected more immediate gratification.

Expectations were fueled by analysts who identified companies whose earnings would grow consistently 15% year-to-year, even quarter-to-quarter. Even more thrilling were new technology issues that doubled in days or weeks and favored stocks that rose 50% or more in a year. Examples abounded in the 1990s. Famously, AOL tripled its stock price in a year.

Now forgotten Exodus Communications, Inc., once known as the backbone of the Internet, is a fine example. Exodus split its stock three times in a matter of months following its IPO. The company's employees were particularly giddy over this development, which seemed to translate into newfound riches. Its CEO's paper wealth was put at over $1 billion. Within a few years, the stock was delisted; its share prices dropped into the low single digits. Obviously, shareholder losses were enormous.

Share owners began watching the daily, then moment to moment, performance of their stocks. TV news and the Internet obliged by carrying continuous market reports to the workplace and home desktops. With minimal programming expertise, investors recomputed their portfolios' total value with a couple of keystrokes. For a while, the market bested porno sites. Both obsessions distressed employers who were paying for the time many employees were glued to images of their portfolios, not the job.

For spice, some investors became stay-at-home day traders. Their strategy: rapid buying and selling. They probably had better odds than the slots in Las Vegas, but it was still high risk. Internet trading offered all the comforts of home plus all the thrills and excitement of casinos. Internet traders entered cyber-communities filled with endless chatter and populated with accomplished con artists running new games that fleeced the naïve. The market was fulfilling the American dream; anyone could become rich. Horatio Alger had become a stock trader.[1]

As we know, the easy winnings became painful losses, very large losses, even total losses. Although many small investors abandoned stocks, the American middle class maintains its interest in stocks—or at least their pension managers do.

Corporate Management's Dependence on the Market

Young companies just before or just after going public are highly dependent on the stock market. More mature, well-established companies are more likely to have the credit standing that permits them to borrow through bank loans or commercial paper or bonds underwritten by investment bankers. However, their share prices are still critical to management for a number of reasons.

Executive prestige is at stake. The company's stock price became the measure of the CEO. Executive status is almost directly proportional to the multiple of earnings; it is seen as a sign of faith in their vision and ability.

During the height of the boom, investors were willing to tolerate no earnings at all well into the future. Many investors didn't know it, because analysts didn't tell them, but the quality of earnings in many of these companies was poor (and their prospects, poorer).

In many high flyers, all or most of the earnings reported were not generated by selling products and services, but by techniques such as acquisitions, brazen overstatements of the value of inventory, not accounting for the cost of employee stock options, or by reporting the now popular "EBITDA."

The Magic of EBITDA

EBITDA, of course, is *Earnings Before Interest, Taxes, Depreciation, and Amortization*—all that nasty stuff that reduces earnings figures. CEOs convinced analysts that in the New Economy, EBITDA was what really mattered. Analysts' evaluations were based on this figure, discounting any significant gap between EBITDA and actual earnings, very considerable in many cases.

EBITDA ended up being a shiny object whose flash obscures sight of the oncoming train. By the end of the 1990s, companies were reporting all sorts of variations on EBITDA, which took

---

inconvenient costs out of the earnings equation. Manipulating EBITDA, and its variants, very effectively manipulated the share price. EBITDA became a major topic of conversation in senior executive meetings.

Remember, all these expenses must be shown in required SEC financial statement filings. EBITDA was a way to back all these numbers out of official statements when a company was being evaluated for investors.

EBITDA eliminated the visibility of interest on massive debt and obscured its often furious growth rate. Executive-owners were also engaged in burying real debt that was supposed to appear on financial statements through elaborate financial structures often involving off balance sheet and offshore entities (located in little known, small foreign countries). Enron created the most fanciful of these types of structures in its many-thousand, amusingly named, *special purpose entities* (SPEs) that were at the core of Enron's fraud.

Company management further manipulated the perception of analysts and investors by the timing of their earnings pronouncements. They realized, with the help of their PR and communications staff, that if an analyst and news conference was scheduled prior to actually filing the financial statement with the SEC, the message could be controlled and financial statement realities could be obscured. This all became known as "Managing the Street" in executive circles.

It got to the point that many analysts and investors didn't bother to take a close look at the financial statements after they were actually filed, instead relying on management announcements to inform their evaluation of companies. Those who did their job and fiduciary duty, often found alarming discrepancies between the picture in the financial statements and the one on the TV or computer screen. Nobody wanted to hear that kind of news, so the diligent few critical voices were marginalized or silenced. Their news fell on deaf ears if they did manage to be heard.

EBITDA was just one of the many techniques used by executive owners to keep the share price afloat in companies confronting financial threats. These techniques allowed those executives to enrich themselves by obscuring the financial picture on which investors were supposed to rely when making investment decisions. Misleading the investing public is among the more serious of charges leveled at corporate wrongdoers.

But more financially stable companies also can be concerned with share price. A company's relatively low share price can attract "undesirable" potential acquirers, even vulture funds. These could gain control and then pick off and sell the more attractive pieces for a quick profit. The converse is also true. A company whose stock is highly valued or overvalued by the market can make acquisitions relatively cheaply by issuing new stock or using stock as the currency for the transaction.

When high-tech companies like Nortel Networks were riding the boom, they could use their overvalued stock to make dozens of "cheap" acquisitions. This was likened to the CEO having a printing press in the basement.[2] Every time the CEO wanted to make an acquisition, he issued stock to fund the transaction. Every time Nortel's CEO did an acquisition, allegedly he also pocketed some cash for himself in the process.

Perhaps one of the more famous (or infamous) examples was America On Line (AOL). Its CEO was able to pull off a merger with Time Warner on terms that had AOL shareholders getting 55% of the new combined company. At the time, AOL was selling for an extraordinary earnings multiple—150 times AOL's annual earnings. It had few assets and had not yet faced the serious competition that was coming on fast.[3]

When a company's share prices are failing to keep up with peers in its industry or the general market, major shareholders, big pension funds, and mutual funds start pressuring management to make changes, and fast. A spate of negative news about the company or its management in the financial press can tempt senior management to become absorbed with damage control. Their more important responsibilities get neglected. Extended periods of relatively low share prices may even lead to the firing of the CEO. This has been suggested as one of Hewlett-Packards's reasons for asking its CEO, Carly Fiorna, to resign.

The Goad of Options

Executive stock options were the factor that truly focused management's attention on the stock market's evaluation of their companies. Highly placed executives became a new elite, a privileged class of shareowners. Executive compensation plans in the past decade have provided for ever-larger option grants. Even when the CEO and other members of top management are not buying or selling company shares or exercising their favorably priced options, they use the going share price to measure the size of their potential fortunes. For some executives, hundreds of millions of dollars are at stake when the share price rises or falls by 10%. Those few pennies more or less in reported quarterly earnings equates to millions of dollars up or down on personal balance sheets.

Making options a significant part of executive compensation was popularized as a way of aligning top management's goals with shareholder goals.[4] It was assumed that giving an ownership stake to executives would make them think like owners. It was assumed that executive-owners would make decisions even more in the interest of shareholders than managers motivated just by a good salary. It is tempting to speculate whose interests executives might otherwise identify with—employees? The community? The alternatives seem somewhat far fetched. But that was the theory.

To be fair, when more generous stock plans were initiated, there were companies with entrenched senior management that had demonstrated lackluster performance over a number of years. Often, they were impressing shareholders by increasing the company's size by acquisitions. (What were their boards of directors thinking all that time?) It could be argued that giving executives very substantial incentives would move them to work more diligently, make better decisions, and hopefully get the company moving toward greater real profitability. As we have seen, the profitability that resulted often lacked something that would make it "real" profitability.

Starting in this same period, corporate boards also began offering much more generous performance bonuses to attract and retain executives. Many of these were tied directly to the company's share price as well as reported earnings. The share price increase with any dividends paid was described as the shareholders' returns. This led to some questionable logic. For instance, if a company had 100 million shares outstanding and the stock went up 10 points in the past year, the annual report might trumpet shareholders gained a billion dollars! With that "gain," an increase in the compensation of those presumably "responsible" for all this (that is, the top two or three executives) getting an additional $50 million compensation was puny. Surely the lion's share to the CEO was well deserved.

CEOs could always quote the figure for the amount of shareholder wealth they took credit for creating. Mention of that changed when stock prices headed south. The president of one company that was tanking fast told a colleague, "I look in the mirror every morning and tell myself that if the stock price goes down, it can't be entirely my fault."

Where Do Higher Earnings Come From? Let Me Count the Ways

Executives found an alternative to the more focused, constructive executive effort that results in both greater earnings and share prices—but usually over some considerable time period. Share prices (and shareholder satisfactions) are very sensitive to short-term reported earnings. Prices respond almost immediately to even hints that a company's quarterly earnings may miss "The Street's" anticipated number by even a penny or two. A dip of 5 or 10% in value is not unusual.

Of course, this kind of over response is irrational. Quarterly earnings ought to be unpredictable within some reasonable range. Presuming that a penny or two is statistically significant and is a measure of real success or failure shows a profound misunderstanding of the real world of business. But funds as well as individuals jump quickly to buy or sell on just such numbers.

With so much riding on those numbers, it is not difficult to understand why executives sought to be more proactive in shaping the reported numbers.

Reasonably honest executives get tempted to have their staff engage in modest "reverse accounting" to bolster the bottom line—especially if some chance factor unexpectedly has hurt short-run profits.

Until a few years ago, only reverse engineering was practiced. Companies would break down a competitor's product to learn how it was manufactured. They would then copy those elements that were not protected by patents and copyrights. Reverse accounting is similar. Management knows what "The Street" is predicting for next quarter's earnings. They then adapt the accounting to meet or exceed those expectations. As Americans have recently learned, a number of these actions do not violate the standards of acceptable accounting.

Realistically, hundreds of uncontrollable variables can cause actual earnings to vary from what might have been predicted several months earlier. But accounting is also "variable" in the sense that some inevitable subjective judgments have to be made.

The inducements to meet the bottom line numbers are so great and the punishments for failure to make the numbers have become severe. It is not difficult to imagine how a senior executive can slip from making very legitimate choices with respect to how the company will account for the last quarter to first stretching the limits of acceptable accounting practice, and then to outright deception to fraud.

Here is a typical scenario.

A senior executive in Company A learns that the upcoming quarter's earnings are likely to fall a few pennies short (per share). In providing "The Street" with earnings "guidance," management was assuming that one of its major customers was going to renew a large contract. Then, those earnings estimates are at risk because the customer was experiencing some credit problems. Its lenders were pressing them for repayment, and they said they were postponing the purchase until the next quarter.

With approval of the customer, Company A's sales department starts shipping merchandise to them and includes profit from the "sale" in the current quarter's earnings, although there is no signed contract and no money changes hands. Or, to be on the safer side of the law, invoices are generated, but with the understanding that there will be no pressure to collect quickly, or ever. In the more extreme cases, the customer is sometimes told that everything can be returned after the quarter has closed.

An enormous array of techniques is used meet earnings' targets that range from very legitimate to quite questionable and illegal. Here are just a few obvious manipulations, which are modest compared to the creative accounting of firms like Enron.

Unneeded, "cookie jar" reserves can be established during good quarters and then drawn on during difficult quarters to boost reported income. Exceptionally good earnings results are hidden in various types of cookie jars inside company accounting systems. Some of the legitimate measures companies can take to save for a rainy day that are allowed for in accounting systems are abused, and some cookie jar practices have tipped into fraud. We have to keep in mind that every loophole in a very elaborate system of rules, standards, and practices for public company accounting has been found and exploited to some degree or another.

Costs can be "capitalized," so that they do not serve to diminish income for that accounting period. At its extreme of fraud, capital cost accounts are used abusively or illegally to hide the true ongoing operating costs of a company. This gives a considerable enhancement to the appearance of efficiency and profitability. Misclassifying expenses in this way was the favored trick of WorldCom, which buried the real cost of doing business in capital accounts that could be depreciated over time. Using this old trick on a vast scale in WorldCom's case had a dramatic effect on its whole industry, as we discuss in Chapter 4, "Black Boxes and Big Black Lies." Capital costs can also be shifted to so-called off balance sheet entities, and these also do not reduce income.

Many companies used, and according to reports still are using, highly generous assumptions concerning how much invested cash in their pension fund would grow in the future. They then take the assumed future gain in the value of existing fund assets as "profit." It is truly a testimony to the power of lobbyists who had such a large role in rigging the system that accounting for public companies allows them to record employee pension funds as if they were liquid assets at the disposal of management or even shareholders.

There has been serious erosion in the property rights that employees have over their pension funds, and the extent of it is revealed here. One of the most common elements in all the financial trickery was this hyper-inflating of the value of pension fund portfolios of assets. Loopholes were available. Employees are participating in retirement programs that have lost all the walls between their pension and their company's control over these funds. Companies resist putting pension liabilities into their financial statements in clear terms and making set payments into their pension fund accounts, and at the same time they claim pension funds as major assets that prop up, or even cook, the financial statements. Some companies have been able to withdraw reserves from what were deemed over-funded plans. They then used these withdrawals to bolster reported income for that year.

It is not hard to imagine how management can be seduced by the inherent and legitimate ambiguities in the calculation of income and costs. Too many managements, over time, begin to move from "stretching the envelope" to outright deception and fraud. After a while, more and more deception is required to make the books "balance."

Just recently we have begun to learn about how insurance companies developed producs that could help companies "beautify" their financials:

> To an extent not understood by investors or regulators, it appears that insurance companies…had profitable little businesses in what might politely be called financial statement beautification. They sold products that had little or no economic rationale, but that were promoted—ever so quietly—as being able to hide losses or smooth earnings. [5]

Privileged Shareholders

Option-rich executives became a new class of shareholder; they were "privileged shareholders." As such, they have the privilege of engaging in truly big-time insider trading. A significant share of their holdings is usually in stock options. One of their privileges is that they don't have to invest any money in their company's stock until the time is "right."

More than anyone, top executives should know when the market is undervaluing their company's stock and when future earnings are about to break out of a slump. They know about the company's new product development efforts that are going to produce a bombshell in the marketplace. They know when new orders are beginning to pile up and their competitors are losing ground. They know when earnings have suffered from some temporary problems that are almost overcome.

Such internal information allows them to know when would be an expeditious time to exercise some of their option hoard. They are allowed this extended "viewing time" because company-issued options don't have the short duration common to the options regular shareholders buy in the marketplace, which may be exercisable for only several months.

These privileged shareholder positions often have another attractive feature. When the options are "under water" for an extended period, that is, the stock has been trading way below the option exercise price, most boards (at management's suggestion) get shareholder approval to substitute options with a lower striking price or give outright grants of stock instead.

Still another privilege, most companies would loan executives the money needed to cash in on their large blocks of options at low or no interest.[6] These loans were the target of regulators and are now forbidden. However, the enormity of their destructive effects should be explained. Executives who accumulated large holdings of options needed cash to finance actually buying the stock the options promised. These transactions involved multimillions of dollars in many cases. After the executive owner takes possession of the stock, he has discretion over what to do with it—keep it or sell it. Enormous lines of credit were opened up to executives by the boards of directors of public companies for the express purpose of facilitating executive enrichment. Ken Lay, former CEO of Enron, for example, made liberal use of his $4 million line of credit at the company in order to cash in $81 million in options in the months before declaring bankruptcy.[7]

The executive loan was expected to be repaid when the executive sold his shares, realizing a profit. New twists were added, however. Executives were allowed to use stock options, which they normally still had plenty of after buying stock, as collateral on loans from their companies (authorized by the boards of directors). When stock prices plunged, these loans were backed by worthless collateral and were often written off. In one remarkable preference extension, John Snow, current secretary of the Treasury, while the CEO of CSX, allegedly returned the shares he acquired through options after the price declined and had his loan cancelled.[8] In a sense, he had a money-back guarantee *after* he had actually bought the stock. That is really no-risk investing.

Obviously, the reverse investment strategy also holds. When executive insiders know that the company's condition is worse, much worse, than the market realizes, they can sell out ahead of the crowd. Thus, Enron executives netted a billion dollars just before non-preferred shareholders were about to lose $70 billion in equity value.[9]

A Really Short-Run Orientation When a Penny or Two Counts

As management becomes more attuned, often obsessed, with stock market evaluations of their company, their focus often narrows to quarterly earnings. Whenever top management is discussed in executive conferences or graduate schools of business, the focus is on strategy, the long run. That is precisely the function of top management. They need to be thinking ahead, asking what business or businesses the company ought to be in, what change is necessary in products, marketing strategy, company locations, and operational procedures.

Why then the obsession with next quarter's earnings? The answer is obvious. Today's stock market is extraordinarily responsive to these very short-run glimpses of company performance; every penny counts.

In terms of what is known about the ambiguity and subjectivity of calculations of earnings over such a brief period, as we have said, this is emotion based irrationality. The personal fortunes of executive owners can undergo major changes with the rise or fall of share prices. Many members of this new class of owners worked for themselves, not shareholders. As we shall see, they had several reasons to focus their attention on what internal numbers would produce what external share price. Their executive bonuses were often based on stock performance, and, of course, the value of their enormous cache of options reflected share prices.

Share prices may go up or down by 10% or more as a result of a penny difference between anticipated and actual quarterly earnings. A company's total worth may tank on the basis of bad quarter. From a statistician's point of view, this is probably silly, an almost random number given the number of variables operating. But from the executive owner's view, anything that affects share price affects his wallet, and therefore gets inordinate attention. Investment analysts exert enormous effort to get the prediction right. Companies have gotten accustomed to feeding this frenzy with regular conference calls and meetings in which "anticipated" earnings get revealed. The investment community has also developed its own "shadow prices"—what sophisticated analysts consider the more likely score when the end of the quarter rolls around.

Americans love scoring. Earnings reports are scores; so are a simple (actually simplistic) number like an SAT, or IQ, or the results of any test or game. The mistake comes from assuming that one number effectively summarizes reality, the characteristics of the student or the company.

Economics has a clear formula for what a company's share is worth. It is the net present value of the future stream of anticipated earnings. Investors, in contrast to speculators or traders, should have as their focus a much longer term than a few months. They are putting their money in with the anticipation of having an asset that will be worth substantially more in several years or even longer. The system relies on considerable trust along with rules and regulations that are meant to run a clean game.

Increasingly, annual report messages from CEOs who are real leaders of their companies seek to discourage short-run evaluations of their company. In annual reports, they carefully explain why a few months' performance is a poor measure or predictor of how the company is going to do over several years. They even warn shareholders to expect some down years to be interspersed with the ups as they focus on long run growth of the company. Shareholders are urged to look ahead, not back.

One of the more negative results of Americans' substantial growth in the public's interest in stocks and the stock market is reflected in obsessions with the very short run. Brokers make their living in part on the basis of their prognosis abilities and on generating fees for the house from the portfolios they manage. Shareholders treat their stock holdings as though they were watching their favorite team play a baseball game. Each "inning's" results are a cause for joy or sadness. Stock investments have become more emotionally involved because there are all these runs and errors to watch, not every few minutes, but every few months. Stock prices are now, more than ever, closely monitored by an extraordinary number of professionals in the money management business as well as by millions of everyday shareholders.

The Executive Challenge

Philosophers and psychologists long ago discovered that we live in the present. It's hard to disagree with that profundity. Keynes said it more painfully: "In the future, we'll all be dead."

But unlike other animals, we can also live in the future; that is, we can anticipate and initiate plans that help shape the future. Only very fatalistic individuals or societies take the position that the future is foretold and nothing will change it.

Management can easily find itself becoming overly responsive to living in the present; that is, to the nearsighted demands of the stock market, the hustling brokers and funds seeking more assets, and gaming shareowners seeking a quick "killing." Not to be forgotten are the seductions of executives' generously dispensed options, company bonus plans, and their own ego needs.

It may well be that performance-based compensation plans are over-weighting the company's most recent share price growth. Of course, shareholders own the company and management's job is to work for their interests. But serving shareholder interests needs to be interpreted as the interests of *all* investors in the company, not just its own executive-owners' interests. The traders and speculators are only marginally owners because they have no intention of maintaining a continuing relationship.

Investor interests get served by building robust organizations that can quickly adapt and constantly innovate in their operations and their products. This also happens to coincide with what builds competitiveness. The current global economy has little patience for companies that can't "hack it," can't keep up with rapidly evolving technologies and fast changing markets.

Ironically, the mantra of "only serving shareholder interests" that surrounds huge option grants and performance bonus plans may work against the investor. Executives are both tempted and pressured to devote too much of their efforts to managing accounting and fretting over the next quarter's report and its impact on the stock market.

A few sophisticated professors of organizational behavior have taught their business students the deleterious effects of single or simple measures of accomplishment (accompanied by high rewards or punishment). Current business experience reminds us that the combination of aggressive target numbers and high stakes leads to a variety of destructive consequences. In nearly all cases, bright human beings learn how to score high, hitting their target in a variety of ways that the scorekeepers never anticipated. Many of these winning techniques are easier to employ than hitting the "bulls eye" in the manner anticipated by those who designed the measure.[10]

Fortunately, leading companies are beginning to make option grants that can only be exercised after a number of years or at retirement. Obviously, this shifts attention away from utilizing executive owner privileges in short-term personal strategies and directs it to longer-term corporate strategy choices. According to some, this will counterbalance the problems of the 1990s that surfaced out of dramatic changes in executive compensation. Or will it?

The problem wasn't just when executive owners could cash in options (often within a few months), it was also the size of the stakes. Potentially, the excesses of stock options that still occur and the fact that executive-owners are in a position to renegotiate the terms of when they can cash in options and have them changed are still serious problems.

At the extreme, companies can become giant lobbyists. They are devoted to lobbying the investment community to obtain its validation of the both the company and the management's worth. They are feeding an insatiable demand for news that will foretell the next quarter's earnings report. These efforts directed at Wall Street need to be redirected to the marketplace.

In brief, corporate management has become too dependent upon and too tightly connected to the investment community. The latter can't be ignored; stock markets are a critical part of our free enterprise. But as the saying goes: Be a bear or a bull, but not a hog. Both executives and the stock market became hogs. The market was knocked back, but too many executives are still at the trough.

We have emphasized the incentives for the CEO to focus on short-term share prices. Beneath them, executives have tough targets to boost earnings and, of course, associated rewards or punishments. Here is just one striking current example. The high-end specialty store chain, Saks, discovered that managers were extracting excessive amounts of so-called "markdown" money from vendors to increase profits.

A true story is an appropriate footnote. A now retired GE senior executive recalls a watershed event at GE. After a long business trip, he was going in for lunch and glanced at the executive bulletin board. It had always been loaded with product and marketing information and updates. This was the early 1990s, and now in a prominent position was a new type of announcement: "Yesterday's closing price of GE stock, Share Volume, Change from Previous Close, Change in S&P for the Day, Change in the Dow."

That says it all. Executives were now energized by a very different universe of activity involving decisions that had immediate effects on their personal fortunes and public image as outstanding corporate leaders.

4

BLACK BOXES AND BIG BLACK LIES

T he more than 2.5 million-year-long evolution of human technology has hit its black box phase.[1] "Black box" has long been applied to computer technologies because just as with a black box, we cannot see their workings.

We are all counting on electrons, invisible to the naked eye, to do our bidding. Most of us haven't a clue regarding how electronic devices actually work. We take these technologies on faith in the notion that somebody, somewhere knows what *they're* doing. Explaining the 1990s can't be done without taking microelectronics into account, making the black box all the more mysterious. In the 1970s, 2,200 transistors on a processor was possible; 30 years later, it's up to half a billion. When we sit down to work on a laptop computer, what's going on behind that familiar typewriter-style keyboard and simulated piece of paper, displayed on a screen filled with icons we may not even understand, is baffling for most of us.

Hieroglyphics are back, and a twist on cuneiform is used to create emoticons—those sideways smiling faces, for instance, in emails, ;-). New slang and shorthand abound. We all struggle to master a common technical language that is still highly unstable, and whole generations of programming languages proliferate so quickly that it's hard to keep track of where we are, fifth generation, sixth? Computer memory capacity and speed are the equivalent of horsepower and zero-to-sixty in the braggadocio of computer owners. In the 1980s, garages filled with a new variation of mechanics who were often as not mystified by the combustion engine now parked outside.

Wonderful things were promised, and some even materialized. Yet new health and safety hazards surface as we spend more of our time sitting in an invisible electromagnetic field in front of screens bombarding us with radiation. We carry electronic devices in our pockets, and hold them in our hands and to our heads. We spend hours straining our eyes while we thumb and click our way through work and leisure activities. Less than two decades ago, only those weird people dubbed nerds considered electronic devices to be playthings. Then, it became cool to be "wired" and some became addicts.

The mysterious gadget we're all staring at these days is largely responsible for the economic expansion of the 1990s, as well as the enormously increased ability of businesses to manipulate their numbers and perpetrate large-scale fraud and near-fraud. Information technologies make it possible to create exceedingly complex accounting systems. Complexity is the handmaiden of financial obfuscation. While new capabilities provide seeming transparency down to the last paperclip, accounting systems are black boxes, the complexities of which few can penetrate.

As the 1990s sped on, great gaps in company information systems were created by all the rapid growth, restructurings, reorganizations, mergers, and acquisitions that were setting records. The manager of systems integration projects in one bank that was quickly acquiring businesses was admittedly overwhelmed by the more than 200 projects he had charge of at the moment. Costly errors can be made, customers can be irritated, and important information is difficult to gather when a company's information systems become chaotic. Mismatched accounting systems, for example, make it hard to ascertain a good and true picture of the company for day-to-day operating purposes. Integrating government information systems in the wake of changes mandated by creating the Department of Homeland Security and recommended by the 9/11 Commission proves no easy task either. It was politically embarrassing when people like Senator Ted Kennedy appeared on terrorist watch lists.

The computer systems of corporations can easily accommodate running two or more sets of books, and often do run a duplicate that can be played around with for a variety of purposes. Theoretically, this

enhances forecasting and planning activities. As accounting professionals have become adept with these new tools, many have stepped more
boldly into prediction and noodling around to see what happens if a
factor (or factors) is changed—now commonly referred to as "what-iffing." Accounting was traditionally an historical exercise. As the pressures have built to focus on the next quarter's numbers, the accounting
profession has come under the sway of its new big brother, finance, and
is pushed to cooperate in earnings manipulations and engage in the
black arts of fortune telling.

It's easy to succumb to illusionary and delusional accounting practices—new technologies make it easy. Because we can crunch more
numbers faster and change an entire balance sheet with the stroke of a
key, we become more confident that we know more. Some became
more confident that they can get away with more. It is easy to perpetrate frauds using a massive number of little transactions that aggregate
into a large number that can provide window dressing for the financial
statements.

WorldCom's fraud was founded on misclassifying a host of transactions
as capital expenditures rather than operating expenses. Thousands of
little transactions added up to the biggest fraud in history. Small billing
"errors" in a company's favor can be duplicated on millions of bills, if
necessary, to puff up accounts receivable. Have you ever known a phone
billing error to be in *your* favor? One systems professional who specialized in medical systems said he had never known a hospital to assign a
high priority to correcting billing system errors that were in their favor.
Or, another little trick is to generate payments for vendors but stick the
checks in a drawer till after quarter-end, so the cash technically remains
in the bank. The illusion of timely bill payment is created.
Unfortunately, small vendors, such as independent contractors, who
don't report to credit raters, are especially subjected to these kinds of
practices, often wasting considerable effort on bill collection.

Because it's so easy to jigger the books, the week or so before a quarter-
end has become a more broadly harried exercise than it used to be,
when it was just the accounting department in a tizzy.

Quarterly Rituals

One executive recounted how the executive team would meet toward the end of a quarter and be told the actual earnings per share number they had from that quarter's operations and the earnings per share number promised to Wall Street. As this quarterly ritual ensued, executives in charge of various areas would promise to ante up a penny here, a few pennies there, in order to make the Wall Street number. They would then return to their respective departments and engage in a frenzy of disruptive activity to deliver on their promises. Senior managers, with profit-and-loss responsibilities, often complained that hundreds of thousands of dollars appeared or disappeared from their P&Ls, and they could never get a straight answer from executives as to what these transactions were all about. Making too big an issue of trying to get to the bottom of these mysterious figures put a person's job at risk. Computers make adjustments easy as their ramifications throughout the balance sheet are posted as soon as the entry is made. It's then easy to readjust an "adjustment," if need be.

Many of Enron's most complex and deceptive special purpose entities were thrown together within a day or two of the end of a quarter. Offshore structures could be created electronically, a flurry of emails nailed down financing commitments, and funds were wired into place in a split second, often just in the nick of time. Over 3,000 of these entities were generated in the space of a few years. It is taking years to unravel Enron's complex financials. It took nearly two years to follow the threads to the serious tax evasion schemes that Enron had buried in its black box.

Accounting systems that emphasize forensics have not kept pace. Even though some in the accounting industry have long called for more forensic training of students, use of forensics in auditing, and better forensic systems, the profession to some extent neglected the potential of new technologies for making the books more, not less, transparent and honest. New technologies make better forensic systems possible, but there has been little demand partly because many people don't realize what the black box can do.

With the technological breakthroughs of recent decades, a new generation of tycoons was spawned and the dawn of a new economy was declared. People left school and secure jobs to join the "gold rush" and some did strike it rich. The American tendency to want to strike it rich led to our recent period of lionizing sports and entertainment figures as the new Horatio Algers. Most of us had the good sense to realize our odds were miniscule, so no time was wasted chasing those dreams. But, when teenagers and college drop-outs began to strike it rich through technological prowess and were made the new icons by the mass media, many thought the odds were more in their favor, as investors, if nothing else. The young thought youth was the best time to gamble; they could return to school or make up the losses if things didn't pan out as they hoped. The middle-aged, who had failed to save adequately for retirement and were realizing there would be no defined-benefit pension plan at the end of their working lives, entered the gold rush initially in a panic to get quick growth out of assets or make a grab for the brass ring while there was still time to make it up if they failed. Old-timers thought in terms of their last gasp or had some money to burn.

Venture capitalists pulled wide open the purse for prospectors, some of whom blew the money even before they made it west, much less opened a mine. The lessons of the folly of funding youthful adventures paved the way for elders to join the gold rush. Venture capitalists started insisting on evidence that at least one "grown-up" was overseeing the kindergarten. Unfortunately, many of the grown-ups regressed and joined in the play or just weren't up to controlling an unruly bunch.

Many Silicon Valley companies brought ex-IBMers in as the grown-ups. More than a hundred thousand IBM employees were conveniently released in downsizings beginning in the 1980s, and everyone thought they could play the "grown-up on hand" part. But many people who had large mainframe computer backgrounds didn't understand the new and smaller black boxes that housed more computing power than the systems they had cut their teeth on as young programmers. And, it was difficult for people who had grown up in a secure giant organization to adjust to seat-of-the-pants new technology firms. Plus, a lot of the grown-ups not only weren't controlling costs but were making the burn rate worse by emulating the lifestyles of big business and new tycoon CEOs and senior executives. First-class travel, handlers, and lavish lifestyles of the executives running big-time organizations were their model, and now their entitlement.

New technologies had given the venture capitalists the tools to calculate their odds, or so they thought. The vast resources of venture capitalists were disbursed under assumptions built into carefully computed failure rates. Operating on the greater fool theory, venture capitalists churned most startups out of their portfolios of businesses for quick returns. A record period of mergers and acquisitions preceded, as it always does, a record period of bankruptcies.[1] For many new entrepreneurs, the name of the game was to get eaten by a bigger fish as soon as possible after an IPO, and soon even big fish were offering themselves as a meal for the biggest fish, well-established, "old economy" companies. People were focused on just prettying up enough for the feast, not on building sustainable businesses. It turned out to be a lot of high calorie, nutrition-empty junk food.

People forgot how many lost their grub stakes in the California gold rush of 1849, how many claims were jumped, how much fool's gold there was, and how many scams were run on unsuspecting prospectors and investors. Americans, as usual, just remembered the good parts of its Gold Rush mythology. As it turned out, perhaps the wrong historical metaphor was adopted. Robber Barons of the Gilded Age might have been more apt. Just as the poverty rate began to go down and employment rates and wages up, the rush was over, leaving the poor quickly poorer and the middle-class financially besieged and economically insecure. Classically, a very small *nouveau riche* class became established, and most of the old-moneyed became richer and more powerful.

The frenzy really hit stride in 1997 when "The Big Lie" got loose.[2] Plenty of big lies were loose by 1997, but most pale in comparison with the effects of The Big Lie. It was truly a whopper. The Big Lie was created through one of the miracles of new technologies, the electronic spreadsheet, which was the basis of the new business pastime—what-iffing.

A WorldCom capacity planner, Tom Stluka, was what-iffing sales forecasts one day and plugged Internet capacity requirements doubling every 100 days into the spreadsheet. Of course, the results of this scenario for WorldCom would be astounding financially. Because WorldCom (and business and the media) were already places "where the distinction between fact and fiction did not exist, where lies were not only tolerated, they were embraced,"[3] The Big Lie quickly took hold and spread.

It took a year for Stluka to realize that his what-if was being quoted by everyone and even the government had taken and run with it. Stluka thinks he even heard a presidential candidate quote it in 2000. WorldCom's 1998 annual report stated that Internet traffic was growing 1,000% per year. The figure was used by Wall Street analysts, the media, other companies, and government officials.

By early 2000, Bernie Ebbers, WorldCom CEO, had a net worth of over half a billion dollars. WorldCom had 88,000 employees in 65 countries, owned 60,000 miles of telephone lines globally, and expected revenues to exceed its $40 billion projection. All this was built on The Big Lie.

Sustaining the lie ultimately led to the biggest fraud in corporate history, the financial destruction of an entire industry, and incalculable taxpayer losses in the form of government contracts and being stuck with the bill for an irrational infrastructure akin to the railroad boom. Thousands of miles of dark fiber[4] encircle the planet. Whole areas of this global backbone of the Internet have massive overcapacity, while other areas have no capacity whatsoever.

Enron believed the lie like all the rest and made massive investments in fiber optics and broadband capacity, which became a big chunk of its dooming write offs in 2001. WorldCom's competitors, wanting to believe the lie's amazing implications for their own bottom-lines and pursuing the winner-take-all scenario, behaved as if the lie was truth. No one bothered to check.

AT&T, for example, was laying cable at the rate of 2,200 miles an hour. As the promise of the lie failed to materialize, competitors thought it must be the fault of their sales and marketing people, or mismanagement of locating their fiber. Internal finger-pointing made for acrimonious meetings. When their numbers couldn't compare with WorldCom's, competitors began draconian cost cutting, gutting long established companies and resorting to more elaborate window dressing for financial reporting, even stooping to fraud and near fraud. Years of this occurred before WorldCom was unmasked as complete fiction. Former CEO of Sprint, Bill Esrey, is left to wonder about Ebbers, "…how you could live a life, knowing the type of things that you're doing, knowing that it's wrong, and also knowing that sooner or later, it has to catch up with you."[5]

Too many executives had become sloppy lemmings fixated on leaders they thought they were following to the pot of gold. Even when WorldCom's audacious capacity projection didn't jive with reality, nobody checked it. Some who were not greater fools were smart enough to get out at the top, lucky enough to get fired before the bust, or wily enough to cover their tracks, and did get their share of the pot and have receded into the background. Even some who quickly amassed fabulous riches turned out to be the greatest fools and lost all or nearly all. For many people, there is a satisfying irony to stories of people who shadily made fortunes only to lose them by investing in other companies run by even shadier characters than themselves.

After Stluka fully realized that the basis for the mantra of the Internet doubling every 100 days was his best-case what-if, he tried valiantly to rein in the lie. He risked sending messages up through the chain of command saying, "I don't think we're reporting the right thing."[6] His effort was futile because "nobody wanted to look at the truth." He describes himself as that guy who told the emperor he had no clothes. American executives long before the 1990s didn't believe there could be such a thing as bad news and would hear none of it. "Don't bring me a problem, bring me a solution!" was a popular, but empty business mantra and off-with-your-head was the fate of messengers who didn't get it. Stluka got nowhere inside WorldCom and didn't take his message public.

Enron, as was its wont, went even further. Enron's own management, industry analysts, and the press described the company itself as a "black box."[7] Enron's "black box" analogy was a convenient contrivance used to push away searching questions. If an awkward question was posed, a condescending response to the effect that you had to be a genius trained in an elite school to see into the black box was the perfect offensive maneuver to change the subject. You didn't need to know how it worked, just believe that it worked, assured Enron management. Louis Columbus, an information technology industry researcher, recalls meeting with vendors selling to Enron, "I asked what their software did at Enron and the term 'black box' came up no less than a dozen times in an hour's discussion."

Enron executives came to expect to be trusted as mythical figures built up by publicity machines. The problem with all this press coverage is that invariably the people in the companies, especially those singled out as celebrities, come to believe their own myths. Mere mortals would never penetrate the complex mysteries of a new economy company like Enron and shouldn't trouble themselves with trying to learn the magician's secrets. Skeptics are retarded, misguided, or crazy. Heretics be damned.

George Soros' bubble theory of boom-bust cycles explains all this very well. Actually, his theory is robust enough to explain a lot more than just economic boom-bust cycles. The self reinforcing *and* self-defeating dynamic of a boom-bust bubble is played out in many human events. Soros' theory is useful because it highlights the importance of the role of false ideology in precipitating the disequilibrium that pops bubbles. Soros describes the bubble-popping moment of truth in the process as being the realization of the falseness of the ideologies associated with booms—a confrontation with reality when irrefutable proof surfaces that can no longer be ignored. When the bubble pops, according to Soros, course correction ensues. That's assuming the bubble actually pops and doesn't just get a bit deflated. In this case, the bubble grew during the record-long economic expansion of the late twentieth century, and companies such as Enron played a major part in puffing up the bubble's boom phase. Market and free trade fundamentalism are major elements of the false ideology of our recent bubble, according to Soros and others.

A former Enron managing director said, "I'll always wonder how much of what we did there was real."[8] The consequences are real enough, though the company turned out to be an empty suit. When the Gordian knot of Enron's structured finance was unwound, it was clear that the company had been bankrupt for a number of years.

The new conventional wisdom of corporate finance is a major prop for visionary schemers. Burying debt for overextended corporations, evading taxation, creating an appearance of profitability and general financial health through various earnings management techniques that window dress reports seems to have become part of the job description for some CFOs. Andrew Fastow, CFO at Enron, certainly thought it was and was proud of the fact that his finance group had become a "profit center."

Many of today's complex, structured finance strategies have offshore havens at their core. Enron's finance group had created more than 3,000 special-purpose entities, which were registered offshore. There is an obvious fix for egregious abuses of secretive, permissive offshore company registration and banking. Public corporations listed on our market exchanges can be prohibited from using offshore registration and banking. We know exactly which principalities to prohibit and yet unfathomably have still not gotten tough on this issue.

Because it doesn't appear that we'll get to some of the systemic causes of these problems anytime soon, investors can take matters into their own hands by withdrawing their money from corporations that engage in practices that are intended solely to move long-term liability off the balance sheet and abusively avoid taxes. In Enron's case in particular, these offshore entities were being used to finagle the company's numbers in a variety of ways every quarter, along with perpetrating Andrew Fastow's over $60 million *personal* fraud.[9] Why would it ever be in an investor's favor to move liabilities off the books, and why would it ever be in the investor-as-citizen's best interest to tolerate tax evasion? The American financial industry is a major enabler in these offshore schemes, including using them themselves. Enron depended on the financial industry's elaborate offshore connections to pull off its quarterly hat tricks.

It is unnerving to realize that it is taking years to understand the role of black box technologies, the depth of deception, and the true (and truly ugly) nature of Enron's black box company. Unnecessary complexity has crept in for the sole purpose of deception and exploiting loopholes.

The perversity of current business practices and IT systems is best high-lighted by the tax shelter scandals. Tax professionals made no secret of the fact that complexity was the key to lucrative tax shelter products, which they were generating by the hundreds. When caught selling abu-sive tax shelters, KPMG quickly promised Congress it would close down this line of products. KPMG is one of the four remaining large audit firms and seems to have been the most aggressive. Many audit firms, legal firms, and financial institutions are caught up in the wide sweep of our tax scandal.

Even though KPMG promised to stop perverting the tax code, the firm apparently couldn't resist. By September 2004, KPMG was under inves-tigation for writing new versions of tax shelters that had been ruled ille-gal. As is becoming so familiar now, the black box yielded up damning email messages dating from the mid-1990s to 2003. The newly surfaced emails show KPMG to be "engaged in exhaustive legal analysis of tax and civil court rulings and I.R.S. rulings to find loopholes in the ever-changing tax code to justify its shelters."[10] In a slide presentation that was stored in KPMG's computer system, one slide stated, "The I.R.S. position of what is 'final' is not 'real world view.'"[11]

> In the late 1990s, KPMG created a giant internal bureaucracy—with layers of departments, sophisticated software, scores of employees and bonuses—to develop and market tax shelters.
>
> The effort included establishing interconnected "laboratories" and idea banks that served as factories to develop tax shelters and even awarded paperweights shaped like light bulbs to low-level employees with tax-shelter ideas.[12]

These tax shelters are real marvels of modern technology and ingenu-ity. Unfortunately, they deprive taxpayers all over the world of billions of dollars in legitimate tax revenue. Absurdly, some companies that have played this game to the hilt have even received checks from the U.S. government that are the equivalent of the tax credits given to very low-income wage earners.

It takes highly trained forensic specialists to penetrate the intricate financial black boxes inside companies. The degree to which penetra-tion can be difficult is highlighted by an incident recounted by an extremely talented and experienced IT professional. An unexpected sequence of events caused his program to crash during testing. He spent days looking for the "bug." Finally, he buried a message deep in the code for any future programmer who might encounter the failure, "If you're reading this, just say softly under your breath, "Oops."

Executives have apparently learned some unfortunate "lessons" about technology from recent events. It is reported that CEOs have curtailed their email use. Many criminal and civil cases have hinged on the long memories of computer systems that destroyed defendants' claims of "plausible deniability." It's a bit like the reaction of one major accounting firm that was found guilty in a case on the basis of a handwritten note. For quite a while, the firm forbade anyone to enter a meeting with a pen.

Predators and their prey co-evolve. If predators don't stay a step ahead of their prey, they don't eat. Regulators, investors, and employees in companies must take a predatory stance toward new technologies, seeing wrong-doings as their prey. The security issues created by new telecommunications technologies are a clear example of how hard it is to stay a step ahead. The Blackberry in your pocket can be picked for all its information. For all its good, information technology is fraught with unintended consequences.

It is sobering to consider the new IT product demonstrations made for the Chinese government: IT warehousing that can create and store extensive dossiers on citizens. Systems for government-issued smart cards that, combined with fingerprint recognition, can track the movement of people along with activities requiring a swipe of the card. As technology moves forward, it will be a real challenge to avoid its pitfalls. If people think black box finances and companies are a concern, what about black box government?

5

THE SHOCKING DESTRUCTION OF ARTHUR ANDERSEN, AUDITING'S GOLD STANDARD

A ccountants often joke that theirs is "the second oldest profession." They're wrong. Accounting is older than prostitution. Documenting economic events on cave walls and incised stones goes back tens of thousands of years. The Sumerians used double-entry accounting 5,000 years ago; Babylonians were still at it a thousand years later. Egyptians were exceptional accountants, as were the Incans, and many others. Rooms full of 2,500-year-old clay tablets written in cuneiform were found at Persepolis, capital of the ancient Persian Empire.

The Persepolis Tablets[1] are the largest cache of ancient accounting records to be uncovered and give a picture of the day-to-day running of a vast empire. The tax collection tablets reveal details about revenue, and another set of tablets reveals how resources were dispersed throughout the empire, right down to allotments of wine provided for workers. We have to wonder if some of those tablets were fraudulent, created so the accountant could siphon off some of the King's resources for himself. Ancient Persian accountants all had to date and imprint each clay tablet with their personal seal, leaving a "paper" trail now followed by archaeologists.

As record breaking, spectacular, and scandalous as corporate failures have been, ultimately, the most historic recent event is the demise of the public accounting firm, Arthur Andersen.[2] Although Enron is our focus now, it will probably become one of history's footnotes, topped by even bigger failures. But putting one of the oldest and largest accounting firms in the world on trial as a criminal, and so putting it out of business, is entirely unprecedented and may never happen again.

Of all the failure points in America's political-economic system revealed by recent events, the failure of the accounting profession is the most serious. Public audits are the linchpin of America's market system. If public auditors are corrupted by resolving conflicts of interest in favor of their personal self-interest or their firm's profits, and if auditors get caught up in greed and hubris, our market system fails. We recently re-learned that lesson. Even if boards, attorneys, and bankers give wrong advice or consent, auditors have to be independent and are charged with speaking up and alerting the investing public to questionable dealings.

The savings and loan industry failure of the 1980s was clearly an audit-based failure that revealed serious weaknesses in our oversight systems that were patched or never fixed. So here we are over ten years later with an even bigger mess. Ironically, Andersen took issue with how savings and loans were doing accounting. Because no client agreed to adhere to what the firm thought were honest accounting standards, Andersen got out of the business of auditing savings and loans before the great crash that cost Americans billions of dollars in bailouts. The firm dropped clients and refused business.[3] But, a lot changed within Andersen between the 1980s and the end of the 1990s.

Public auditors, like those in Andersen, are specialists within the accounting profession. No more than half of all accountants are Certified Public Accountants (CPAs). Of those who are CPAs, only about ten percent are doing attest work, which is the only accounting work that is regulated by the government.[4] We might ask ourselves why, if accounting is a profession, all accountants should not meet the standards of the CPA, whether doing public audits or practicing within government and business. In other professions, all practitioners are licensed, but not in accounting.

To be a CPA, an accountant must pass a licensing examination and agree to uphold the profession's code of ethics. If a CPA doesn't keep up with continuing professional education, the license lapses and must be reinstated. An independent practitioner or accounting firm that does public corporation audits must be registered with the Security and Exchange Commission (SEC). Like other professions, anyone having a felony conviction is excluded from obtaining a license and loses the license to practice if a felony conviction occurs. Auditors' licenses are suspended or revoked if they violate the profession's code of ethics, independence rules, or generally agreed upon accounting principles and audit standards.

Public audit firms are required by the SEC to be partnerships partly to avoid the conflicts of interest that could arise if firms were corporations, thus having outside investors and a need to "make their numbers." Requiring audit firms to be partnerships also removes the corporate "shield" that protects public corporation executives and board members from personal liabilities in the face of civil or criminal litigation. As an organizational form, partnerships force more individual and collective responsibility among the owners—the partners. It is very easy to file a civil or criminal suit against the entire partnership for an offense committed by one of its members. That is just what the Department of Justice (DOJ) did to Andersen. The entire U.S. firm of Andersen was indicted on one felony count of obstruction of justice. No single individual in the firm was named in the indictment.[5]

When the SEC was created by the Securities Acts of 1933 and 1934, there was a choice to be made. The SEC could either take direct responsibility for the conduct of the independent financial audits mandated by the Securities Acts or it could effectively give a franchise to accounting firms to do this work. The latter was chosen.

Firms registered with the SEC were deemed qualified to perform the independent audits that public corporations registered with the SEC were forced to buy. Public auditors were essentially functioning as extensions of the federal regulatory apparatus charged with protecting the investing public's interest and the integrity of U.S. markets. Public auditors ultimately work for the American public to protect the public interest. Auditors are charged ethically to "speak without fear or favor."

This public audit system worked reasonably well, until lately. The power of the Securities Acts actually gives the American people a lot of options in terms of how the public interest is to be protected in our market system. There has always been the threat to auditors that if this approach failed, they risked losing their very lucrative franchise. Over time, that threat diminished as interests became entrenched and the SEC's real power was chipped away. By the 1990s, the idea of having the U.S. government take a more direct role in public audits wasn't taken seriously by anyone. By that time, corporations had effectively "captured" the regulatory apparatus and were calling the shots.[6] The revolving door between auditors and their clients was whirling steadily with little monitoring as auditors and their clients got cozier and cozier. Audit firms began agitating for less restrictive independence rules and waged pitched battles against the SEC on behalf of client causes as well as their own industry's. Audit firms lobbying on behalf of clients is against SEC rules.

The franchising solution did put a big stick in the hands of the people. But it was never used, until the Andersen case. Convicting Andersen of a felony meant that the firm lost its SEC registration status, its franchise, and so could never again engage in public auditing. Public audits had decreased as a proportion of the firm's business over the course of time. For years, public audits had been a commodity, business to be won as the lowest bidder or used as a loss leader to sell other consulting services. Even though the firm might possibly have survived financially through revenues from its other services, losing the right to conduct public audits put a stain on the firm's reputation from which the majority of partners believed it could not recover. As events unfolded, it was also clearly possible that the firm would be bankrupted by investor litigation.

The firm vigorously fought the criminal felony indictment, and then tried desperately to settle with the DOJ to preempt the indictment. It failed. The U.S. firm of Andersen was indicted on one felony count of obstruction of justice. The brief indictment, unsealed on March 7, 2002, lays out the situation clearly. It is presented in its entirety at the end of this chapter.

Andersen was one of the world's biggest audit firms, known at the time as the Big Five, and now, the Final Four. The firm's partnership structure was complex. Partners in each country in which the firm operated belonged to a country-specific partnership. The country-specific partnerships were rolled up to a worldwide partnership agreement in which nearly 3,000 partners participated.[7] There were two classes of partners: those belonging only to a country-specific partnership and those belonging to the worldwide partnership, which was highest status.

Technically, the DOJ only indicted the U.S. partnership, which represented 28,000 employees. The worldwide partnership consisted of 85,000 employees, with 350 offices in 84 countries, serving 100,000 clients, including governments and multinational corporations. The firm's former competitors shared the $9 billion annual revenue that had once gone to Andersen. Andersen's demise was a global event of considerable import, and for its competitors, it was a windfall.

Even before the U.S. firm was indicted, the loss of its reputation as American business scandals unfolded caused many non-U.S. partners to remove themselves from the worldwide partnership. Most often, this was done by switching their allegiance to another of the major U.S. accounting firms operating in their country. Some non-U.S. partners were reluctant to sever their relations and hung on till the indictment. As the scandal was unfolding, Andersen was revealed as an auditor not just of Enron, but also of WorldCom, Quest Communications, Inc., and Global Crossing. A number of clients tried to weather the storm and not change auditors, which can be a big nuisance, but finally, most had to defect for the sake of their own reputations.

When the indictment was filed in March 2002, the remaining partners did not hesitate to do the inevitable and began closing down the firm. The indictment alone put them out of business, and they knew it. By the time the jury rendered a guilty verdict in mid-June, the firm was down to only about 3,000 people, and as of this book's writing, 200 remain to finish it off.

At the first suggestion of a criminal indictment, Andersen partners and their attorneys told the DOJ that indicting the firm would "kill" it. Andersen's partner in charge of the entertainment industry organized demonstrations in which local office personnel marched on state capitols and in Washington, D.C. It is reported that Michael Chertoff, the DOJ attorney in charge of the Andersen case, now head of Homeland Security, was only irritated by what he considered to be defense attorney histrionics and public relations efforts to use the media to put pressure on his office.

Andersen did attempt to try the case in the court of public opinion, and had some strong advocates, such as Lou Dobbs, who editorialized extensively in the firm's favor on his television news program. Dobbs also invited representatives of the firm onto his show to make their case directly to the public. Andersen charged publicly that the DOJ was abusing its power and was about to effectively execute the entire firm for the criminal actions of a small number of its members.

This only made Chertoff more furious. Chertoff, who made his reputation prosecuting mobsters, considered Andersen the worst kind of offender—a recidivist. From Chertoff's perspective, Andersen had a string of highly publicized bad audits through the 1980s, including a major fraud case, Waste Management, Inc. Among other things, Waste Management was assigning garbage trucks 40+ years in asset lifespan, then claiming they were worth $30,000, when they were realistically worth $12,000. How could an auditor miss that one? The SEC and the courts didn't think an auditor could or should miss that one, and the firm had signed a cease and desist order just as Enron was erupting. Technically, in the Enron case, Andersen could be guilty of violating that cease and desist order along with any violations stemming from Enron (then the other cases).

Afterward, when the firm essentially was no more, some former partners speculated that Michael Chertoff may truly not have comprehended that the ultimate consequence of the indictment alone would be to put the firm out of business entirely. Afterward, the firm was often characterized by former employees as "murdered." Recently, an article authored by a former member of the firm, published in *Critical Perspectives on Accounting* was titled, "Rush to judgment: the lynching of Arthur Andersen & Co."[8] Andersen's appeal was heard by the Supreme Court in May 2005 because lower appeals courts upheld the guilty verdict. Even though a reversal of the verdict would not bring back the firm, it would restore some of its reputation for posterity. A reversal might also make a difference in the outcome of dozens of lawsuits that are still outstanding.

At the end, the firm reverted to its basic value system, from which it had drifted over the course of several decades, as did the profession. Only a small portion of the partners who closed down the firm saved themselves before doing their utmost to ensure that the lower-level members of the firm were taken care of first. A vast majority of the partners gave dignity to the last days of the firm's existence by taking care of employees and clients first, making no attempt to weasel out of obligations such as office space leases and using all the firm's assets to pay fines and claims of litigants adjudged by authorities. All this was done in an orderly fashion with astonishing speed.

Had it not been for the trend among professional partnerships toward becoming Limited Liability Partnerships, which the firm followed, individual partners' personal assets would also have been sacrificed. Professional partnerships are intended to put partners at considerable risk. Until the adoption of a Limited Liability Partnership structure, individual partners' personal assets would be subject to claims on a partnership. Perhaps if that had still been true, people would have been more careful. Most professional partnerships in the U.S. have adopted the more protective Limited Liability Partnership form, which drifted across the Atlantic after becoming established in Europe.

The Andersen diaspora in 2002 resulted in 85,000 people going into other firms, going out on their own, or retiring. Some changed careers by going into academic, government, or corporate jobs. Those switching out of public auditing altogether had decided the changes in the profession compelled by the Sarbanes-Oxley Act would make a career in public audit firms far less lucrative and exciting. Irrespective of what happened to them, former Andersen employees are people who have learned a hard lesson and could be important assets in thinking through larger, systemic issues, and developing better oversight.

The 5,000 or so retired Andersen partners are a major resource to the American public. Retired partners lost everything in the firm's retirement account; pension checks and benefits stopped.[9] Having suffered the most, and having the perspective of change over a long period of time, most retired partners are not shy about speaking their minds in terms of where the profession, and their former firm, went wrong. We can learn as much from failure as from success, and sometimes, we can even learn more. Like Enron, Andersen "has it all" and will go down in accounting and business history as much more than a footnote. Hopefully, there is much to learn from this case, and we will make an effort to learn it.

In hindsight, one former partner said the partners lost sight of their personal risk and began behaving more like CEOs and vice presidents in corporations. As partnerships like Andersen rapidly expanded and became more complex, they did indeed become more like corporations than partnerships. Despite many internal and external structures that would appear to manage risk to protect the public interest, a significant proportion of partners were willing to circumvent these ultimately weak oversight mechanisms.

There is a striking parallel between Enron's risk management regime and Andersen's. Both had created risk-management groups staffed with specialists. Both bragged about the extent of their risk-management systems and used them to provide assurance to outsiders, especially regulators, that this provided protection from mistakes and wrongdoing. But in both cases, risk management was marginalized, effectively powerless, and easily manipulated.

In Andersen's case, a core element of the risk-management program was its *Professional Standards Group* (PSG). The PSG consisted of the firm's most talented auditors. Its charge was to analyze the most difficult accounting questions, brought to the group by its fellow partners who were conducting audit engagements. The PSG was the keeper of the Holy Grail and rendered opinions on making the often tough calls on ambiguous technical issues. A primary role of the PSG was to keep the firm and its clients out of trouble with regulators and within the bounds of law, initially both in spirit and technical compliance.

Audit partners brought their problems to the PSG and the PSG resolved them. It was custom for the audit engagement partners to follow the PSG's opinions, so it was assumed unnecessary to issue a rule to do so. If, in a rare case, an engagement partner took issue with the PSG opinion, presumably he would take it up with the PSG and serve notification of actions contrary to the PSG opinion and a rationalization of his decision. The management structure above the engagement level would adjudicate a difference of opinion between an engagement partner and the PSG. It was unthinkable that audit engagement partners would act contrary to the PSG without their fellow partners, who shared risk equally, knowing about it. Yet, that is exactly what happened in the Enron audit.

One former partner expressed a feeling of complete dismay when he found out David Duncan, Enron's lead audit partner, did not follow PSG opinions, and more importantly, that both Duncan and his immediate boss, Michael Odom, head of the firm's energy practice, had not notified the PSG of their rejection of the PSG's advice. Members of the PSG had said in no uncertain terms that the firm could not support Andrew Fastow's shenanigans—right from the get go, with Fastow's first special purpose entity scheme being roundly criticized as unthinkably riddled with conflicts of interest.

"Conflicts galore" was the opinion stated in a memo written by Carl Bass, the member of the PSG assigned to Enron. Regarding one of Fastow's bolder schemes, Bass wrote, "I did not see any way that this worked. In effect, it was heads I win, tails you lose."[10] The transaction Fastow was proposing was a sham and violated accounting rules, and Bass called him on it. Apparently, Duncan and Odom not only ignored Bass's opinion, but "inaccurately wrote that Bass and others had agreed"[11] with their decision to go along with Fastow's scheme. It later came out that Enron people were making claims that Andersen had blessed accounting treatments without Andersen having ever been consulted.

Carl Bass became a thorn in Fastow's side, so he demanded that Andersen remove him from Enron's account activities. It had always been an important matter of independence that auditors not cow-tow to client requests to remove partners and managers who didn't see things their way. At the time of Enron's removal request, Andersen was making over half of its $52 million in annual Enron fees from consulting services. The firm was projecting that Enron would soon become a $100 million a year account, with all the growth coming from consulting.

Andersen removed Carl Bass from the Enron account in March 2001. He and fellow members of the PSG were furious and they said so. It was a shocking thing to do. It was also very symbolic. When the PSG was first established, the office of the head of the group was just steps away from the CEO of the firm's office. By 2001, the PSG was seven layers down in the Andersen organization. It was a politically difficult slog for a PSG member to get in front of the CEO of the firm, Joseph Berardino. There was a very similar situation in Enron, where its touted risk management group was effectively a toothless tiger at the margins of power.

The accounting profession, like others, has a self-regulatory system, and even before Enron, some accounting professionals and outside critics believed that system had failed.[12] At a professional conference in November 2000, one panel participant, Donald J. Kirk, a member of the Public Oversight Board, stated

> ...I believe we've been through a critical phase in the last two years involving a very significant failure in self-regulation—the failure to police compliance with our own rules on independence dealing with financial interest in clients. Our own policing of those regulations fell far short of what was necessary.[13]

Over time, big accounting firms became increasingly like the businesses they audited—they went corporate. Even though there were no outside investors to please quarter-to-quarter, and Wall Street wouldn't dare ask partners about the firm's financial matters, the big accounting firms began restructuring using the same models and approaches that became popular in corporations. Some consulting partners in big firms began considering the prospects of taking their consulting businesses public. IPOs were hot and generating windfalls of cash.

Perhaps most importantly, large audit firms adopted and implemented the latest corporate notions about public relations, sales, marketing, and corporate communications. This was one of the bigger nails in Andersen's coffin. In 1972, the Federal Trade Commission lifted the ban on soliciting business that had applied to the accounting profession. (Attorneys, doctors, and dentists were all similarly banned until the 1970s.) Accountants could not advertise or directly ask anyone for their business. The ban was put in place 50 years earlier over concerns that the cutthroat competition among accountants at the time was bound to compromise audits. Now, 30 years after lifting the ban, it would seem we have re-discovered the reason to have it.

Public audit firms became sales organizations oriented toward marketing their consulting services, often using the audit business as a loss leader. In Andersen, the old and new styles of partners were labeled the Merchants and the Samurai. By the 1990s, the Samurai clearly ruled within Andersen. Harvey Kapnick, who had been head of the firm between 1970 and 1979, was a vocal critic of the direction the firm was headed during his retirement. Kapnick "...believed that the dilution of standards at his beloved firm could be traced to the rise of the auditor-salesmen and the poisoning effect its drive for profits had on Andersen's famous independence."[14]

Accounting firms were both creating and following fads in corporations. For example, public accounting firms were certainly major players in developing the business re-engineering, enterprise IT systems, financial engineering, and structured financing fads of the 1990s. Public accounting firms were paid big fees to help companies like Enron do mergers and acquisitions, restructure operations, set up special purpose entities, use off-shore financial structures and business registrations to best effect and for greatest tax advantage. Big public accounting firms are also responsible for developing many of the computer systems that run many of the major corporations and governmental entities. Andersen became the largest computer consulting firm in the world in the early 1970s. It was Andersen that designed and installed EDGAR, the public corporation financial reporting system used by the SEC.

During the past 30 years, the major public audit firms have come to be about much more than just doing the public's audits. All sorts of business, management, and information technology consulting were bringing in most of the fees by the 1990s, far overshadowing public audit revenue. In 2000, the Standard & Poor 500 companies reported paying $3.7 billion in non-audit fees to auditing firms while paying only $1.2 billion in audit fees.

In one case, Sprint Corp. paid Ernst & Young $64 million for consulting and only $2.5 million for its audit. Arthur Levitt, chairman of the SEC at the time, remarked, "I have to wonder if any individual auditor, working on a $2.5 million audit contract, would have the guts to stand up to a CFO and question a dubious number in the books, thus possibly jeopardizing $64 million in business for the firm's consultants."[15] Levitt tried, and failed, to use the study to make the case for restricting public audit firms' consulting activities.

In 2002, the Sarbanes-Oxley Act finally prohibited auditors from doing non-audit-related consulting work for audit clients. A problem that had clearly been growing alarmingly for decades was resolved, but it took colossal business failures, billions in losses, and weeks of bad press for politicians to get it done.

Within the profession, some expressed concerns about the degree of cozy entanglement auditors had grown to have with clients. Conflicts of interest were growing alarmingly over the course of decades and intensified during the 1990s. The SEC had regularly raised these issues, and efforts had been made over the years to get at the systemic cause—the proliferation of non-audit consulting to audit clients. Each time the SEC made a move to deal with this most serious conflict of interest in the audit profession, it was beaten back, sometimes viciously.[16]

The relationship between the big accounting firms, like Andersen, and the SEC grew contentious. Firms increasingly aligned themselves with clients on major accounting issues, such as whether or not employee stock options should be treated as expenses on corporate balance sheets. Firms acted as allies for corporations by spending heavily on political campaign contributions and lobbying politicians to take positions favorable to their corporate clients. They helped argue the corporate case for or against legislation and regulations by rendering professional opinions for large fees.

Public audit firms like Andersen were expanding by setting the same kinds of growth targets expected by Wall Street of public corporations, and this produced the same pressure-filled environment found in the corporate cases of failure. Some firms put partners into Management-By-Objectives programs with large sales targets, and these programs were tied to individual bonus compensation and promotion. For a little while, this spurred growth, but as these approaches played out the reserves they initially tapped within a few years, partners described the destructive effects of these programs as becoming unbearably unrealistic and stressful. In one case, partners in one office who did not buy into or achieve targets were threatened with being "counseled out." Many did resign, "observing that public accounting had increasingly become 'a young man's business' in which only the young think they can 'do twenty percent more every year.'"[17]

Partners had always effectively been the sales force of their firms, but their sales role became increasingly central; good sales skills were valued over good technical expertise. Like many corporations, Andersen adopted the popular Client Service Team model for large accounts, such as Enron. Ideally, the team would coordinate delivery of all the various services performed for the client.

The Enron Client Service Team included a marketing staff person with whom David Duncan had special meetings to cook up sales strategies to sell more services into Enron. A lot of Andersen staff's bonuses, indeed, their very careers, were riding on Enron. It was the firm's second largest client, and more importantly, was a trophy client getting a lot of positive press. Losing Enron's fees would not be a financial crisis for the firm, but losing the cachet of being Enron's auditor would be a PR blow.

In 1989, Richard Measelle became head of the Arthur Andersen business unit when the firm restructured to make Andersen Consulting a more autonomous entity. Arthur Andersen consisted of the traditional audit, tax, and accounting practices, along with offering some consulting services. The consulting services to be offered by Arthur Andersen became a source of bitter contention with Andersen Consulting partners, and the partnership agreement between the two entities was officially dissolved in 2000. Measelle was described as behaving like a corporate CEO in terms of style and initiatives. Not all partners were comfortable with his leadership. In Andersen's case, each partner had an equal vote on significant matters, such as who would be their CEO. Not all partners might have been comfortable with Measelle, but a significant portion must have been comfortable because he was elected.

Under the reign of Measelle as CEO, the Partner Purge of 1992 occurred.[18] Measelle directed every office to undergo a performance review based on the yearly number of billable hours the partners supervised. The plan assumed that each partner should handle about 20,000 hours of work per year. If an office billed 100,000 hours and had 10 partners, that was five too many, and they had to go. Low individual performers were asked to leave or retire. Measelle justified the actions, saying, "The firm and its competitors were only facing up to the fact that they were not immune to the laws of economics."[19]

The ruthless purge was unprecedented. Partners in firms were much like academics with tenure. At Andersen, it took a two-thirds vote to oust a partner, including David Duncan when the time came. Virtually all the partners in the firm had never worked anywhere else. To them leaving the firm that they "loved"[20] was tantamount to leaving one's wife and family.

Many of the old guard within the firm did not believe in the new sales orientation and were not prepared to leave without a fight. One senior partner who was told to purge said, "I thought their arithmetic was a rather simplistic way of looking at things, and I told them so."[21] The purge eliminated many partners with strong technical skills and older, more experienced partners. The Purge of 1992 destabilized the partnership by elevating economic insecurity among partners, and that would prove fatal.

In the next chapter, we explore the Andersen case further as we discuss some of the major outstanding issues in the audit profession. The four remaining large audit firms are still being linked to business scandals despite the lessons many believed making an example of Andersen would teach.

Supreme Court Overturns Andersen's Conviction

On May 31, 2005, as this book was going to press, the U.S. Supreme Court handed down its decision to overturn the 2002 felony conviction of Arthur Andersen. The decision hinged on a technicality and leaves the door open for the Department of Justice to retry the case. An addendum at the back of the book (see page 249) discusses this turn of events.

INDICTMENT FILED: MARCH 7, 2002

UNITED STATES DISTRICT COURT

SOUTHERN DISTRICT OF TEXAS

UNITED STATES OF AMERICA,

against –

ARTHUR ANDERSEN, LLP,

        Defendant.

THE GRAND JURY CHARGES:

I.   ANDERSEN AND ENRON

1.   ARTHUR ANDERSEN, LLP ("ANDERSEN"), is a partnership that performs, among other things, accounting and consulting services for clients that operate businesses throughout the United States and the world. ANDERSEN is one of the so-called "Big Five" accounting firms in the United States. ANDERSEN has its headquarters in Chicago, Illinois, and maintains offices throughout the world, including in Houston, Texas.

2.   Enron Corp. ("Enron") was an Oregon corporation with its principal place of business in Houston, Texas. For most of 2001, Enron was considered the seventh largest corporation in the United States based on its reported revenues. In the previous ten years, Enron had evolved from a regional natural gas provider to, among other things, a trader of natural gas, electricity and other commodities, with retail operations in energy and other products.

3.   For the past 16 years, up until it filed for bankruptcy in December 2001, Enron retained ANDERSEN to be its auditor. Enron was one of ANDERSEN's largest clients worldwide, and became ANDERSEN's largest client in ANDERSEN's Gulf Coast region. ANDERSEN earned tens of millions of dollars from Enron in annual auditing and other fees.

4.   ANDERSEN performed both internal and external auditing work for Enron mainly in Houston, Texas. ANDERSEN established within Enron's offices in Houston a work space for the ANDERSEN team that had primary responsibility for performing audit work for Enron. In addition to Houston, ANDERSEN personnel performed work for Enron in, among other locations, Chicago, Illinois, Portland, Oregon, and London, England.

II.   THE ANTICIPATION OF LITIGATION AGAINST ENRON AND
      ANDERSEN

5.   In the summer and fall of 2001, a series of significant developments led
      to ANDERSEN's foreseeing imminent civil litigation against, and gov-
      ernment investigations of, Enron and ANDERSEN.

6.   On or about October 16, 2001, Enron issued a press release announcing
      a $618 million net loss for the third quarter of 2001. That same day, but
      not as part of the press release, Enron announced to analysts that it
      would reduce shareholder equity by approximately $1.2 billion.
      The market reacted immediately and the stock price of Enron shares
      plummeted.

7.   The Securities and Exchange Commission ("SEC"), which investigates
      possible violations of the federal securities laws, opened an inquiry into
      Enron the very next day, requesting in writing information from Enron.

8.   In addition to the negative financial information disclosed by Enron to
      the public and to analysts on October 16, 2001, ANDERSEN was aware
      by this time of additional significant facts unknown to the public.

      • The approximately $1.2 billion reduction in shareholder equity
        disclosed to analysts on October 16, 2001, was necessitated by
        ANDERSEN and Enron having previously improperly categorized
        hundreds of millions of dollars as an increase, rather than a
        decrease, to Enron shareholder equity.

      • The Enron October 16, 2001, press release characterized numerous
        charges against income for the third quarter as "non-recurring" even
        though ANDERSEN believe the company did not have a basis for
        concluding that the charges would in fact be non-recurring. Indeed,
        ANDERSEN advised Enron against using that term, and document-
        ed its objections internally in the event of litigation, but did not
        report its objections or otherwise take steps to cure the public
        statement.

      • ANDERSEN was put on direct notice of the allegations of Sherron
        Watkins, a current Enron employee and former ANDERSEN
        employee, regarding possible fraud and other improprieties at
        Enron, and in particular, Enron's use of off-balance-sheet "special
        purpose entities" that enabled the company to camouflage the true
        financial condition of the company. Watkins had reported her con-
        cerns to a partner at ANDERSEN, who thereafter disseminated them
        within ANDERSEN, including to the team working on the Enron
        audit. In addition, the team had received warnings about possible
        undisclosed side-agreements at Enron.

- The ANDERSEN team handling the Enron audit directly contravened the accounting methodology approved by ANDERSEN's own specialists working in its Professional Standards Group. In opposition to the views of its own experts, the ANDERSEN auditors had advised Enron in the spring of 2001 that it could use a favorable accounting method for its "special purpose entities."

- In 2000, an internal review conducted by senior management within ANDERSEN evaluated the ANDERSEN team assigned to audit Enron and rated the team as only a "2" on a scale of one to five, with five being the highest rating.

- On or about October 9, 2001, correctly anticipating litigation and government investigations, ANDERSEN, which had an internal department of lawyers for routine legal matters, retained an experienced New York law firm to handle future Enron-related litigation.

III.   THE WHOLESALE DESTRUCTION OF DOCUMENTS BY ANDERSEN

9.   By Friday, October 19, 2001, Enron alerted the ANDERSEN audit team that the SEC had begun an inquiry regarding the Enron "special purpose entities" and the involvement of Enron's Chief Financial Officer. The next morning, an emergency conference call among high-level ANDERSEN management was convened to address the SEC inquiry. During the call, it was decided that documentation that could assist Enron in responding to the SEC was to be assembled by the ANDERSEN auditors.

10.   After spending Monday, October 22, 2001 at Enron, ANDERSEN partners assigned to the Enron engagement team launched on October 23, 2001, a wholesale destruction of documents at ANDERSEN's offices in Houston, Texas. ANDERSEN personnel were called to urgent and mandatory meetings. Instead of being advised to preserve documentation so as to assist Enron and the SEC, ANDERSEN employees on the Enron engagement team were instructed by ANDERSEN partners and others to destroy immediately documentation relating to Enron, and told to work overtime if necessary to accomplish the destruction. During the next few weeks, an unparalleled initiative was undertaken to shred physical documentations and delete computer files. Tons of paper relating to the Enron audit were promptly shredded as part of the orchestrated document destruction. The shredder at the ANDERSEN office at the Enron building was used virtually constantly and, to handle the overload, dozens of large trunks filled with Enron documents were sent to ANDERSEN's main Houston office to be shredded. A systematic

effort was also undertaken and carried out to purge the computer hard-drives and email system of Enron-related files.

11.   In addition to shredding and deleting documents in Houston, Texas, instructions were given to ANDERSEN personnel working on Enron audit matters in Portland, Oregon, Chicago, Illinois and London, England, to make sure that Enron documents were destroyed there as well. Indeed, in London, a coordinated effort by ANDERSEN partners and others, similar to the initiative undertaken in Houston, was put into place to destroy Enron-related documents within days of notice of the SEC inquiry. Enron-related documents were destroyed by ANDERSEN partners in Chicago.

12.   On or about November 8, 2001, the SEC served ANDERSEN with the anticipated subpoena relating to its work for Enron. In response, members of the ANDERSEN team on the Enron audit were alerted finally that there could be "no more shredding" because the firm had been "officially served" for documents.

THE CHARGE: OBSTRUCTION OF JUSTICE

13.   On or about and between October 10, 2001, and November 9, 2001, within the Southern district of Texas and elsewhere, including Chicago, Illinois, Portland, Oregon, and London, England, ANDERSEN, through its partners and others, did knowingly, intentionally and corruptly persuade and attempt to persuade other persons, to wit: ANDERSEN employees, with intent to cause and induce such persons to (a) withhold records, documents and other objects from official proceedings, namely: regulatory and criminal proceedings and investigations, and (b) alter, destroy, mutilate and conceal objects with intent to impair the objects' integrity and availability for use in such official proceedings.

6

AUDITING THE PUBLIC'S AUDITORS

P ublic auditing has to be fixable. Public auditing is *the linchpin* of our enterprise system. It is supposed to keep companies honest in how they do their accounting and reporting, safeguarding the public's interest in terms of both investing and taxation. Public auditing is important to public corporations as well as governmental entities required to be publicly audited. Its role should make the financials more than transparent. Auditors should also be in a position to alert management, the board, and investors to unexpected consequences of decisions that have been implemented, sometimes hastily.

An auditor's seal of approval assures the shareholder that the numbers are real and not an infomercial, not PR or a marketing tool. It also assures citizens that taxpayer money is not being misappropriated, embezzled, or squandered. The case of Andersen illustrates many of the issues we take up in this chapter. Andersen, once a leader in the industry, the gold standard, is now a cautionary tale.

All the large public auditing firms, and especially Arthur Andersen, got into the business of designing and installing sophisticated corporate and government information-technology–based financial management systems and were handsomely paid to do so. Arthur Andersen developed the first computer business application in the 1950s—a payroll system for General Electric. IBM's founder, Thomas J. Watson, had predicted the business market for IBM's new computer to be five units before Andersen demonstrated its potential.

While many business and government information technology systems are state-of-the-art, some even leading edge, or as they sometimes would have said at Andersen, bleeding edge, it is clear they don't work very well to prevent abuse or detect fraud. It is up to humans to perform qualitative oversight. But, we don't train auditors well enough to attend to telltale signs and catch whiffs of stench beneath the surface.

Arthur Andersen, the man who founded the firm in 1913, exhorted his staff to get the facts behind the figures, and trained them to do so. The founder's motto became the firm's motto, "Think Straight, Talk Straight." But that was during the early half of the twentieth century. Arthur Andersen was a man whose integrity was beyond reproach in a time before black box electronic technology. He had founded the firm in 1913 and died in 1947 at the age of 61. Comptometers were the big productivity boon to auditors of the founder's era.

Public auditors are to have the run of the place; no hard-drive, file drawer, or office is beyond their reach. Auditors chase paper trails to their origins, including contacting customers and vendors to help them verify that transaction and financial reporting systems are honest. Auditors have certainly been creating electronic systems that help them do audits and came to rely too heavily on computer sampling techniques and doing computerized systems' tests of a client's accounting programs. Everything about the arrangements between external auditors and their clients has worked against auditor independence and initiative. Relying on computerization is one of those arrangements. It is easy to feel satisfied when a machine ticks the boxes for you and provides convenient evidence that an auditor did his job because he hit the start button on a computer program.

Auditors are too reluctant to follow up on, much less seek out, qualitative indicators that something is not quite right. Qualitative techniques need to be incorporated into audit practices more extensively—there needs to be more "smell" testing. One well-known businessman in Houston steadfastly refused to invest in Enron because he said it didn't pass his smell test. If he smelled something fishy, it is hard to imagine how auditors with full access to Enron's offices and books didn't get a whiff. At peak times, there were as many as 100 Andersen professionals occupying office space inside the Enron building, working cheek-by-jowl with Enron staff.

Price pressures on audits have contributed to heavy reliance on running some sophisticated computer programs to test the client's computer systems—a bare bones approach. It has become clear that many corporations were spending a laughable amount on their audits by the end of the 1990s. Some at the SEC were beginning to suggest that low audit fees were a serious concern.

Auditors are somewhat loath to act as spies for the public, although that is clearly their role. Auditors are also reluctant to make waves that could send the clients out shopping for a new auditor more amenable to seeing things their way.

Auditors are also conscious of a serious responsibility to balance the possible consequences to the health of a company against any actions they might take. If an auditor doesn't give a clean opinion on the state of a client's books, or if a firm walks away from a client's business, eyebrows go up at the SEC and in the markets. An auditor's opinion letter can affect share prices and launch investigations.

To meet the challenge of balancing their obligation to protect the public interest against their obligations to clients, auditors usually first try to work with a client to "cure" the books of any ills discovered by an audit. Efforts are made to minimize the damage to a company that restatements or public announcements of accounting problems can cause. Unfortunately, these efforts were taken to the level of covering up in some cases, such as Waste Management.

Audit firms were also thinking of their own risks in these situations and their own profitability. Sometimes, it takes threats to go to the SEC to get a client in line with an audit firm's recommendations for a cure, and if a rogue auditor is found conspiring with clients to cook books, audit firms are expected to self-report to the SEC. Audit firms did sometimes report finding what those in the industry called black-hatted CPAs, those within their ranks willing to bend or break the rules. Too often, this move was resisted until it became incredibly obvious that one of their own conspired with a client to commit fraud or mislead investors, was negligent, or just plain incompetent. Andersen went through the motions of self-reporting in the Enron case after partners realized that the media would make Andersen auditors' part in the scandal obvious.

Auditors are inspectors ethically obliged to blow the whistle. Unlike attorneys, who claim to have issues with reporting wrongdoing tied to client privilege, auditors' clients have no such privilege. Auditors are representatives of investors and investors have every right to know if a company is keeping its books honest. Honest and transparent books are essential for making good investment decisions and maintaining trust in America's market system.

Auditors have long described members of the profession in terms of "white hats" and "black hats." Within the population of over three hundred thousand members of the *American Institute of Certified Public Accountants* (AICPA), we can assume that some are incompetent, negligent, corrupt, even criminal black-hatted CPAs. The profession's self-regulation regime is supposed to make efforts to screen out unsuitable candidates, ensure that CPAs stay professionally current, and deal with offenders by suspending or revoking licenses. The SEC is responsible for ensuring the efficacy of the self-regulatory system of the accounting profession, and civil and criminal courts have jurisdiction over those with the blackest hats.

While certainly the majority of auditors wear white hats, it would seem too many hats were becoming dingy or turning black. Getting mixed up with Enron's outlaw band proved Andersen's downfall.

Andersen's Partner Purge of 1992 disproportionately got rid of auditors with white hats who would stick to their guns on tough issues and were not awestruck by clients. One of the partners culled in the Purge was Mike Gagel, who always saw his responsibility as being "to the shareholders, not the management."[1] Gagel, who had always seen his profession as a "higher calling," was told bluntly that "the decision had been made" that he would retire.[2] Gagel was only 50 and had never considered an early retirement.

At his retirement party a few months after he was told to retire, Gagel's staff presented him with a framed caricature: It showed him passing through Andersen's trademark wooden doors for the last time, briefcase in hand and a white cowboy hat perched above his eyeglasses. 'Mike Gagel,' the caption read, 'One of the good guys.'"[3]

There are plenty of white hats among the ranks of retired auditors. Many of Andersen's own retirees are vocal critics of the firm and the profession. Some were among the critics who expressed alarm at what was happening under the guise of the "new economy." Everyone knew a bubble was developing and it was clear to many that unscrupulous accounting was becoming standard practice. Auditors in white hats apparently were outnumbered and outgunned not just by CEOs and CFOs standing to make millions of dollars in personal bonuses and stock options, but by their own gang members who were putting self-interest above professional ethics.

Clearly, auditors were too much under the thumb of Mythic CEOs and had no clear channel of communication directly into boards of directors. The Sarbanes-Oxley Act has made significant changes directed at the problem. It is now the responsibility of the board of directors' audit committee to hire or fire the auditors. Sarbanes-Oxley also mandates that auditors have direct communication with the board without the CEO's presence. The change in communication channels for auditors could be very meaningful, if the CEO doesn't control and manipulate the board. In many corporations, that is still a big "if."

Large, sophisticated computer systems process millions of transactions with lightening speed, but these systems have significant limitations. Even the best forensic systems are currently reactive by nature. Business systems capture history to which forensic techniques can be applied, but those applications can be circumvented. Forensics is a predator-prey game. Those hunting down fraud and abuse are routinely out-foxed and have to add new tactics for catching on faster next time.

Many within the accounting profession have been agitating for more training in forensics in college programs and more forensics built into the audit through standards and practice changes. These ideas have been successfully resisted by others in the profession. Many in the accounting industry did not want to take more responsibility for finding fraud and abuse.

Because investor litigation began naming audit firms in legal actions charging fraud and negligence in the 1970s, the accounting industry has used "it's not our job" as a primary defense. Based on the premise that auditors could be fooled by a determined management, auditors constructed elaborate procedures to prove they were fooled in case of a lawsuit. Risk management in audit firms was largely oriented toward managing the risk of lawsuits by focusing on plausible deniability protections for audit firms. This orientation is hardly likely to encourage auditors to be alert to early warning signs.

While it is laudable that the American system permits legal remedies in the case of negligence or conspiracy in fraud on the part of public auditors, the reaction of public auditors to civil and criminal liabilities has been legalistic posturing. On the advice of attorneys, firms began embedding legal defenses in audits. Always conscious of preserving work papers related to audits, auditors had tended to err on the side of saving and retaining documents beyond regulatory requirements. As litigation became more of a risk, document retention and destruction policies shifted toward doing the minimum. The profession also carefully circumscribed the scope of audit activities to limit legal vulnerabilities. Risk management in audit firms was directed as much, if not more, toward managing legal risks as toward ensuring honest audits.

One of the partners who had been found culpable in Andersen's Waste Management, Inc., audit failure, Robert Kutsenda, was barred from doing audits for one year.[4] Because it had become a point of principle to "stand behind" professionals in case of legal troubles, partners who were barred from practice in the course of lawsuits were not fired. Instead, some actually seemed to thrive; one, Dick Measelle, even went on to become CEO of the firm. Because he couldn't be assigned to audits, Kutsenda was given the position of being the partner in charge of the firm's global risk management. It's easy to see the logic of putting someone who has supposedly learned the hard way in charge of preventing future troubles. Unfortunately, the lessons taken were more along the lines of legalistic defensive tactics than improving audits.

Under the aegis of Kutsenda, the risk management group promulgated a new Document Retention Policy, which had been issued just prior to the Enron debacle. Considering how often audit firms encountered difficulty defending themselves because of stray documents and hand-written notes, the new policy instructed Andersen personnel to destroy any documents not directly related to supporting the firm's audit opinion. This was the policy Andersen's in-house lawyer, Nancy Temple, was referring to in her email to David Duncan, which triggered the destruction of over two tons of paper and thousands of electronic files.

It was later found that Duncan had not destroyed key documents and the firm helped recreate anything required for investigations. The jury did not convict Andersen of obstruction of justice based on any documents that had been destroyed. Instead, the firm was convicted on the basis of an email from Temple to Duncan that suggested an after-the-fact wording change in a message to Enron from David Duncan, and she asked that her name be removed from the distribution list of this critical email. To the jury, this smacked of cover-up and led to the guilty verdict. For all the millions of dollars spent on risk management, it was again a single stray document that hoisted the firm by its own petard.

If the resources that Andersen, and the accounting profession, has plowed into defensive tactics and education programs directed at explaining that fraud and abuse detection is not their job had been invested in learning from mistakes and developing better forensics, the 1990s might have been a different story. If the enforcement apparatus had done more than slap the wrists of audit firms in SEC and criminal cases, the 1980s and the 1990s might have been a different story. Despite the profound seriousness of audit failures steadily piling up at the SEC and in the court system, firms and individual auditors are routinely allowed to settle cases "without admitting or denying" the charges. The self-regulatory apparatus that has control over CPA licensing almost never revokes a CPA's license. A CPA found culpable in civil or criminal proceedings might, at most, have their license suspended for one, three, or five years.

The fines levied on firms and individual CPAs were easily affordable. Just as Enron was melting down, Andersen was paying the largest fine levied against an auditor by the SEC to date—$7 million for the Waste Management, Inc. case. It wasn't the fines that were a problem for firms; it was the multi-million-dollar settlements in investor lawsuits that were a problem. Professional liability insurance costs went the way of other professions—skyrocketing. The big firms got together and formed their own insurance consortium to cope with this financial exposure. It was bankrupted by Andersen's cases. Regulators weren't putting serious pressure on firms, but investors sure were. America's public protection laws giving investors standing in courts are all that stood between a massive failure and a complete breakdown in the American market system.

After an $80 million civil litigation settlement in 1980, Andersen's risk management program included ranking clients on their potential to go bankrupt. It became an annual routine to do risk assessments on clients to determine whether or not to continue doing their audits. Enron was in Andersen's highest risk category.

In February 2001, 14 partners performed the annual risk assessment for Enron and concluded that Enron should be kept as a client provided that certain actions were undertaken to reduce Andersen's risk. The risk assessment group relied on David Duncan's evaluation of Enron, and it was clear later that Duncan had severely distorted the Enron situation. The risk assessment concluded there was still high risk to the firm, but that it was "intelligent gambling" on Enron's part.

Most shocking of all are the old tricks that corporations were using to dupe auditors. WorldCom, for example, was burying its basic operating expenses in capital accounts, which made the company look far more cost effective in its operations than it was. The ripple effect of WorldCom's bogus operating cost numbers was enormous. Competitors made ever-more eviscerating cuts in their own operations trying to match WorldCom's performance. Heads of competing companies expressed their profound dismay at realizing what they had done to their own companies in their race to keep up with WorldCom.[5] The fraud perpetrated by WorldCom is one of the oldest tricks in the book, yet it was not detected by internal or external auditors.

Many believe that by the 1990s auditors were simply too naïve or just in over their heads. One executive described the situation by using an example of an auditor requesting contact information for a random sample of the company's clients. Auditors are expected to contact a sample of customers and vendors in the course of an audit and use sophisticated sampling programs to identify candidates for thorough follow-up. The executive recounted what happened when the auditor asked for the contact information in order to conduct interviews with clients. The auditor was stalled. Company executives said they would need time to provide the information and used the delay to call the clients on the auditor's list. Clients were offered special services and deals in exchange for giving the auditor a glowing report.

By the 1990s, the power and prestige of auditors had waned. Senior executives who were counterparts to auditors in all the large bankruptcies were multimillionaires and celebrities. By comparison, the power and prestige of partners in major accounting firms was greatly diminished. Joseph Berardino, CEO of Andersen's worldwide partnership, was reported to make about $3 million a year, a pittance in the 1990s. David Duncan, the lead partner on the Enron account, was reported to have made $600,000 a year in contrast to his direct counterpart, Enron's chief accounting officer, Richard Causey, who exercised over $13 million just in stock options between October 1998 and November 2001. Gone were the days when auditors were feared and respected.

Andersen staff who worked on the Enron audit are described as geeks excited to be invited to a cool frat party.[6] But beyond that, Enron was a bully, and Andersen's auditors were hardly part of the in crowd. The young Turks who rose to power in Enron bullied and cheated fellow employees, those in the old-guard within Enron. They bullied competitors, regulators, analysts, bankers and attorneys, and even their own customers.

One account of Enron's bullying tactics describes how an Andersen auditor was held hostage in a conference room by Enron employees.[7] After the Andersen auditor entered the room, a chair was slid under the door and he was told, not so jokingly, that no one would leave the room until Enron got an opinion letter from him. The opinion letter meant $270 million in tax credits for Enron. "...Enron employees threatened, cajoled, and badgered the Andersen employee...the Andersen auditor, thoroughly upset by the heavy-handed tactics, agreed to produce the letter."[8]

Auditors might well have been naïve, but there are limits to this explanation given the fact that young Andersen staff at Enron was referring to Enron's accounting as "shambolic."[9] Clearly some of Andersen's peoples' noses were working.

During the 1990s, youth ruled. Andersen and Enron were no different than many organizations. Older workers were pushed out of positions of authority and the reins of business were going into the hands of ever-younger, more highly educated youths. David Duncan was made lead partner on one of the firm's largest and riskiest engagements at the age of 37. He was given the assignment in part because he was the same age as his client counterpart, Richard Causey, who was the chief accounting officer of America's seventh largest public corporation. In hindsight, some former Andersen partners admit Duncan was too young and inexperienced to stand up to a bullying client like Enron. While the brashness and inexperience of youth doesn't explain everything that happened, it does explain some of what happened.

Andersen had always been known for giving its people a lot of responsibility early in their careers. Clients started joking that the Andersen team arrived in yellow school buses. Andersen's partners wanted very much to be considered "with it" when it came to new economy companies where teenagers and twenty-somethings were often CEOs. Tremendous fee potential existed in the 1990's gold rush and Andersen wanted its share. Enron was heavily covered in the media as the harbinger of the new economy company, and the marketing cachet to be gleaned from being Enron's auditor was incalculable, but certainly very large.

One retired Andersen partner summed up the three questions we need to be asking ourselves: Who makes the rules? Who owns the audit? How are auditors compensated?

Who makes the rules? Critics of the accounting profession say the crux of our problems lies in the fact that corporations took over the rule-making process. When the rule-making procedures were established, it was deemed fair and sensible to have public corporations be part of the process. However, this arrangement requires balance to maintain the fundamentally crucial independence of regulators.

Public corporations pay for the entities that regulate them more directly than is usually the case. Fees assessed by the SEC and contributions made to the accounting profession's rule makers were intended to pay for public company oversight. Public companies were given seats on boards of accounting rule-making bodies. Critics of this system point out the dangers of being financially dependent on the group a regulatory apparatus intends to oversee. A similar problem has surfaced in the Food and Drug Administration. The Vioxx scandal revealed the role of corporate fees paid to the FDA in corrupting its independence.

When the *Public Company Accounting Oversight Board* (PCAOB) created by the Sarbanes-Oxley Act was financially structured to rely on corporate assessments for funding, some sounded an alarm that this would just be more of the same. Jaws dropped when the first act of the five members of PCAOB was to vote their chairman a salary of $560,000 a year and set the rest of its members' salaries at $452,000 per year—salaries greater than that of the president of the United States. The head of the SEC only earns $142,500 a year. The chairman of the Federal Reserve Board, Alan Greenspan, only takes home $166,700 a year.

The PCAOB is charged with an active role in setting accounting standards and is intended to take a more proactive role in oversight. The PCAOB will audit the auditors by performing inspections. In theory, inspections will finally provide a proactive mechanism for earlier detection. Firms that audit more than 100 public companies will be inspected annually. Firms that audit 100 or fewer pubic companies must be inspected at least once every three years.

The PCAOB got off to a slow, rocky[10] start and completed its initial, admittedly limited, inspections of Final Four audit firm audits in August 2004. Inspection of about 16 audits in each of the four largest firms found "significant audit and accounting issues."[11] Nineteen companies involved in the inspection were required to restate their earnings for 2003 because of errors discovered by the PCAOB. That result is both encouraging and discouraging. Inspections did catch problems, but they also found too many problems.

William McDonough, chairman of the PCAOB, promises "tough love" for the accounting industry and believes that even though the first reports are discouraging there is only a "remote" chance that another big firm "will be found to be as poorly managed as Arthur Andersen" and have to be forced out of business.[12]

It's a bit early to tell whether the standard setting power granted the PCAOB will bring significant reform. To many, it is discouraging that the issue of accounting for all employee stock option expenses took so long to resolve. Rule making seems as cumbersome as ever, and despite some rumbling in the early days of scandal about seriously considering a shift toward principle-based standards rather than the current rule-based system in the U.S., that talk seems to have died down.

Other countries have principle-based oversight, but the U.S. has stuck to a rule-based approach. Some say corporations prefer rule-based systems, which offer more opportunities for circumvention. Americans were shocked to learn that many of the practices that misled and effectively defrauded investors were technically legal, even though they violated the spirit of the laws and regulations that were in place. America's generally accepted accounting guidelines contain over 100,000 pages of rules. America's financial scandals compromised the U.S. accounting profession's claim to have a superior system, which has stalled efforts to harmonize international accounting systems for decades. The solution to international standard setting probably lies in a system that combines principles and rules.

Who owns the audit? Before the SEC established a mandate for public companies to submit an annually audited set of financial statements, companies owned their audits. An auditor might be retained to certify a company's books in the course of developing a public offering, to value a company for sale, or for banking purposes before the SEC was established.

A story about the early days of Arthur Andersen tells a heroic tale of how the founder stood up to a client who had the firm do an audit for a prospectus. Arthur Andersen found the company was materially misstating its financial position and issued a qualified opinion to that effect. When the owner of the company demanded the firm go along with his version of his company's finances, Arthur Andersen refused, saying it was his firm's name on the opinion and he would not risk the firm's reputation on a lie. Andersen took the bold step of claiming that the audit opinion belonged to his firm, not his client. The client fired Arthur Andersen, but taking a stand served Andersen well. The firm became known as the gold standard in the industry.

With the advent of the SEC in the early 1930s, it is clearly intended that the American public owns the audit where public companies are concerned. The issue has been muddied by the fact that the companies being audited happen to pay the bill. Auditors act as public servants and are entrusted with protecting the public interest. We should be concerned that some auditors still don't "get it." A Vanderbilt University study released in October 2003 concluded that: "…audit firms under pressure from major clients bending the rules are still prone to produce inaccurate audit opinions—if they think they won't be caught."[13]

How is the auditor compensated? The fact that the company being audited hires and pays its independent auditor is a known flaw in the investor protection system. Shifting responsibility for hiring, firing, and paying auditors to the audit committee of a public company's board of directors may prove helpful, or it may prove to not be an effective enough measure for making auditors more independent. The extent of reform that would make more significant changes than this is dreaded by all concerned.

Retired Andersen partners have angrily pinpointed greed as the primary cause of the failure of the firm and the profession. As one retired partner put it, "Somehow management lost sight of its 'core' and greed destroyed what I valued as a partner for 22 years."[14]

Perhaps the most serious issue at hand is the question of how auditors are compensated by their firm. Each year, partners divvy up the profits. At Andersen, partner pay adjustments were made every two years. Partners are strongly encouraged to keep costs down and have to make investment decisions that will directly affect their compensation and the firm's future profitability. Andersen was proud to claim that the firm's partners invested about ten percent of its revenue in professional development, boasting that it had the number-one ranked training and development center. Large investments such as this directly affected partner compensation and could be contentious matters put to a vote.

Not all Andersen partners received the same amount of compensation. It depended on what they did. As mentioned, the CEO of the firm received $3 million for his role. Increasingly, as the firm shifted toward a sales orientation, partner compensation depended on salesmanship. Average partner annual compensation at Andersen jumped from

$130,000 in the early 1980s to $450,000 in 2000. In addition to annual compensation, partners built up equity in the firm, all of which they lost when the firm shut down.

Andersen partners were paid on the basis of getting credit for revenue, and a bonus system was instituted that could make for big differences among partners. Aggressive revenue and profitability targets were set for partners and were tied both to rewards and punishment threats made very real by the Partner Purge of 1992. Andersen had created a toxic compensation system that led to constant internal fighting over who got credit for revenue.

In contrast to Andersen's system of credit for revenue, PriceWater-houseCoopers had a partner compensation system in which revenue could be counted toward more than one partner's performance. At PriceWaterhouseCoopers, one partner might get credit for the sale of services and another partner would get the same amount of credit for doing the work. This was a system that could promote cooperation among partners. At Andersen, that couldn't happen. Pitched battles over who got credit for the revenue occurred with every sale that had to involve other partners. Internally, this was referred to as the "good old Arthur Andersen Fee Fuck."[15]

Throughout the 1990s, a rift grew between the Andersen Consulting partners and the Arthur Andersen partners as they squabbled over compensation and had turf battles over selling consulting services. At the beginning of the 1990s, when other big firms were merging, Andersen split its partnership into two firms—Andersen Consulting and Arthur Andersen—held together by an umbrella partnership agreement: Arthur Andersen Worldwide.

The firm's consulting division had agitated for more autonomy and parity in power with the auditors for years, and this division into two firms was the attempted solution. Hundreds of Andersen Consulting professionals turned in their CPA licenses in a gesture to make it clear to the SEC that theirs was now a separate firm and that they were not in the audit business. The SEC came to agree with that position and did not impose regulations on auditors that applied to Arthur Andersen on Andersen Consulting.

This new organizational structure created a major distraction within the partnership as acrimony grew over compensation issues. The worldwide partnership agreement called for revenue sharing between the partners of Andersen Consulting and those of Arthur Andersen. If either firm brought in more revenue than the other, the agreement called for a transfer of 15% of the difference be paid to the firm with lower revenue. The revenue transfer clause proved to be a poison pill.

An example of the effect of this clause in the worldwide partnership agreement was that Andersen Consulting partners transferred $173 million to Arthur Andersen in 1997. This amounted to an average of $150,000 from each of the 1,100 Andersen Consulting partners to Arthur Andersen. It translated to $100,000 average gain for each of the 1,700 Arthur Andersen partners. Andersen Consulting partners were known to make cracks to Arthur Andersen partners suggesting they be thanked for making it possible for the Arthur Andersen partner to buy himself a new BMW.

In 1997, the arguments between Arthur Andersen and Andersen Consulting came to a head and both firms filed with the International Court of Arbitration to dissolve the worldwide partnership that yoked them. In August 2000, the court granted the dissolution. Andersen Consulting became Accenture and changed organizational form—it is now a publicly held company registered in Bermuda. Arthur Andersen announced that it would now simply be known as "Andersen" and that its worldwide partnership structure would now be called "Andersen Worldwide."

Andersen was dealt a severe financial blow by the International Court's arbitrator, who ruled against Arthur Andersen's claim of $14.6 billion in damages, which was due under the terms of the worldwide partnership agreement. Andersen Consulting partners were only ordered to pay the $1 billion in revenue transfer payments and damages that had accrued between 1997 and 2000. When the partnership dissolution was initiated, Andersen Consulting partners began putting the revenue transfer payments into an escrow account. This had the effect of denying their Arthur Andersen counterparts access to that revenue for three years. In August 2000, Andersen partners faced a future without the contribution of revenue from Andersen Consulting or the $14.6 billion they had felt sure would be granted in the dissolution.

The turmoil of the dissolution took more than a financial toll on Andersen. Leadership was distracted and Andersen Worldwide operated with an interim CEO from 1997 until early 2001 when Joseph Berardino became CEO. Berardino had only been CEO of Andersen Worldwide for a few months when Enron blew up, and many felt he made a mistake by not letting the head of the U.S. firm deal with the charges of the SEC and the U.S. Department of Justice. Instead of trying to do damage control by making Enron a localized U.S. problem, Berardino believed the CEO should make it his problem, which he did.

Between the aggressive sales targets, a toxic revenue credit system, and the leadership and financial consequences of an acrimonious split with Andersen Consulting, there is the audit caught in the crossfire. It is no wonder Andersen had more than its share of the major failures—Enron, Qwest Communications, Inc., Global Crossing, and WorldCom.

Compensation programs within audit firms need to be made an issue for the new PCAOB as it pursues its regimen of investigations of audit firms. In light of the findings of the PCAOB's limited first investigation that there are still deep problems in the nation's audit system, compensation should move to the top of the list of issues to get resolved. Audit firms should put their compensation systems under internal review and take steps to ferret out conflicts of interest they may have built into their organizations. Business practices in general, and compensation in particular, within public accounting firms need to get considerably more public scrutiny given all the examples of continuing failure that we discuss throughout this book.

A Final Thought…Really Public Auditing

Largely because Arthur Andersen initiated government audits by offering to demonstrate their value, the American public has an extensive government audit system, with its own standards and practices. At all levels of American government, we have both internal auditors and *external public* auditors charged with performing the same function of oversight on government audits that they do for our publicly registered corporations.

It is the public audit requirements we built into the economic system that give confidence in the American market's honesty and transparency. Additionally, America's system of government auditing puts confidence behind government bonds and promises of payments. At least it did, but we cannot be so sure now.

The structures of governmental auditing largely mirror public auditing. The equivalent of the FASB is the GASB,[16] and the rest of it was largely constructed using public corporation auditing as its basic model. Accommodations for obvious differences were made as government external auditing systems and requirements were established. Independent external auditing of a government's finances is a relatively recent development intended to force transparency for the public and prevent fraud and misuse of public funds. The government also has other oversight mechanisms, such as inspector generals, citizen oversight bodies, citizen watchdog organizations, and the federal government's *General Accounting Office* (GAO), which was initially designed to be independent, not subjected to partisan pressures, and able to speak "without fear or favor" throughout successive administrations.

Among the disturbing revelations in congressional investigations this past year was that Medicare's chief actuary, Robert S. Foster, was pressured to fudge his numbers in a report to Congress giving the estimated costs for adding prescription drug benefits to Medicare. Understandably, actuaries play a major role in calculating the cost projections in the Social Security and Medicare programs. Calculating something as important as the cost of a new and very large entitlement was put in the hands of Medicare's chief actuary, and he came up with a number projecting a $534 billion cost that should have been used in the Medicare bill put before Congress for a vote. Medicare's chief actuary is required by law to provide nonpartisan counsel to legislators. He had established the $534 billion number five months before the bill was submitted to congressional debate. The bill submitted by the Bush administration contained a knowingly incorrect cost figure of $400 billion.

The bill barely passed in the House in a vote of 216 to 215. Had lawmakers known the true cost of the bill, everyone agrees it would have failed to pass on a bipartisan basis. A number of Republicans didn't like the bill as presented, especially the cost-benefit analysis of the expenditure. In the judgment of many, senior citizens did not stand to significantly gain from the program in proportion to its cost. Democrats criticized the bill on the basis of not significantly helping seniors and giving the pharmaceutical industry too much power and aid by prohibiting governmental negotiation on price and seniors from purchasing drugs in other countries with better prices. When the real cost number was revealed after the bill had passed, there was an uproar. Reports were commissioned and hearings held.

The most deeply disquieting revelation in this incident was that Medicare's chief actuary was silenced by a threat of "severe" personal consequences if he tried to get his real cost number out before congress voted. He was ordered to withhold the information, even if Congress asked for it.[17] This was the equivalent of the CEO in a publicly held company telling his public auditor what numbers would or wouldn't be used in financials filed with the SEC and expecting the audit firm to keep its mouth shut if it didn't like it and to issue a clean opinion letter anyway. This goes to the heart of a well-working public audit system by destroying auditor independence. Foster reported, "I was threatened—with my job if I released this information, particularly to members of Congress who are getting ready to vote on it."[18]

In another government-related incident, a former employee in Fannie Mae's controller department, Roger Barnes, blew the whistle on questionable accounting practices there. Fannie Mae's $9 billion financial restatement scandal reveals how much quasi-governmental entities can abuse the public trust. Similar to the public audit profession being given the franchise to perform the auditing function of the Securities and Exchange Commission, Fannie Mae has been given the mandate to ensure that as many Americans as possible have financial access to home ownership. In this arrangement, Fannie Mae is able to operate as a publicly traded company, listed on the stock exchange.

Fannie Mae, and its not-quite-so-evil twin, Freddie Mac, which also recently experienced troubles, are unique, government-chartered mortgage-finance companies. Freddie Mac and Fannie Mae's regulator is the *Office of Federal Housing Enterprise Oversight* (OFHEO). In an unusual twist on misleading financials, Freddie Mac got into trouble for not reporting its earnings success. Earnings were underreported in order to create "cookie jar" reserves that would smooth earnings over time, thus making Freddie Mac appear to have steady growth over time. Fannie Mae is a whole other story.

OFHEO issued its report on the preliminary findings of a special examination into Fannie Mae's operations. Among the many echoes of Enron, the report said Fannie Mae had a "dysfunctional and ineffective process for developing accounting policies, an operating environment that tolerated weak or non-existing internal controls...and an executive compensation structure that rewarded management for meeting goals tied to earnings-per-share, a metric subject to manipulations by management."[19]

The report was also critical of the concentration of power in the hands of Fannie's chief financial officer who the report says, "failed to provide adequate oversight to key control and reporting functions." You could just substitute Enron, or any of a number of the business failures, for Fannie Mae pretty much all the way through the report.

OFHEO's report stirred a furor. Executive greed on the order of magnitude in publicly held corporations was driving Fannie into highly risky territory. If immediate emergency measures were not taken, this gigantic financial entity could quickly collapse. Among other things, Fannie was ordered to boost its capital reserve by 30 percent to cushion the risk that the bank had taken on through complex transactions involving derivatives and the financial instruments used to hedge against interest-rate and other risk. OFHEO ordered Fannie Mae to recalculate all these types of transactions for all quarters going back to 2001—a $9 billion restatement.

The September 2004 report sent a shock through the markets and raised an unthinkable specter of a massive failure with the prospect of dire consequences for the economy. Fannie Mae and Freddie Mac were created to "pump money into the home mortgage market by buying billions of dollars of home loans each year from banks and other lenders, then bundling them into securities that are resold to investors. Their stock and debt—Fannie Mae's is nearly $1 trillion—are widely held by investors in the United States and around the globe."[20]

Creating the newly mandated capital reserve will require making difficult choices. To raise the money, Fannie Mae could issue new stock, but that could weaken the share price. It could sell assets from its investment portfolio, which includes much more than just mortgages, such as aircraft leases, for example. It could even scale back its purchases of home mortgages to be resold as bonds on Wall Street, which would likely reduce the supply of home loans for prospective buyers and make rates and terms harsher. The increase in capital reserves has to be made no matter the consequences to investors or the general public. Otherwise, they risk a failure that would require untold billions of dollars in taxpayer bailouts, a collapse in the financial market, and serious consequences to millions of homeowners and prospective homeowners. The CEO was forced to retire and the CFO was fired.

Fannie Mae's troubles are described as one of several "elephants in the room" with significant potential to hurt the American economy. Debt, deficit, derivatives, deflation, demographics, *accounting*, oil, and terrorism are some of the other "elephants" mentioned by experts. Heaven forbid they should stampede.

7

DIRECTORS: WHY THE WEAK OVERSIGHT

The spotlight has been on boards of directors that facilitated corporate corruption and executive misdeeds. New legislation, the Sarbanes-Oxley Act, specifically assigns explicit audit responsibilities and penalties to boards for oversight failures. These responsibilities and penalties have begun to change boards' passive view of their responsibilities. However, it is worth examining the sources of past failures not just to explain board ineffectiveness, but because some of these perversities persist.

There is an apocryphal story of the mother who asks her bright youngster what he wants to be when he grows up. After he has muttered something about the attractions of becoming a basketball star or movie director or rock musician, the mother interrupts his recital of childish dreams...

> *"Now listen, Billy. You probably have never heard of the job corporate director. But it is probably the best, the absolute best job in the world. The hours are short, sometimes as little as one or two hundred hours a year. Yes, you heard me, a year. Obviously, you can do any of those other things you like in your 'spare' time.*

> *"Then there is the pay—maybe a hundred or even two hundred thousand per year. Often, lots of other benefits that you probably won't understand now. You know, some directors earn several times that! And some of the work hours are spent at luxury hotels, eating the best food, and often with golf included. Everything is paid for; the travel is usually first class.*

"It is a little like being asked to join an exclusive club. The other members are usually fine people. Some will be important contacts that will help you make money or get a better 'outside' job. Everyone you meet will be nice to you and very friendly; in fact, they will go out of their way to please you and provide whatever you need while you're at the club. If you play your cards right, you can even become a member of as many as a dozen of these clubs. What a life!

"Remember, these wonderful clubs have no dues; instead, they pay you. Let me tell you son; it's a paradise. No other clubs like that...anywhere!

"Start thinking about it. I want you to learn how you get one of those great jobs; sorry, I meant to say directorships."

Of course, that little tale is fiction. However, in the recent past, most director "work" had modest actual work requirements. Reports are mailed in advance of the meeting and might only require a few hours of reading. There are usually no more than five or six formal meetings per year. Some members "attend" by telephone, thus avoiding the need to travel and its time and effort. The meetings often take place on weekends (so that they don't interfere with anyone's regular work pursuits). In many companies, there is a tradition of having at least one meeting a year at a resort with fine golf courses, spouses invited. Of course, all travel and living expenses are "on" the company's tab.

In 2004, directors' pay rose 13% to an average of $176,000 in the 200 largest U.S. companies.[1] Given their estimated hours worked a year, average compensation works out to be close to $900 an hour, plus various perks Many directors also get stock options for their company's stock. In 2003, an MBNA director, a Columbia University professor of Romance Languages, made $4.5 million on his MBNA options.[2] A mutual fund, Strong Equity, formerly had a professional football player on its board who received $139,000. [3]

With options, Enron directors were clearing a million dollars a year. Currently, the large, well regarded data storage company, EMC, gives its directors 60,000 shares in their first few years of service. (That is currently worth almost ¾ of a million dollars!)

Much Power; Little Influence

A naïve business student or the general public may find the actual role of directors puzzling. Legally, a director plays a powerful role in corporate governance. The board can and does fire the CEO, usually when earnings have been anemic, or more recently, when scandal erupts. They are then responsible for hiring replacement CEOs. Boards must approve most major corporate investment decisions and top management's compensation. The board is supposed to be self-perpetuating; that is, the board replaces any openings on the board.

The board's primary fiduciary function is clear: to protect shareholder interests using these legally mandated powers. A major part of this duty is coping with the inevitable potential for clashes of interest between the company's executives and the shareholders. [4]

Effective boards also can provide valuable, less formal services. They are a source of expert counsel to top management that is not tinged with vested interests or the desire to ingratiate oneself with the "boss." (Remember, many paid consultants seek to give advice that will lead to additional consulting fees.) Ideally, their diverse backgrounds, years of experience, and confidence born of successful careers provide a rich mix of ideas and a sound critique of the CEO's proposals.

Intel's board is, or, at least, was a superb example and a rare exception. Its board had a thoughtful, talented chairman, the former co-founder and CEO Andy Grove. He has written about the consequential contribution the board makes to Intel's strategic thinking. He lauds their ability to grill top management on both intended new initiatives and past successes and failures in product development and marketing. Board members make site visits and get a real feeling for company operations, according to Grove. It is significant that he, the former CEO, not the current one, runs the board and has shaped its culture. [5]

Large numbers of important boards are not effective, nor have they been diligent or conscientious in protecting shareholders. That seemed to be of all the boards in companies accused of accounting deceptions and executive looting. Their boards surely did not act as a check on the CEO.

Many boards have pampered their CEOs with incredible salaries, bonuses and an enormous variety of other forms of current and deferred compensation, pension supplements, enormous retirement and severance packages, and baskets full of options. After the fact, many board members have admitted they didn't understand the complexities and financial implications of the executive compensation plans they approved. Often, these were prepared and endorsed by a well-paid compensation consultant who advised the CEO.

Rubber Stamped Payout?

Newspaper stories suggest that the highly controversial payout of $140 million to Richard Grasso, the former head of the New York Stock Exchange, was approved with two members of the compensation committee absent and on the basis of an agenda item added at the last minute. The board was only given a two-page "cursory" summary of the pay arrangement. Later, some board members asserted that they didn't really understand what they were approving.[6] Most surprisingly, but indicative of board involvement, the former comptroller of New York State, chairman of the compensation committee, admitted he had not realized how much additional income was being voted Mr. Grasso in his last contract. [7]

Corporations like Enron engaged in a multitude of obviously illegal shareholder deceptions that were rubber stamped by a board of distinguished professionals. The head of Enron's audit committee, Dr. Robert Jaedicke, was a famous Harvard Business School Professor of Accounting who had become Dean of Stanford's Business School. No published accounts of Enron's failure suggest that he had objected to Enron's highly irregular accounting.

In 2002, a Senate committee found that Enron's board "knowingly" went along with Enron's high risk accounting and off-the-books deception, "...They waived Enron's code of ethics when [they] allowed CFO Fastow to run an outside partnership that was buying Enron's assets." [8]

Members of the board certainly did not seek to penetrate Enron's deceptive and extraordinarily convoluted financial dealings.

After a period, Enron executives became so confident that their board was indifferent to the "goings on" that they stopped submitting many of their decisions that required board approval. Apparently, there were no complaints. [9]

The former CEO of Time Warner, Jerry Levin, has been widely criticized for substantially overpaying to merge with AOL. Even the usually outspoken member of Time Warner's board, Ted Turner, voiced only a weak objection. AOL's early successes were the result of having been an early player in providing Internet access for PC users, and it was clear its edge was gone by the time of the merger.

Apparently, Levin's board did not subject his decision to debate or close scrutiny. Time Warner shareholders only got 45% of the combined company. AOL had been a market favorite but was, by then, wildly overpriced. In fact, before Levin's deal, AOL had tripled in price in one year, but also had one of the highest earnings multiples ever recorded. A few years after the merger, AOL was performing so poorly that the corporation removed AOL from its name and wrote off most of the original value assigned to AOL on its books. Time Warner shareholders took an enormous bath. [11]

Levin had little respect for his board's views on this or any other subject and was determined to get AOL at any cost to bring his company into the Internet world. This is the conclusion of a finely detailed study of Time Warner and AOL's merger. Levin's relationship to his board of directors is described by Nina Munk:

> He didn't go out of his way to seek their [the board of director's] advice…giving them as little information as he could get away with…He generally made it clear that his decisions were a *fait accompli* and that they were well-paid rubber stamps(!).[12]

Although the board had many experienced executives, they appeared uncritically compliant.

It should have been obvious that Levin needed to have his wildly calculated assumptions challenged. He was extrapolating the extraordinary growth AOL had experienced when competition was slight and assuming that their Internet competency could "transform" the staid magazine, cable, record, and movie businesses of Time Warner. There was enormous risk in that assumption.

Recent scandals involving the mutual fund industry stimulated the disclosure that their boards never questioned egregiously high management fees. These substantially reduced shareholder returns. They ignored the growing evidence that many popular funds were allowing a favored few investors to engage in trading, fast in and out buy/sell orders, that violated the rules of the fund. (In one notorious case, the directors turned a blind eye to a fund that had redemptions that were 800 times average net assets.) Many boards appear indifferent to the "kickbacks" to brokerage firms that push their funds. In the wake of scandals, the SEC ruled that mutual fund boards have to be chaired by an outside director.

We could find no evidence of directors resigning in protest over the accounting irregularities or compensation plans that decimated shareholder interests. In reality, few directors ever resign; they are forced to leave their boards when they reach the mandatory retirement age. Even then, many directors feel they are being pushed out, deprived of a highly attractive position just because of age.

Director resignations, even for no stated reason, would likely have been at least a red flag that encouraged closer scrutiny of the accounting of many of the corporations that had abandoned the rules. No directors were whistle blowers or came forward voluntarily even after incriminating disclosures were made. After companies that were some of the worst offenders in fraudulent financial practices were forced by creditors to change managements, board members had to be pressured to resign.

Why the Passivity?

Something was obviously wrong with the way boards functioned. Why do corporate boards appear to have failed so completely to live up to their fiduciary duties to shareholders? Until recently, no one seemed to notice. Shocking as it may seem, Enron's board was ranked among the five best functioning boards in America by a distinguished group of business school academics and corporate executives.

Many board members have just not taken their positions that seriously. Their behavior and the record suggest they rarely accepted their legally prescribed function as the guardian of shareholder interests. They devoted relatively few hours to the job, and meetings were part social events. Most dutifully looked at the reports mailed to them before their infrequent meetings but rarely, if ever, grilled executives or dug deeply into the business matters brought to them. The serious charges made by Sherron Watkins, the VP at Enron who brought Andrew Fastow's deceptions to the attention of Ken Lay, were only superficially investigated by Enron's board. They appear to have engaged in white washing these matters.

Unquestionably, the company paid insurance that appeared to protect them from any liability fostered this casual approach to responsibility.

Most directors likely believed that landing a director's job was good fortune and not to be put at risk by asking tough questions or appearing obstreperous. Being on a large company board brings prestige and cachet (your name featured in the annual report). Not to mention the generous compensation for limited hours and tender care by the company's officers. It is a soft job. No need to feel stressed over tough decisions. No requirement to produce carefully reasoned reports. (Witness the complaints of "overwork" after the Sarbanes-Oxley Act was passed.)

These have been good, very part-time jobs for retired executives, military officers, academics, or politicians. Some favored board members get much more than the published annual salary. A few examples follow.

Tyco paid one director a $20 million fee for providing some aide in arranging a merger. (He later returned the fee.) Another had the company buy his Florida house for $2.5 million. Richard Perle, former head of the Defense Policy Board, headed a venture capital fund that received a $2.5 million investment from Hollinger International when he was a board member.[13] Several Hollinger directors got big grants for their favorite charities from the company treasury. [14]

Some corporate directors were getting large loans guaranteed by the company. Some Enron directors cleared well over a million dollars a year with their option grants. A well-known retired member of Congress serves on seven boards, and all the boards provide substantial fees to the law firm of which he is a partner. This, in fact, is quite a popular exchange.[15] It was not unusual for a director to also receive high consulting fees. Some rather obvious conflicts of interest, not to mention self-interest, were trumping directors' fiduciary responsibility.

Many boards were and still are very large and unwieldy with 15 or more members. Enron had 14 board members. Members are often selected to demonstrate the many important people who can be called upon by the CEO. Many of the most important of these can be absent or participate by telephone. It is difficult to develop a consensus that is contrary to the usual "go along" posture and even a split vote is considered inappropriate.

Very small boards have another problem: group loyalty and norms that discourage rocking the boat. New members quickly get socialized into a passive view of their role.

Although direct evidence is lacking, it is likely that board members were reluctant to be vociferous in opposing the CEO and perhaps endangering their own tenure. CEOs usually exercise great influence over board member selection. Board membership typically required the continued support of the CEO.[16] New members were chosen to be compatible with the CEO.

Who Gets on Boards?

Most shareholders give little or no thought to who was being nominated as the directors of the companies in which they were invested. They ignore the proxies and the bios. Directors must face re-elections, but companies can seek to rule out any shareholder revolts by manipulating the rules such that only a third are elected each year.

It was obvious even to the most naïve stockholder that the *elections* in which they were asked to participate were farcical. There is always only one "Russian style" slate, and they almost always win with more than 90% of the votes cast in their favor.

More recently, shareholders are taking their voting power more seriously. Among several notable examples of attempts of shareholders to exercise power more directly is the case of Disney. The presumed failures of Disney CEO, Michael Eisner, received a great deal of publicity. Shareholders were distressed that Disney stock lagged its peers, yet Eisner had collected a billion dollars in compensation over the past years. So shareholders revolted, and an almost unheard of 43 percent voted against the re-election of Eisner as Chairman of the Board to demonstrate their lack of trust in his leadership. [17]

Questions have been raised regarding whether some board members find their positions and the emoluments so attractive that they over-commit themselves. For example, Shirley Ann Jackson, the president of Rensselaer Polytechnic Institute (RPI) and a distinguished scientist, served on ten boards in 2003 while managing this prestigious science/engineering university in upstate New York. Among those boards were Federal Express, AT&T, and Marathon Oil. [18] Troubled, Canadian-based Nortel Networks selected as a new board member Admiral William Owens, who was also serving on more than a dozen other boards. [19] Mutual fund board members often serve simultaneously on dozens of boards within a single, large family of funds.

Now, some companies are making new rules for membership. Florida Power and Light, for example, has a new rule: None of their directors can serve on more than five boards. That is still a large number.

Currently, the SEC is considering various proposals that would, under certain circumstances, allow shareholders to nominate some candidates for board membership. Such nominations would probably come from institutional investors (pension funds and large mutual funds). For example, Fidelity and the pension funds of state employees, such as the California Public Employees Retirement Fund (CALPERS) have huge positions in many companies. A few unions with large pension funds are pressuring to get approval for easier shareholder nominations of board positions.

CALPERS is perhaps the most active pension fund seeking improvements in corporate governance. New York State's equivalent state pension fund recovered 6 billion from investment banks that had sold it and other investors "bad" Worldcom bonds.[20]

So, who gets on boards?

1. In smaller companies, and some large corporations, boards consisted largely of friends and often cronies: golf partners, friendly local businessmen, even relatives. ("Friends and family" as one cell-phone company advertises.)

2. More sophisticated CEOs select impressive names or "trophy directors." "Trophies" are former members of Congress, ex-senior military officers, senior government officials, prestigious professors, or better yet, current or former college presidents. All serve to dress up the annual report and score points against other CEOs. It seems unlikely that trophy directors, such as Henry Kissinger, will devote substantial effort to representing shareholders.

3. Experienced professionals from Wall Street and law firms often serve on boards, some or all of whom might have provided past services to the company.

4. Representatives of other companies who have made major investments in the company. (They might be exploring a future merger or just seeking to protect their investment.)

5. Executives of acquired companies, usually growing out of a merger agreement

6. Favored senior executives who get rewarded by having a board seat.

The stock exchanges have recently adopted rules requiring half of all boards to be made up of non-insiders. The purpose is to provide more independent judgment by those, in theory, not dependent on the CEO.

The Role of the CEO in Board Selection

In theory, the board is independent of and the "superior" of the CEO. In actual practice, it is rare for someone to get on the board who does not have the approval of the CEO. It is assumed that a board member who loses the confidence of the CEO will not be re-nominated. Usually the CEO expects to be chairman of the board, which puts him in the cat-bird seat.

This creates governance problems. As Chairman they become adept at getting personal supporters on the nominating committee for board membership. The board's responsibility to protect shareholders obviously is ignored when CEOs and the business press frequently refer to "my" or "his" board. As we have said, most boards also feel that new members should meet with the approval of the CEO.

Given the power of the CEO to influence board selection decisions and the high value board members place on the emoluments that come with continuity, it becomes clear why there has been limited open criticism of CEO actions or strategy…or compensation. Self-interest trumps duty.

Increasingly, boards that are becoming more responsible hold meetings that exclude the chairman. This is a very positive development.

The Sarbanes-Oxley Act specifies that nominations for new board members must come from the existing board's nominating committee. Of course, they can still check out the CEO's views and are not likely to propose new members to whom the CEO has an aversion.

The feared and tough new requirement introduced by Sarbanes-Oxley is that the head of the board's audit committee "accept legal responsibility" for the accuracy of the company's financial reporting. The CEO and chief financial officer must do the same. That law also gives the audit committee of boards the independent right to hire outside experts to assist them in the evaluation of complex financial reports and transactions.

Director Risks

The board member who chairs the board's audit committee must now be accounting and finance "literate" and can no longer excuse financial statements that are deceptive or inaccurate by claiming that the auditors and the CEO gave their assurance that the reports were valid. (Cynics referred to this as a board's stay-out-of-jail card.)

Both because of legal requirements and the embarrassment of accusations of board lassitude, board members are now receiving big packages of detailed material to read. Much of this relates to financial matters and control procedures. Unfortunately, a cursory examination suggests these are highly legalistic, turgid, and almost impenetrable documents, often reading like "boiler plate." Their major purpose appears to be avoiding future legal challenges, not identifying issues worth exploration or debate.

There are now complaints that some directors may have to work as many as two hundred hours or more a year![21] For the first time, there are fears that board members may be subject to legal charges for failure to exercise their fiduciary responsibilities, and real penalties have been assessed in a couple of high-profile cases.

Companies report that there is a shortage of candidates for audit committee openings. A candidate must have a reasonably good accounting/finance background and be willing to accept this new liability. Consulting firms that specialize in ferreting out potential board candidates are scurrying to find those with substantial accounting knowledge who now appear in short supply. But overall, there is little evidence that fearful board members are resigning or that there is a shortage of other candidates.

There are a large number of civil suits against directors involved in companies that "cooked" their books. Interestingly, over the years, there have been almost no personal penalties levied against board members for dereliction of duty. As just noted, companies carry officer and board member liability policies for just such purposes. (The major underwriters are beginning to be more cautious about writing these policies, and premiums are going up.)

Exceptions to this safe haven are occurring. To settle one investor lawsuit, ten former Enron directors recently agreed to collectively pay over $13 million in addition to the $155 million proceeds of their director's liability insurance.[22] To put that contribution in perspective, it is worth recalling that some of these board members, with options, were clearing millions of dollars a year. The $13 million figure was arrived at by calculating a ten percent gain from selling Enron stock over time. Eleven former WorldCom directors were also ordered to personally pay a total of $20 million out of their own pockets as a result of legal pressures initiated by New York State's activist comptroller, Alan Hevesi.[23]

High-profile, "trophy" board members used to endorse or legitimate a company with limited resources might encounter publicly embarrassing financial troubles. It would be easy to assume that such risky companies could not be able to attract people with consequential reputations.

A Telling Example

Judge William Webster is a distinguished public official. He has been head of both the FBI and the CIA, impeccable credentials. He was recruited in 2000 to head the audit committee of the board of U.S. Technologies. They were a very small, struggling, Washington, D.C., firm that provided venture business services. Its major subsidiary handled outsourcing from companies wanting the cost advantage of using prison labor to make furniture. It hadn't earned a profit for six years, and its cash on hand was down to $9,000 when Webster joined. There was nothing very promising about its future prospects. In a short time, the company's stock price declined to pennies. Shareholders took a bath. [24] He might have thought he could help a struggling company and his reputation does not appear to have suffered. He was appointed vice chairman of the Department of Homeland Security's advisory council.[25]

With few exceptions, there has been little reputation risk in assuming a board position. Only rarely is publicity given to board members associated with a company in trouble. The New York Stock Exchange, Disney, Enron, and WorldCom being notable exceptions.

Putting Directors to Work

Boards can play a useful role in corporate governance. But they will continue to be ineffective even with the reforms that have been put in place. More radical reform is required.

Boards represent latent power. It is painful to consider how many of those corporate corruption debacles and losses to shareholders might have been avoided or ameliorated if boards had not been handmaidens of the CEO or "out to lunch." The fact that there are only limited examples of boards that probed their company's financial health or the implications of major financial commitment is a worrisome state of affairs.

Change requires boards to begin working. Until now, the director's job has resembled the infamous "no show" positions created by strong craft unions. Pay changes hands, but there is little work in return. These much-sought-after positions were sinecures. Re-nomination was almost guaranteed until a director reached some prescribed retirement age. It is an ideal, prestigious position to intermix with retirement leisure or to provide a stimulating change away from one's own office.

To be fair, boards are now moving more aggressively to replace deficient CEOs and finding replacements. Most recently, the board of American International Group forced the resignation of the CEO who had built this financial powerhouse. Most were "handpicked, long serving close friends of Mr. Greenberg, the CEO. But they feared that the company's reputation was at risk and pushed aside their long standing loyalty.[26] In the last year, the boards of HP, Disney, and Fannie Mae have also acted to remove CEOs whose performance they deemed inadequate.

To date, improved board functioning has emphasized certifying (and being legally responsible for) the accuracy of the company's publicly audited financial statements. In a sense, in addition to making sure the board takes its job seriously, this is a check on the effectiveness and candor of the external public auditors. The requirement suggests that some of these costly public auditing firms are either incompetent or unduly influenced by corporate management to approve questionable choices. Regrettably, the redundancy may be a necessary safeguard.

Improved controls have auditors also reporting to and questioned by the board's audit committee without the CEO present. Auditors would be asked to detail management decisions they found questionable, even though these were approved. Boards can be much more involved in assuring themselves of the future solvency of the business. In the past decade, many corporations saddled themselves with debilitating debt under the questionable assumption that they could accurately predict their future income and cash flow. Unfortunately, neither auditors nor chief financial officers were impediments to the growth of onerous debt levels that eventually led to the need for asset fire sales, bankruptcies and enormous shareholder losses.

Boards should be grilling the chief financial officer and the auditors about the risks of inadequate cash flows with ever greater debt leverage. Off-balance-sheet accounts were used to hide critical financial information from the public and shareholders. Numerous off-balance-sheet items and complex derivatives complicate the board's audit responsibilities. Excessive complexity should be a warning sign. If the audit committee or the compensation committee, or anyone on the board for that matter, can't understand transactions or contracts, that should be a warning signal.

As noted earlier, many "desirable" board members serve on a dozen or more boards. Leading companies are now seeking to severely limit the number of outside boards on which their executives or directors can serve as a means of getting more serious attention.

Advice and Dissent

Boards should not be chosen to contest the CEO's capability or remake the CEO's decisions. But board members need to act like the peers (and occasionally superiors) of the CEO—the CEO's only peers off the golf course.

Inevitably, a hierarchy impedes criticism; it is not easy to tell bosses they are misguided, need to consider a broader range of variables, or should rebalance their trade-offs. Most subordinates try to please or, worse, favor decisions that improve their promotional opportunities or the status of their units. Most recently, senior managers are often preoccupied with survival in intensely competitive executive teams or engaged in desperate measures to achieve Wall Street expectations.

Board members are not bucking for promotion or defending their turf and should be able to speak freely. However, board members won't speak up if they are fearful about risking the CEO's ire or have conflicts of interest.

No matter how bright, experienced, and wise the CEO, like any leaders coping with ambiguous information and high-risk decisions, benefits from hearing diverse opinions. A good board will have members with significant experience in areas relevant to problems facing the company.

Effective boards provide a wealth of tough and relevant questions that stimulate the thinking of the CEO. They bring ideas, experience, and insight from diverse cultures: technology, law, government, and the social and economic worlds.

Tougher Boards

Probing questions combined with a board member's relevant experience and knowledge should be a major part of the content of board meetings:

What assumptions are you making in setting forth on this course? What tough tradeoffs among competing possibilities did you make? What alternatives to the X decision got considered and why were they dropped? What unanticipated events could derail your plans? Where are the greatest uncertainties, risks you have factored in? How much of your planning represents a straight-line extrapolation of the past?

How well established and viable is your succession plan? Where is the company dependent on the loyalty and continued good

---

> health of one or two key employees? Which of your recent appointments and promotions are you worried about?
>
> Other than getting an investment banker's evaluation of the terms of this acquisition (merger), how can it be justified to us and to our shareholders? How hard and realistic are the projections (and with what assumptions)?

The relationship of the board to the CEO should be one of mutual respect, not friendship or loyalty. Board members may think it is unrealistic to be both the judge of the CEO's performance and also be a trusted source of wise counsel. What makes the two compatible is the board member's ability to demonstrate a serious commitment to the welfare of the organization and its shareholders. Otherwise, it is too tempting for the CEO to denigrate critics.

Spending serious time and effort to really understand the business, its competition, and challenges conveys the image of a board member's commitment. Raising insightful, timely questions that convey knowledge of the company legitimates the director. Without these, board discussions are vacuous and board members are tolerated, not respected. Andy Grove's policy of having board members actually visit corporate locations—and hopefully speak directly with some local managers (who are not pre-selected) would be a step in this direction.

Unfortunately, directors sometimes speak to impress one another. Not surprisingly, their questions receive polite, platitudinous responses. "Grandstanding" and ego trips at board meetings provide the CEOs cues that there is no need to take these people seriously.

Boards larger than eight or nine members are less likely to have useful, intense, focused discussions of strategy issues. (Remember Enron's 14-member board.) Any subject, other than a merger or acquisition, gets short shrift. Obviously, "trophy" directors who serve on numerous boards can't demonstrate that level of commitment, nor would it be expected. CEOs are unlikely to take seriously board members who demonstrate little preparation and prefer to participate by phone.

The board earns the confidence, and the ear, of the CEO by being neither self-serving nor disengaged. It is a mistake for a board member to accept CEO largesse: consulting assignments for the company, for example, or loans or apartments or trips that are largely vacations. All have been typical board benefits. (The Sarbanes-Oxley Act has proscribed some of the most obvious conflicts.) Nor should a board member's other affiliations—law partnerships, charities, vendors—receive the favored treatment they have in the past.

CEOs who have confidence in the board's commitment to the future of the company share more sensitive information about the company, its vulnerabilities, and problems that are worrisome. With serious premeeting preparation, directors are more likely to ask the right questions about the right issues. Directors need to assure themselves that most of their time is not consumed by the dissemination of carefully vetted, "censored" formal reports to and from the company's key officers.

The introduction of a lead director is a positive step. It is easier for some purposes to have one director to communicate the board's concerns to the CEO. Policy as well as personal issues can get more candid treatment. What would otherwise be an unacceptable challenge to the CEO's autonomy becomes a legitimate, collaborative effort at problem solving rather than escalating into mortal combat. The CEO can learn that his or her performance is under some question in the privacy of a meeting with the lead director.

Because only the board is in a position to terminate a CEO whose performance is unsatisfactory, requesting increased meetings without the CEO can appear to be a sign of big trouble. If private meetings are the norm, and the CEO is not Chairman, corrective steps can more likely be taken, when necessary, before it comes to unleashing the turmoil of asking the CEO to resign.

The core of being a good board member, rarely talked about, is being able to handle the inherent contradictions of the job. To be effective, each director should be seen by the CEO as a legitimate, potentially helpful advisor as well as someone who is a conscientious critic. Board members must be constructive critics in the context of the welfare of the company.

REQUIRED CHANGE;
Historically: Low Expectations;
Even Lower Performance

Even a medium-sized company can spend several million dollars in direct costs for its board. Then there are the indirect costs. There is the value of time spent by senior executives preparing for the meetings and supervising the preparation of reports that will be distributed. In the past, board meetings had been a costly ritual. Ritualistic is the operative word. Boards have been sleep-walking through prescribed steps that symbolize their power to challenge top management and represent the corporation's shareholders. The ceremony represented by the pre-scribed meetings typically goes off without a hitch. Board meetings are treated with respectful attention and some energetic preparation as is due this consequential ritual. But, too often, little gets accomplished.

Boards are an important part of corporate governance. By law, they provide legitimacy to transitions in top management. They provide some assurance that neither nepotism nor favoritism determines who will replace a CEO. In theory, their oversight function is also critical. Who else can confront the CEO with tough challenges to his or her decision to make a major acquisition or to incur a significant increase in the debt load of the company?

Diverse, well-chosen boards can also be a partial substitute for consult-ants eager to sell their favorite solutions and expand their billings. Board members should be better informed than these outsiders and more committed to the shareholders' best interests. In sharp contrast, "star-studded" boards function narrowly to provide legitimacy and endorsements to the importance of the CEO.

There is little evidence that boards have served their primary function well: protecting the interests of shareholders. Their record for taking fiduciary responsibility seriously leaves everything to be desired. In addition to having an almost perfect record of not identifying illicit financial maneuvers, they failed to deter or even discourage the accu-mulation of catastrophic debt in many companies. Adelphia's board allowed the Rigas family to borrow billions of dollars with little or no collateralization. Those, and many other kinds of board failures, are now familiarly associated with many-billion-dollar debt levels that led to bankruptcy or years of asset fire sales.

The evidence suggests that board positions are very attractive, too attractive, to incumbents. Board members go to great lengths to hold on to their jobs. When two companies combine and the boards are merged, it is difficult to get the resignations necessary to bring the new board down to a reasonable size. Resignations are rare even when a company appears to be engaging in fraud.

The implications are worrisome. Board members' apparent timidity has its source in concern that appearing critical to the incumbent CEO threatens tenure or is unseemly. Incredibly this deference is endorsed in a Harvard report on boardroom dynamics. As quoted by a financial journalist, it concludes that when a board "expresses skepticism about management's proposals, it undermines the supportive climate that is important for a CEO to succeed." [27] As we now know, a board's failure to express skepticism can cause the company to fail.

Historically, boards are dominated by the CEO, whether he also chairs the board or not. The CEO typically handles the agenda, speaks most, and clearly controls the board's functioning. When board members use the phrase, "It is your board," when speaking to the CEO, that confirms the legitimacy of those anxieties.

Enron had an illustrious board including the former head of the Federal Energy Regulatory Commission and a distinguished account- ant, also a Stanford Dean. But they are described as not seriously chal- lenging the outrageous financial shenanigans that allowed the company to appear both profitable and breathtakingly path-breaking in its busi- ness strategies. The board even approved allowing their chief financial officer, Andrew Fastow, to establish a private company and negotiate on behalf of that entity with Enron as to what Fastow and his partners would get as profit!

On its part, management did not feel compelled to be forthright with the board. Why would they "tell," that is, provide more complete reports that might be incriminating to a compliant board—a board that never "asked?"

Purposely or not, boards demonstrated the self-protectiveness of CEOs who could claim that they had no personal knowledge of any wrong doings. Shareholders didn't come close to getting their money's worth from boards that remained uninvolved in the affairs of the companies whose shareholders they represented.

Structural Change to Improve Effectiveness

As we have said, more companies are separating the CEO job from that of chairman of the board. Many believe that CEOs too often hold too many positions—chairman and CEO or chairman, CEO, and president or chief operating officer. Wearing these many hats has contributed to creating what some now refer to as the Imperial CEO.

An independent chairman puts some further distance between the CEO and the board. Hopefully, with that separation, the board no longer would be "his" or "her" board. Board members should then be willing to speak up, to be critical, and to disagree with one another. A diversity of opinion and healthy conflict, within bounds, and by people who are committed to the welfare of the organization, can help avoid catastrophic decisions.

Selection criteria need to go beyond those traditionally employed: PR worthy, a "name," existing lawyers or bankers with whom the company has a relationship and, of course, attractive to the CEO. Board consultants who are told not to seek "trophy" new members will also find a bigger pool.

Rarely do board members get outside the well-insulated meeting rooms and the carefully crafted senior management presentations. Board members need to be encouraged to take Andy Grove's (Intel's former CEO) advice about visiting corporate sites individually (not en masse in a guided tour) to get a feel for the organization and its people.

Rethinking Boards

The well-kept secret is that boards of directors have been prestigious, secretive "clubs" providing comfortable sinecures for the fortunate chosen. They are rather similar to the imaginary mother's description in this chapter's introductory fiction piece. In their priorities, job retention outranked protection of shareholders; it wasn't even close. For that, it was important to stay on good terms with the CEO.

Good corporate governance will not occur until priorities get reversed and board members are not afraid to put their positions on the line. In fairness, there obviously have been great numbers of conscientious and able board members who have made consequential contributions. At times, they have saved the CEO from a potentially disastrous acquisition or excessive debt or a questionable new initiative that would be a serious diversion of energies and resources.

Again, relying on the financial press, some boards appear to be more responsive to shareholder concerns about their CEO's failure to drive earnings increases and excessive executive compensation requests. For example, the PeopleSoft Board, a prominent software company that competes with Oracle, fired its CEO after a year of disappointing earnings.[28] (He had also given inaccurate financial information at one meeting with analysts.) More recently, Hewlett-Packard's board did the same.

There is a risk here. Boards can become too responsive, too impatient, and short-run oriented to the potential detriment of investors. Longer-run strategies can be impeded by the need to demonstrate straight-line quarterly earnings increases to "The Street" and the big funds. As we have shown, this overemphasis has as its byproduct the incentive to play games with numbers, creating infamous "cooked books" and, of course, starve critical longer run initiatives.

Board members must cope with the contradictions of being a constructive critic, who fire an inadequate CEO, and a respected source of wise counsel. After all, they are the only ones not beholden to the hierarchy.

CEOs have tended to increasingly short tenures. It is the shareholders who are supposed to have long-run interests in the strength and growth of the company. The current climate that encourages less passivity and more vigorous emphasis on short run shareholder returns as the major criterion of a CEOs effectiveness may have unanticipated consequences. CEOs that deliver substantial share price increases will get these well-publicized outsized compensation packages Those who fail this test in just a few years may be ousted.

A new CEO can face many "legacy" corporate problems. A variety of external factors can hurt performance in the short run. It is easy to shed people, projects, and whole divisions. Many of these quick fixes may have deleterious longer run implications (Remember, just a few years ago, some U.S. oil majors eagerly disposed of what was deemed excess refinery capacity.) Powerful incentives induce pushing the limits of financial "engineering" and corporate accounting.

The new world of hyper global competition will not favor companies or nations with excessive nearsightedness and accounting mischief. In protecting shareholders, boards need to mediate pressures for immediate returns with the needs of long term operating effectiveness and growth.

If boards can return to their legal responsibility to represent the real interests of shareholder investors, not trader, they will help restore the tarnished image of American business.[29]

8

TOO SILENT CRITICS: JOURNALISM

fter a slight hesitation, the Dutch businessman replied, "Because they are too smiley."

He had been asked by American-based marketing staff why he was critical of the use of "success stories" as sales collateral. It had become all the rage in the U.S. to use professionally written stories as a way to both flatter important clients and convince prospective customers. He went on to explain that these stories came across to the Dutch as too unrealistic and contrived. To him, the stories even seemed a shade dishonest.

"You mean to tell me the Dutch are not mindless positivists?" asked one of the Americans. The Dutch burst into laughter, vigorously nodding.

There is a difference between the can-do optimism Americans are famous for and the mindless positivism that sometimes makes Americans "too smiley." Optimists believe problems can be solved; mindless positivists don't believe there are problems. "Don't bring me a problem, bring me a solution," they thunder. Consultants assure, "No problem." Academics declare, "Problem solved."

Many business journalists and academics complied, bringing only good news, not problems, to the public during the 1990s. Breathlessly reporting hype spoon-fed by their brethren, the public relations specialists in corporations, journalists played a significant role in puffing up the bubble of the 1990s. Management scientists in academe cried, "Eureka, I have the simple formula!" or wrote smiley case studies. Management began believing its own press, forgetting how much they control and manipulate the access of journalists and academics who investigate them. Mixed in with some genuinely fine CEOs worth learning from were the CEOs who were fictions, creatures of their own PR department.

A few journalists did play their critical, unbiased investigative role well. Enron's questionable dealings were finally exposed by journalists. Oddly, the exposure of Enron is recounted as a heroic tale of great courage on the part of the journalists and their publishers (Bethany McLean of *Fortune*, and Rebecca Smith and John R. Emshwiller of *The Wall Street Journal*). It's a bit disturbing when professionals who do what is expected from their profession on a daily basis, to protect the public interest, are so rare that they are lionized.

Journalism was drawn into the business scandal. Journalists were shown to be the willing dupes of spin-doctors within companies and to have a pack mentality of promoting only "good" news. A number of prominent journalists were revealed to be on Enron's payroll as "advisors"—a story that disappeared almost as soon as it surfaced. Quasi-journalists on financial and news TV networks failed to reveal their conflicts of interest when touting companies in which they had personal investments or other ties. Now that they are forced to, they often do so sniggering, "tongue-in-cheek," minimizing the idea of a conflict of interest. More recently, information revealing possible conflicts of interest is displayed as graphics, eliminating the need for individuals to verbally make required declarations to the investing public.

Quickly on the heels of early revelations, journalism really was scandalized. Journalists who were outright frauds, or on the take as PR consultants, and publishers that were caught inflating circulation numbers in order to command higher advertising prices embarrassed the profession even further. In journalism, as in business, scandals continue unfolding years later. In late 2004, Armstrong Williams and others were exposed as accepting payments from federal agencies to promote the Bush Administration's policy initiatives, a type of bribe taking for propagandizing. Dan Rather, a pillar of the journalistic community, retired under a cloud that included firing several top CBS News executives. The illustrious *New York Times* issued an apology to the American public for its failure to serve the public's interest in the run-up to the Iraq War. There is increasing talk of propaganda, a frightening specter for any American.

Americans' confidence in their free press is compromised. Confidence of journalists in their own leadership has declined, and there is a widening morale problem in newsrooms.[1] At the national level, "the number of journalists who feel that news reports are increasingly sloppy and inaccurate is rising."[2]

We're not always sure who thinks they are bound by journalistic ethics. Those writing for newspapers and appearing on clearly news programs surely define themselves as within the profession. But, are writers for news and financial magazines professional journalists? Where do writers reporting in industry, trade, and financial publications put themselves in terms of ethics? Then there is the Internet, which blurs lines further. Some major newspapers admit to having different standards for their Internet publications. Journalists themselves often deny they are professionals, saying instead that they practice a "craft." This creates a dangerous mindset. Any employment that has "protecting the public interest" at its core is a profession, so independence and ethics are essential. While writing may be a craft, journalism is a profession.

Corporate executives, coached and trained by their public relations specialists, are experts at manipulating the media. Journalists are rewarded and punished with access. Some are flattered by being made part of the in-crowd that would be invited on special retreats with celebrity executives. Some executives even personally pay public relations experts to get stories placed that will raise their profiles. Enron put media notables, especially pundits, on $50,000-plus annual retainers. Armstrong Williams, a prominent broadcast commentator and newspaper columnist, was accused of ethics violations by taking $240,000 in payments from the Department of Education that were funneled through a PR agency he was part of, to shill for the government's No Child Left Behind Act. "In an interview, Mr. Williams said his mistake was thinking like a businessman, without worrying enough about journalistic ethics."[3] Mr. Williams said he probably shouldn't have done it, but refuses to return the money.

Journalists, eager to get their bylines, wrote smiley stories about executives and companies that were revealed to be frauds. Dutifully printing company press releases without digging into claims or checking with critical sources, journalists confirmed the opinion many PR professionals have of them—that they're lazy. PR experts make journalists' jobs easier by doing as much of their work for them as possible, even offering pre-written stories in addition to carefully crafted press releases and announcements.

There is a whirling, revolving door sending former journalists into well-paid PR positions. PR has become a field in which practitioners are carefully trained to control the message and to coach others to stay "on message." Like government regulators valued for insider contacts and knowledge, journalists move into industry and consulting with ease.

Journalists offer rationalizations for their failure to protect the public's interest in the 1990s. Competing with tabloid journalism, 24/7 news channels, "infotainment," and the Internet caused corner-cutting in the rush to publish. Their corporate parents wanted more with less. Journalists became like any other employee in corporate America where expectations focused on the bottom line, and short-term metrics had to be achieved.

Like other industries, the media was being deregulated and consolidated into vast global empires. Within these empires, the level of conflict of interests steadily rose, as they did in other professions and our political system. Not only were a few major corporations forming large chains of newspapers, but deregulation was allowing these to be part of conglomerations of all types of print and broadcast media, including the movie industry. Even General Electric made media part of its empire. Most of the news Americans get is projected from corporations squarely in the entertainment industry. No industry is better than this one at sliding down slippery slopes.

As increasingly bold acquisitions concentrated media ownership in fewer hands, "synergy" was the promised future benefit to shareholders. When people began to question the effect of this synergy on the independence of journalists now caught up in these large corporations, they were assured that journalistic ethics would protect the public.

Well-established luminaries claim they cannot or will not be censored by their own corporate executives, but people are already starting to wonder what will happen when they retire. Two of the three major network news anchors, Tom Brokaw and Dan Rather, have now retired. Also, Bill Moyers, anchor of PBS's *NOW*, retired, so we shall soon see what happens with the changing of the guard. Other retirement worries include Jim Lehrer of PBS's *News Hour* and Brian Lamb of CSPAN. Many watch their protégés closely for signs of hope when the inevitable comes.

Journalists regularly participate in self-analysis, as do most professions these days. At press clubs, professional associations, and academic events, speakers and panels of well-known publishers and journalists air dirty laundry and discuss the difficulties of preserving independence and meeting ethical obligations to serve the public. Most disturbing was one candid revelation when a famous journalist was asked if there was a problem with corporate executive editorial interference and censorship. The reply was that interference and censorship were rarely overt because journalists had begun self-censoring, anticipating the corporate position and preferences of their parents. A recent book about journalism, *Killed: Great Journalism Too Hot to Print*,[4] takes up editorial censorship and self-censorship issues, especially among freelance journalists.

Careerism dominates in journalism just as elsewhere, and the payoffs can be huge. Worldwide fame and gobs of money are there for the chosen few. As journalists became stars and were paid accordingly, the profession began its glide down the slippery slope. Stories about the Bush tax cuts enacted in 2001 often include smirking jokes in front of audiences pointing out the fact that well-known journalists are among the high-earning beneficiaries, describing themselves as "in the club."

There is tremendous intrinsic power in being a journalist, even the small town variety. In addition, power from associating with the powerful is heady stuff. Business majors in some schools are learning how to "capture" the media with techniques including flattery. Students of public relations learn how to coddle their media contacts and pitch ideas that will get a journalist's attention.

Budding journalism students learn their trade through corporate internships more often than by working on independent newspapers and locally owned broadcast stations, now few and far between. Cub reporters idolize and emulate the rich and famous, and sometimes, infamous, in their profession, as well as the honest and trustworthy. Some journalism school-run student newspapers have drifted into corporate models, run more from a profitable business perspective than from a public-service perspective.

It's difficult to imagine eager young students flocking to journalism schools because they burn to be a financial news reporter, but perhaps more do these days. Journalists covering the business beat are routinely getting front-page bylines and loads of book contracts.

There are so many books about Enron, mostly written by journalists, that books on Enron are even referred to as a genre. Some of the best accounts of recently failed companies such as AOL, Nortel, and Enron,[5] have been produced by journalists. Journalism is great for chronicling contemporary history—telling the tales in compelling, succinct, and we hope, fact-based, ways. The public benefits enormously when publishers give journalists time to develop the full story. The enormity of the story of business failure, implicating themselves along with everyone else, shook many in the profession into a keen sense of needing redemption to restore the public's decreasing trust. Many are more probing and skeptical these days.

At the same time the journalism profession began worrying about restoring public trust, the big media conglomerates made a power grab. In 2003, the *Federal Communications Commission* (FCC) ruled in a decision split along partisan lines to allow further concentration of media ownership into the hands of six entertainment and media industry giants. The force of the public's reaction to this move by the FCC caught politicians by surprise. People realized America's famed free press was threatened.

It proved no easy task for politicians to get the industry giants an increase in the face of public opposition. Citizens expressed displeasure and alarm in petitions, demonstrations, letter writing and calling campaigns organized by a motley assortment of special interest groups that took up the cause as an assault on the public interest. Rather than the originally generous change, big media owners had to settle for a compromise increase that just ensured Rupert Murdock was within the bounds of FCC regulations, which he had already violated before the rule change. There seems to be nothing like a compromise for dampening public outcries, so perhaps this was the outcome sought all along.

Unfortunately, in the heat of battling to stop the increase in media ownership in local markets, the real point was missed. The percentage of ownership in local markets was too high before the increase was proposed. Most average Americans had not realized the extent to which big corporate media had taken control of markets already, and many were shocked and wondering how this had happened. It happened because the media that was benefiting by these changes in ownership conveniently neglected to report the story along the way. The 2003 public battle should have been about reducing the market ownership percentage below the pre-increase levels. Now Americans are stuck with the problem of beating back the new, even higher figure, a seemingly hopeless task given that an increase passed despite one of the most concerted citizen efforts since the Vietnam War. Few events have revealed the extent of corporate capturing of America's political system than this one, which resulted in further diminishment of our free press's freedom.

The repeal of the Fairness Doctrine by the FCC in 1985 is another event that slipped by Americans and has had significant consequences. The Fairness Doctrine was established in 1949 as an attempt to ensure balanced, fair coverage of controversial issues. Broadcasters licensed by the FCC were deemed "public trustees" with obligations to provide contrasting viewpoints on controversial issues of public importance. The public owns the airwaves and has every right to include non-monetary demands, as well as monetary payments, in license agreements. Similar to the more recent attempt to have Congress override the FCC's decision to increase allowable media market share, both houses of Congress voted to override the FCC and put the Fairness Doctrine into law in 1987. President Reagan vetoed the legislation. The effort of Congress to revive the Fairness Doctrine was initiated during George Bush the elder's presidency, and the legislation was passed again. Bush vetoed it. The consequences of losing this public protection are clear 20 years later. Journalists, including those covering business, are under less pressure to ferret out the other side of a story. Broadcasters, such as Clear

Channel and Fox News, are openly considered among journalists themselves to be propaganda pipelines using the public's own airwaves to misinform them.

The *State of the News Media 2004 Report* gives little comfort. Like many in other professions, journalists know what needs done, but are caught in bad systems, which they now believe have "problems that seem more structural and protracted."[6] The survey report says a number of disturbing things:

- Although their worries are changing, the problems journalists have with their profession in many ways seem more intractable than they did a few years ago.

- News people feel better about some elements of their work. However, they fear more than ever that the economic behavior of their companies is eroding the quality of journalism.

- In particular, journalists think business pressures are making the news they produce thinner and shallower. They report more cases of advertisers and owners breaching the independence of the newsroom.[7] Clearly, what's needed is akin to the ChineseWall that must exist between an investment firm's analysts and traders.

The survey also asked journalists about their confidence in the public's ability to make good decisions. "Ultimately, journalism is predicated on [journalists'] faith in the public. Here, journalists' views have become dramatically more pessimistic."[8] We can only wonder what will happen in a profession charged with serving the public when those in the profession lose faith in the public.

This crisis of faith is considered troubling by the report authors, who speculate, "Is it possible that market research data is persuading journalists today that they understand their audiences better and also that those audiences are dumber than they thought?"[9] The report contains an important lesson for us all: "A cynical view of the public becomes a self-fulfilling prophecy that leads journalists to produce a shallower product because they think the public cannot handle anything else."

As the role of market research has expanded and become based on seemingly sophisticated statistical sampling techniques using the latest technologies, we forget that this kind of research is deeply flawed by subjective bias and the problems of measuring "human subjects." Focus groups, used along with surveys, are attempts to correct for the pitfalls of over-reliance on quantitative methods, and the problems there are group-think dynamics and a dependence on skilled, unbiased facilitators who resist the temptation to shape the outcome.

USA Today began prominently featuring a variety of polling, and research results and market research showed this was liked by readers. Despite the fact that this data is often unscientifically generated and/or have margins of error that should set off alarm bells, readers quote what they read, overlooking the margin of error in fine print. Polling has become a daily feature of many TV newscasts and Internet sites; Internet technology makes this possible. By the end of the show, the results are in and viewers have been driven to the Web site. Journalists might question the degree to which the public is not well served by trends like this. It is a type of disinformation campaign that does indeed have a certain degree of self-fulfilling prophecy power behind it.

In addition, many news magazines have taken up the task of ranking. Anxiously awaited lists ranking everything from universities, hospitals, CEOs, and CFOs to Most Powerful Women, Best Places to Work, and Best Boards are published. People and organizations become preoccupied with pleasing those who control rank. Knowing the criteria and methods used, individuals and organizations can manipulate the process, but more disturbingly, the process manipulates them in turn.

Some ranked lists may have some public interest value, but are these efforts honest enough in terms of the resources applied to develop them? One of the major issues facing journalism is the same as everywhere else. Staff and funding cutbacks are said to put a strain on the basic functioning of day-to-day operations, and journalists fear this is compromising quality. Rank lists, no matter how loosely developed, must translate into sales or they would not have proliferated as they did. It's easy to convince people that methods are rigorous and the right measures are used when you can readily generate lots of quantitative data.

Given the fact that Enron and the other big failures made the top of just about every list published in the business press, this list-making seems questionable. Enron was the top company on many lists. Enron's CFO, Andrew Fastow, had just made the top of the Best CFO list when his frauds were exposed. Enron's board of directors was ranked among the best. Rebecca Mark, CEO of Enron's international group, which struck some of the most colossally bad deals in business history, was on *Fortune's* list of the 50 Most Powerful Women. Many of those we saw being arrested over the last few years made the top of various lists, which no doubt served to grow their power and compensation.

Many of the executives headed for jail can wile away their time by poring over their press clippings from the glory days. Gazing at their pictures and reading their glib quotes, some might even feel remorse or at least a sense of irony. Journalists looking back over their portfolios might be doing the same.

Meanwhile, Americans and leaders within journalism must face the daunting task of reforming the media. A free press is considered a critical part of democracy's foundation, so this is a political issue first and foremost. No matter what political or personal views an American may hold, the recent fight against increasing the percentage of market share held by big media conglomerates demonstrated that the media is a public issue that transcends many boundaries, going to the heart of having a well-functioning democracy.

Political action that breaks up the concentration of mass media power in the hands of a few giant corporation executives is imperative. Assessment of the consequences of killing the Fairness Doctrine is also in order. Interestingly, the Internet, so often blamed for the deterioration of journalism, is turning out to be a boon to the kind of activism required to put pressure on the American political system. Americans are just realizing the political power of this new technology and are still learning how to use it.

Within the journalism profession, leaders will have a hard struggle to take back the high ground of their chosen profession. Making principled decisions, speaking out, taking a stand, and drawing lines in the sand are not easy when such high-income personal stakes are involved.

But that is what real leaders do. There most certainly are journalists who work hard, report honestly and fairly, and take their professional responsibilities seriously. These people need to be in a position to change their profession and should be role models for students and interns so their numbers grow.

Fortunately, stories that dig deeper surface more frequently these days. One example is an exposé of executive retirement plans, which have become the new "stealth compensation" in CEO pay packages now that stock options get uncomfortable attention. The reporter dug into these more obscure, less divulged parts of executive pay, and his hard work paid off for investors.[10] Again, the public was shocked by the continuing brazen greed of executives.

As one IT industry columnist put it, "Without a truly impartial press, who can you trust? No one."[11]

9

TOO SILENT CRITICS:
ACADEME

Some university business programs have taken to offering "jail-house seminars," which include a field trip to jails in order to understand ethics. Students get to interact with "white collar" criminals and supposedly will learn from their mistakes. Described as a variation on "scared straight" programs meant to deter juvenile delinquency, one would think these seminars might also include a field trip to general population prisons. That way, students can get an idea of what might eventually happen to white collar criminals of the future.

Students are expected to learn "the danger of making incremental compromises with principle"[1] by talking with inmates. Hopefully, they will not be talking with the newest batch of white collar criminals, who insist on innocence or ignorance, believe they have been persecuted, and show little in the way of remorse. Perhaps there is little danger of this because there will be proportionately so few going to jail. Those who do, won't be there for long.

Out of possible sentences in decades or even beyond a human lifetime, actual sentences are far short of the maximum, and everybody seems to know how short they really are. Sam Waksal, disgraced founder of ImClone, is expected to only serve slightly more than six of a seven-years-and-three-months sentence for insider trading. Ken Lay, former Enron CEO, is facing a 175-year maximum sentence, and we know that won't be enforced if he is convicted. There is the rare example of a long sentence, such as that of a Dynergy tax accountant who got 24 years, causing the media to prematurely declare a new era of harsh sentences.

Maybe students in the Class of 2020 can have a chat with him. The former vice-chairman of Rite Aid received a ten-year prison sentence that seemed harsh because he was 76 years old. His case involved witness tampering for which there is little room for mercy.

Andrew and Lea Fastow were both able to plea bargain for comparatively short sentences; Lea served a one-year sentence. Andrew Fastow has pled to two of the 98 counts against him and agreed to serve a maximum sentence of ten years. The Fastows have also agreed to forfeit more than $29 million. That seems like a lot, but it is reported that when Fastow cashed out of the fraudulent partnerships he had created at Enron, his total take was $60.6 million (not including his Enron compensation and stock).[2] Any first-year business student can do that math.

To be fair, these cases involve real prison time. Just recently, two Merrill Lynch high-status investment bankers each received about 3 years of prison time for work they had done for Enron. (They had been involved with the now infamous "barge deal," where Merrill had pretended to buy these with a significant profit for Enron. Enron had guaranteed Merrill that they would not lose money in the deal.) Many graduate students in business consider investment banking their most favored career.

If business students are faced with a choice between doing the right thing and making millions of dollars for themselves by skating on or over the ethical edge, will they reflect on a field trip, or will they have role models like Michael Milken and Ivan Boesky to follow? Sure, they did a little time, but look how wealthy and prominent they were after getting out of jail. Perhaps these nefarious characters from the 1980s really were the role models for the 1990s. Milken and Boesky certainly seemed to offer a low-risk/high-reward strategy for fortune building. The fates of executives caught in criminal and civil litigation in this round of scandal will serve as models for students just as earlier cases have over time.

Many business programs still don't even require any coursework on ethics or social responsibility. Some in academe argue that by the time students get to business school, their moral foundation is already formed. That may be true for some students, but can't be true of all, and why would there be any harm in reinforcing scruples that students may have already acquired? Beyond that argument, the fact that students have reported leaving business schools with diminished moral grounding compared to when they entered provides a case against those academics not wishing to waste time on ethics. It is deeply concerning that some business schools are found to be actively working against students' moral inclinations.

When courses on ethics or social responsibility are offered but optional, some students report avoiding these courses believing their appearance on a transcript sends the "wrong" message. More typically, students don't want to waste time (and big tuition dollars) on courses that do not seem to have direct relevance to future careers and compensation.

Students are taught that markets are amoral. This is simply not true. All economic systems have a very real moral dimension, the nature of which matters a great deal. More recently, the market and free trade fundamentalism taught in most business schools takes this view to new extremes. Students are even taught that these amoral markets will actually be better at creating social justice than any social mechanisms have been in the past. Jeffrey Skilling, Enron's CEO, believed firmly in that idea. So did his traders, who presided over the market manipulations that created California's catastrophic energy crisis.

When business schools do consider teaching ethics and social responsibility, they wrestle over whether this should be done in specialized courses or by embedding this topic throughout the curriculum. This is an argument that hangs up the process of initiating programs. The all-too-obvious answer is both.

Back in the late 1950s with help from the Ford Foundation, Courtney C. Brown, Dean of Columbia University's Graduate School of Business, initiated a pioneering required course which provided a broad view of the role of business and business executives in society. The materials forced students to explore the dilemmas faced by executives contending with market, political, and social responsibility issues. The course integrated American business history and the logics of private capitalism with contemporary events and institutions. It forced students to make tough trade offs with no easy wins and to balance short-run expediencies with long-run survival and growth.

Sadly, the course no longer was required after the late 1980s. Both students and faculty were demanding more time in the curriculum for the increasing quantity of technical materials, particularly in the finance field. Post-Enron, the current Dean of Columbia's graduate school announced a resurrection of ethics in the curriculum, as have some other schools. The Ohio State University, for example, initiated a program in 2004 in which all 800 incoming students were given a book that dealt with ethical issues. This was followed up by having the book's authors speak to the students, and presumably individual teachers worked the book's lessons into their courses.

Simulations featuring business games in which competing student teams confront tough problems with some kind of award for the winning team have become popular. Faculty are amazed at the intensity of competition generated. Not infrequently, students use deception and trickery in order to win, which allows for later discussions of motivation and ethics. Sensitive faculty can also use the actual tactics and strategies of student teams to examine issues around the priority given to cooperation versus competition in seeking "rewards." *Experiential learning*, as it is called, is a more powerful way of teaching ethics than simple lectures and discussions.

Executives of tomorrow are the product of business school selection. The experience of Jeffrey Skilling, former Enron CEO, makes an interesting case.

Harvard had some doubts about accepting Skilling. Its interviewer of marginal candidates asked him point blank if he was smart. Skilling shot back, "I'm *fucking* smart."[3] If Harvard was considering the character of its applicants, one would think this would have sent him packing. Instead, he was accepted.

Skilling believed more than most in the popular, social Darwinian view that markets are the ultimate judge of right and wrong. He thrived at Harvard, becoming one of its Baker Scholars (those in the top five percent of their class).

One former classmate recalls a class he attended with Skilling. Students discussed a product that "might be—but wasn't definitively—harmful to consumers."[4] Students were asked, "What should the CEO do?" "I'd keep making and selling the product," replied Skilling. "My job as a businessman is to be a profit center and to maximize return to the shareholders. It's the government's job to step in if a product is dangerous."[5]

The anecdote doesn't go on to provide the professor's reaction to Skilling's answer. That is the crucial information in terms of the role of business professors in developing new members of the executive class, especially the most elite members. The textbooks, cases, and exercises chosen by professors are important, but what goes on beyond that in classroom discussions is key. Professors also hold the reward of grades which send the most powerful signals about right and wrong.

Given Skilling's mindset and the rewards and reinforcement Harvard bestowed upon him, it is worth noting that he went on to join one of the most influential management consulting firms in the world, McKinsey & Co. He then became the CEO of America's seventh largest company, Enron, which he drove to wrack and ruin.

We can only wonder how people, such as Skilling, get through prestigious schools and what those schools promote and value when we read descriptions of Skilling as a manager. He is said to have had "dangerous blind spots, appalling management skills, no understanding of people, distaste for the details of execution, and slowness to recognize when reality didn't match theory."[6]

Instead of recognizing Skilling's apparent narcissism for what it was, Harvard not only tolerated Skilling, it promoted him as a role model for other students by making him a Baker Scholar. Skilling's demonstrated lack of conscience and giant ego were confused with something very different—leadership potential.

Many business schools in America are public institutions, supported by tax dollars. The prestigious, mostly private, elite schools, for good or ill, serve as models for the others. Jeffrey Skilling got where he was in large part because of Harvard's reputation, and the school extolled him and Enron in quite a number of their famous case studies. Its influential publication, *Harvard Business Review*, published an article in

January 2001 featuring Enron as a major case example in a discussion of strategy.[7]

Business school faculty have little incentive to expose deleterious corporate practices. Their status is derived from published research and their acceptance by industry as highly paid consultants or lecturers in corporate executive development programs.

Increasingly, academic journals publish research based on quantitative studies. These usually utilize numerical data that can be derived from published reports or survey questionnaires mailed to a large number of companies. Both the design of large questionnaire studies and the motivation of respondents combine to reduce any possibility of surprising disclosure. Rarely does publishable research require intensive field work which might surface company-specific data on questionable corporate behavior.

Less-academic publications, magazines, encourage academics to simply describe and endorse current management fads, usually with colorful diagrams and graphs. The professor gets his or her name in print, and the article may give credibility to organizational techniques like those used by the "Enrons" of business.

Many faculty develop course materials and lectures that are really "beta tests" of carefully honed ideas that will be salable for either consulting or executive development programs. Faculty members make their reputations by publishing "new ideas," but there is often a reluctance to challenge what is currently accepted wisdom. For example, it might be hard to imagine, but some management scholars never thought enlarging senior management ownership with massive stock options was a good idea.

University professors and administrators are allowed to moonlight. They can do private consulting and serve as paid members of boards of directors. Informal prestige rankings within these schools demonstrate that consulting, particularly with high-visibility corporations, adds to the status of faculty both with students and within the faculty itself.

In many cases, schools have rules about the percentage of faculty member's time that can be devoted to this lucrative moonlighting. Unfortunately, enforcement of these rules has become very lax in some schools. Although somewhat extreme, the case of one professor at a large public university is instructive.

Several years ago, a business school professor who received his doctorate from a top-ranked university was among a number of people charged by the SEC with insider trading. The case is not yet resolved, and he has denied the charges. However, in the reporting on the case, two things came out:

- This professor was serving on six boards of directors. He earned $125,000 during one year alone from board memberships.

- In the course of his decades-long career as a business professor in a publicly funded university, he had branded himself and established a successful consulting business along with lecturing for fees and earning book royalties. He added this to his nearly $100,000 salary as a professor (salaries at the most prestigious business schools are now much higher). He is estimated to be worth around $10 million and was able to buy the naming rights to a university building by pledging $7 million to its building fund.

In official documents filed with his university, he claims he spends "100 hours—twelve-and-a-half workdays—annually" for his consulting firm. This is the maximum amount allowed by university policy.

Enron's CFO, Andrew Fastow, also claimed to only be working a few hours a week in his capacity as an executive in control of some of Enron's SPEs. Enron's board of directors had made an exception to the company's ethics policies to allow Fastow to also act as an executive in these entities. Fastow's moonlighting was normally prohibited because it created conflicts of interest. He would be in a position of negotiating deals with Enron on behalf of the entities he headed. The SPEs were where Fastow made his fraudulent personal income, and, contrary to what he reported to the board, this was actually consuming most of his time and energy.

To their students and to the public, faculty can appear somewhat indifferent to ethical issues that might be involved in their consulting. Years ago when industrial unions were waging major organizational campaigns, some business school faculty consultants helped companies find ways to resist unions. In December 2004, Stephen A. Ross, an MIT professor of Finance and Economics, became the subject of an SEC investigation. He is alleged to have accepted a $1.3 million investment for his consulting company from Ernst & Young, the auditor of TIAA-CREF, for which Ross was a Trustee (equivalent to a board director).[8] Current law makes it illegal for an auditor to offer any kind of payment or relationship to corporate officers or directors.

Several years ago, Harvard was threatened with the loss of a major government contract to work on privatization implementation in Russia. It was alleged that a faculty economist on the project with his spouse had engaged in profit-making activities in Russia using the project's status and knowledge. In another case, a distinguished professor at Columbia University devoted an entire floor of his sizable home to a market research company that he owned. His graduate students might engage in projects that were relevant to their course work with him that contributed to his consulting projects.

A more garden-variety case surfaced at Yale's School of Management. The head of its International Institute of Corporate Governance was fired for double billing $150,000 on his expense accounts. He was billing Yale as well as the sponsors of events who had invited him to speak. One newspaper editorial quoted experts on corporate governance saying this was another case of leaders failing to lead by example.[9]

Tenured senior faculty in prestigious universities can develop hubris and arrogance similar to the management style and sense of entitlement of CEOs responsible for some of the corporate scandals that have shocked Americans over the past half a decade. Business faculty routinely make considerably more than many of their counterparts in other departments of the university. Many add to this their moonlighting gains and model ostentatious living for students. These practices are rationalized by fallaciously arguing that those who teach would be lost to industry. If you tell a businessman that, he laughs.

As in medicine, there may be legitimate reasons to allow for "clinical" experience. The consultant gets exposed to the complexities of the real world whether it be the human body or organizational behavior. This provides useful case material for classroom use and may well instruct the educator about the shortcomings of current theories and the real complexities of implementing organizational change. A limited amount of this experience has a legitimate place in a professional school. Some professors engage their classes in solving real business problems, and this can be truly enriching experience for students. The question is always one of payment.

Just as the SEC questioned the toxic effect of non-audit consulting on the part of public auditors, there is a question about the toxic effect of too much outside consulting in academe. Regrettably, business in contrast to medical "consulting" is likely to involve communicating (selling?) currently popular ideas and techniques to clients more than learning from clients.

In very fundamental ways, business consulting is not research. Consultants must please their clients, are often viewed with suspicion and resentment by employees, and usually do not get to follow the results of what they do for clients. Research requires objectivity and a critical perspective. Research cannot be controlled completely by management and should be focused on consequences in the long and short term. Academics are the guardians of a scientific method that allows testing of the claims, tacit assumptions, and beliefs of the everyday work world. They are supposed to be removed from the pressures of the marketplace, which assures us that their findings are not biased by personal interests and are protected by academic freedom.

Business school professors have generated piles of papers, books, and case studies that laud now-disgraced companies. They contribute to the creation of individual and company celebrities as much as journalists do. For a truly surreal experience, read a *Harvard Business Review* article on strategy featuring Enron as a case study that was published just months before Enron was exposed.[10] Then, read *The Smartest Guys in the Room*[11] to find out how thoroughly duped the authors of the article must have been. The book reports that Enron was crawling with academics writing case studies. At least five were done by Harvard alone; after all, Skilling was one of their own, so this garnered PR for the school.

Much of the academic publishing as well as the popular business press became too "smiley" because these activities served as PR for many academics' consulting sidelines. Offering canned formulas and quick fixes with "new" theories was the way to get consulting gigs and large speaking fees from industry. Playing to management, not the public or workers, gets you into the executive suites and boardrooms from whence big fees flow. Featuring executives and their companies as smiley success stories surely curries favors.

If you like surreal experiences, try another one. The April 2004 issue of the *Harvard Business Review* features an article offering to teach people "The Hardball Manifesto"—five *killer* strategies for trouncing the competition. "The idea is to ruthlessly devastate a rival's profit sanctuary, raise competitor's costs, and deceive the competition." The authors, in this case both affiliated with a consulting firm rather than a university, suggest "questions to ask before taking action that could cross legal or social boundaries." And, they warn, "A hardball playbook won't do you any good if you feel squeamish about using it."[12]

If there are business school professors delving into ethics, social responsibility, and workers' experience, they are often few and far between, marginalized, and tolerated, just barely. Those in other disciplines who might ask tough questions about American business are easily stonewalled and even co-opted by occasionally getting a nibble at the consulting pie.

During a meeting to discuss the conduct of a required course on international business, one teacher raised the issue of incorporating the tough issues of fairness and social responsibility into the course. When the teacher indicated a belief that it was important for business students to know the harm that can be done by unethical corporations and understand how unintended consequences can emerge that require corrections and tough trade-offs, including against high profit, he was interrupted.

The senior professor in the group smiled coyly and reminded the bleeding heart that "We are, after all, *pro-business* here."

The unveiled message was clear. The popular textbook's cursory attention to the dark side of international business and facile justifications exempting business from responsibility were not to be challenged by any extra discussion of these tangential issues. Business students should not be made to feel uncomfortable about the morals of their chosen field. Being *pro-business* meant not being critical of contemporary dogma and the status quo.

Universities are not enforcing their own rules that are intended to curb moonlighting abuses. The number of boards a faculty member can sit on and the amount of time that can be devoted to consulting should be carefully considered. Whether it is even appropriate to allow outside consulting where fees are paid to the faculty member, rather than perhaps the school itself, is a question. There are other models. For example, in Germany, professors are entirely prohibited from moonlighting and risk losing their jobs and their pensions if they break the rules.

Although it would be nice to think that business school faculties are doing some serious soul searching about their role in creating the executive class, significant change is unlikely unless the moonlighting incentives are taken out of the equation. People just don't bite the hand that feeds them.

Conclusion

This chapter has looked at business school faculty from which Americans expected critical investigations and some real improvements. Surely, tenured academics should be the least cowed. Regrettably, conflicts of interest and self-interest trumped the responsibility of academics to search out signs that some parts of one of our most important institutions were beginning to degrade. Recent events make it obvious that academe also became "too smiley" and lost their essential critical perspective. Academics have far more capacity for change from within and at the individual level. Academics also have far more responsibility to society. They handle something much more precious than money. They have charge of the next generation of businessmen not just going into American businesses, but into businesses globally.

The well known economist, Robert Shiller, provides a sharply candid view of the relationship of business education to what happens to student behavior when it becomes executive behavior: "Education molds common assumptions and conventional wisdom. When it comes to the business world, our universities—and especially their graduate schools of business—are powerful shapers of our culture. Business ethics is just another academic specialty, and can be seen as remote as microbiology to those studying financial theory."[13]

10

FEES GALORE

F ees for this, fees for that—pretty soon, it adds up to real money. Professional service firms grew and sprang up through the 1980s and 1990s, and individuals hung out their own shingles in the wake of downsizing. Service providers proliferated their products. A host of middlemen surfaced to broker deals for independent contractors, and outsourcing became popular. Internal accounting systems now routinely track internal "funny money" fees or cross charges within the company, often referred to as "internal consulting."

Here, we discuss trends in the use of services by corporations and the enormous outflow of cash that accompanied these trends. Traditional service providers, such as auditors, attorneys, and bankers, offered a host of new services that we now know introduced conflicts of interest that compromised their independence as "trusted advisors" or protectors of the public interest. All sorts of boutique services came into the market, such as compensation and image consulting, and recently, personalized coaching. We also look at how the SEC uses fees for services to fund our capital market's regulatory regime.

Consulting certainly has a legitimate place in business activity. There can be great value in getting an outside opinion or not keeping highly specialized experts on staff if the need for their services is not constant. Judicious use of consulting services can greatly benefit a company. However, shareholders should be alert to excessive use of consultants and understand how the consulting industry works.

The consulting boom started in the 1980s, escalated in the 1990s, and then hit a rough patch in the general economic downturn that followed. During the boom period, the consulting industry was changing and among the changes was "productizing" its services. This strategy involves packaging up boiler-plated service offerings that can be sold like mass-produced widgets.

One example of the rush to create products was the 500 active tax products KPMG had for sale in 2003. Legal and accounting firms treated opinion letters as "products" earning as much as $100,000 or more a pop, aggregating into fee generation in the millions for issuing the same opinion letter over and over to different clients. Law firms made millions of dollars on opinion letters alone in the various tax evasion schemes revealed in the wake of Enron. Whenever executives, like those at Enron, were challenged by the press, investment analysts, credit rating agencies, the SEC, or the IRS, they could haul out their expensive opinion letters in defense of their actions.

In addition to Enron's inside legal staff, Vinson & Elkins, the company's outside legal firm was billing $35 million annually. The law firm charged as much as $1 million for a tax shelter review and opinion letter. Banks could get as much as $15 million for their role in tax shelter transactions for Enron. Enron's tax department was essentially a profit center constantly trolling for ideas. We now know how shady some of these shelters were in the wake of tax evasion investigations of Enron.

Enron's investment banking fees ran to $235.7 million in 1999 alone. Merrill Lynch took $40 million of that pie in 1999, including a $25 million charge for handling Enron's Asurix IPO.[1] As Enron was coming undone and desperate for cash, JPMorgan Chase and CitiGroup together agreed to extend $2 billion in unsecured credit to keep Enron afloat. As part of the deal, Enron was to mandate use of JPMorgan Chase and CitiGroup as strategic advisors with an initial retainer of $15 million each up front to put the deal together. Another $45 million in fees were due upon closing the deal. The $2 billion promise of credit was withdrawn, but not before both banks had received their $15 million fee payments.

Professional service firms focused on "maximizing the practice," which translated to boosting revenue and profit. Large firms targeted large companies to make their aggressive numbers, which triggered bonuses. Enron was spending about $750 million annually on consulting and professional services just before going bankrupt. As of mid-2004, $665 million in fees to lawyers, accountants, and others have been generated by the Enron bankruptcy proceedings.

Many professional firms became "multidisciplinary firms," branching into new service areas as rapidly as ideas could be hatched and packaged into products. Fees for services exploded in the banking, investment, legal, and accounting industries. In addition, independent research firms, such as Gartner, which provides research services to the IT industry, got into consulting, despite critical opinions that this would compromise their independence.

Clients were also driving trends in the consulting industry because they wanted a one-stop shopping experience. As client-consultant relationships became more complex, consulting firms began using "client service teams" to coordinate the relationship. Client service teams, a seemingly sensible idea all around, however, became focused on marketing more services. As we discussed earlier, in the case of Andersen, Enron's audit firm, a client service team was headed by David Duncan, Enron's engagement partner. Duncan's team included a marketing professional with whom he had regular special meetings to develop strategies for selling Enron more services. In 2001, Andersen charged Enron $25 million for its audit services and another $27 million for a host of other services. Andersen expected Enron to soon become a $100 million per year account by selling it more non-audit services.

The consulting boom is at the center of the massive conflicts of interest that arose in the economic system during the 1990s. All the professions were corrupted. In addition, the "promise" of consulting, lobbying, and speaking fees down the road had a corrupting influence on some politicians. As mentioned in Chapter 8, "Too Silent Critics: Journalism," Enron even paid journalists advisory fees of as much as $50,000 per year, creating a conflict of interest in their coverage of Enron. Everyone seemed to have their hands out for a fee of some kind.

There are some good reasons to hire consultants, and there can be good reasons not to hire consultants. Boards of directors should serve an important function in making this determination. Boards should consider whether consultants are being used to rubber-stamp management wishes, as ready scapegoats for management failures, or even to perform management jobs making the consulting fees redundant to executive salaries. Consultants can provide useful expert knowledge, outside perspectives, and specialized skills if properly managed, but these relationships can easily slip into the cart-leading-the-horse if consultants become too involved in management decision-making.

Companies like Enron use elite consulting firms, like McKinsey & Co., for their public relations value and to give assurance that management knows what it is doing. Elite firms use the publicity value of marquee accounts like Enron to market their services. Keeping marquee clients happy is a priority in consulting firms. If anything goes wrong in a marquee account that threatens its continuation as a client, consulting firms go into full-tilt emergency states.

Enron was McKinsey's top client with $10 million per year in billings. Enron was used to validate McKinsey's brilliance. After all, Jeffrey Skilling, Enron's CEO, had been a McKinsey consultant to Enron prior to taking a position with the company. In fact, as Skilling gained power within Enron, he began shaping it into the McKinsey model. McKinsey published extensively on Enron, calling Enron employees "petropreneurs" and touting Enron's McKinsey-promoted practices, such as loose-tight management and Skilling's "asset-light" strategy. Skilling was said to use a "good McKinsey trick" to avoid analysts' questions—dump a ton of data on them.[2]

Many management consulting firms are kissing-cousins to academe (discussed in Chapter 9, "Too Silent Critics: Academe"). Firms that rely primarily on hiring people directly out of college into collegial organizational cultures have particularly close ties to academe. Consultants are under pressure to stay ahead of their clients and to be up on the latest ideas, always on the leading edge. New theories keep consultants in business and provide opportunities for new services (and products).

Introducing a need for change initiatives on the part of the client means more fees if a contract for implementation, and now outsourcing, will follow. The consulting industry has hit upon a way to really marry into the client organization for the long haul—outsourcing. During the

1980s, the sales model for consulting services was refined. First, get a contract to do feasibility or strategic consulting, often a break-even project or even a loss leader. The product of these exercises includes recommendations for a large project broken into a series of individually priced stages to avoid sticker shock, sometimes with alternate scenarios and pricing. Or, if the client is cash poor or a hard sell on a big project, a more modest proposal is made, usually with the hope that it will lead to more "follow-on" work. Finding follow-on work became an intense focus in the consulting industry. Andersen's Enron client service team was looking for follow-on opportunities as much as coordinating services for the client. In the late 1980s, the consulting industry began working on the next piece of the sales model—outsourcing—and it was to become a huge piece, the Big Enchilada, as Jeffrey Skilling liked to say.

AOL is an extreme example of how service providers might approach a client. AOL salespeople first investigated the finances of prospective clients for advertising services and then worked backwards to take as much of the cash as possible. Startups funded with venture capital were wrung dry.[3]

Like any business, consulting firms are focused on their revenue stream. Outsourcing solved the persistent problem of boom-bust financial cycles within consulting firms as discreet projects came and eventually went. Stabilizing revenue by locking in steady cash flow from long-term outsourcing contracts was the miracle the consulting industry needed to service its own pressures for double-digit growth. Consultants began toasting success at deal-closing parties and announcing long-term contracts worth hundreds of millions to the press. Their dream of fields of cash cows came true. Enron pursued this strategy, offering to manage the energy of companies and governments right down to changing the light-bulbs. Multi-year, multimillion-dollar contracts were announced that had Enron changing light-bulbs all over the world.

Although there have always been some good reasons, both cost and efficiency-wise, to outsource routine operations, clients in large outsourcing deals quickly found it was more costly and ultimately less efficient or effective to outsource more complex functions.[4] After the initial honeymoon, many bitter divorces ensued. But the trend goes on because the consulting industry has found ways to make client books look better and give the client an appearance of adaptability to analysts by outsourcing, along with using more contract labor of all sorts. On the part of the client, outsourcing contracts give the appearance of stabilizing costs and keeping up with the Joneses. Announcements are made to the press that make clients look smart, and the issue of whether these arrangements actually do stabilize costs or keep clients on the leading edge is usually not re-visited in the press. Change-order fees can quickly mount up as a client tries to actually get what it needed, wanted, or expected from the deal. Consulting firms have also honed the ability to extract fees out of the cancellation of carefully crafted contracts.

Enron was an extreme case of what happened as some companies began to offer outsourcing. It was unprepared to follow through on these contracts. Enron was worse than most because it was an entirely undisciplined, chaotic environment that was not bothering to control its own costs or smooth its own operations. Key executives within Enron had no interest in day-to-day operations; in fact, anyone who did exhibit an interest in the mundane was a much poorer, second-class citizen. There was no money to be made in bonuses or increased stock options from actually making Enron work as a company. Nonetheless, Enron took on major contracts in which commitments to operate client functions were made and then ineptly executed or not kept at all. Enron's energy outsourcing contracts, among other things, called for Enron to pay the client's bills for them, and then clients were appalled when they were put into collections by vendors that Enron had neglected to pay on time.[5] In Enron's case, this wasn't just a matter of ineptitude; the company had almost no cash.

Although Enron is an extreme case, a lot of the consulting companies offering outsourcing struggled with coming to terms with the reality that they had actually diversified into a very different kind of business. Consultants naively jumped into very different types of businesses on the assumption that this would just be an extension of what they already did. IT hardware and software companies took on large outsourcing commitments and then had to learn to live with their own hardware and software on a day-to-day basis. This was a far cry from dropping off products or heading out the door when an IT system had been converted. Misguided assumptions were the foundations of multi-year contracts that ended up in big financial losses and operational disruptions for many consulting firms and their clients.

The IT industry was particularly susceptible to assuming that anything related to IT should be easy. Hardware and software companies launched consulting services in the 1980s and outsourcing in the 1990s. These consulting units were grafted onto the traditional business even though consulting required a very different business model to be effective. One CFO of a large hardware manufacturer openly voiced his adamant objection to getting into the consulting business as too risky, but the company plowed ahead anyway, losing millions and alienating clients in the process. Beginning in the 1980s, the IT sector was no longer content with offering to integrate computer systems, but was pushing to integrate and then re-engineer entire businesses around new technology. IT consulting firms began offering their own brand of software products and aiming at new consulting markets, such as strategic and management consulting. Many, like Andersen, were McKinsey wannabes. IT consultants soon learned that being in the software business was not easy, and ongoing support was costly.

As clients became dependent on consultants, resentment grew over the disparity between employee and consultant compensation, employees felt increasingly threatened with job loss, and executives started demanding more detailed billings from consultants as costs mounted. As consultants' personal compensation became more dependent on clients, they became more compliant, but also focused on protecting their secrets in order to keep clients dependent. Consultants learned to sit patiently through brow-beatings by frustrated clients. In the 1990s, consultants suffered through the tantrums of teenagers heading start ups. One mature consultant described keeping a change of clothes on hand in order to dress "hip" for young clients who didn't trust people in suits. He also saved one foul-mouthed tirade that a teenage CEO delivered on his answering machine, which he played for people to show how far things had gone. The young CEO's father called later to apologize for his son's behavior.

Enron represented the kind of bullying client that arose when millions were at stake. Remember the incident mentioned earlier in which

Enron employees enticed an Andersen auditor into an office, stuck a chair under the doorknob, and badgered him for 30 minutes, telling him he couldn't leave until he agreed to deliver an opinion letter immediately in support of a tax scheme that meant millions of tax savings to Enron. The beleaguered auditor complied.[6] Many at Andersen suffered through Enron tirades.

Consulting became a high-stakes, cutthroat industry as all types of consulting organizations began cross-competing. Pure consulting firms had all kinds of competitive threats from entrants into their field. New markets for services were created as the industry grew larger and more complex. One of the more insidious developments in the industry was the rise of executive compensation consulting. Along with their use by boards of directors, executives hired them personally to give advice on new ways to beef up their pay and tighten up their contracts. Compensation consultants are pinpointed with central responsibility for ratcheting up executive pay and slipping complex compensation contracts past boards. Their fees were a small price to pay, either with company funds or out of their own pockets, for executives reaping the benefits.

Public relations consultants were also in on the bonanza of the 1990s. Like compensation consultants, they were hired personally by executives for whom the company PR machine was not generating enough publicity. Racking up a list of speeches, being quoted in the media, or better yet, getting a picture out, was the way up the corporate ladder and the way to negotiate better compensation contracts. Image consultants, executive coaches, and a host of other boutique services surrounded the occupants of executive suites, paid for both by the company and themselves. In addition to internal resources, companies like Enron paid fabulous fees to PR and advertising agencies.

Lobbying firms are a variation on the consulting theme, and this sector of the industry has had a considerable role to play in recent events. Enron was among the corporate leaders in campaign contributions and lobbying activities. Well-known figures, such as Henry Kissinger and James Baker, were on the payroll. Enron executives were also, as private individuals, leaders in political contributions and campaigning. Along with political party involvement, Enron hired political consultants, such as Ralph Reed, former executive director of the Christian Coalition, and Republican pollster, Frank Luntz. Political consultants helped Enron devise strategies to push its agenda of deregulation, bend accounting rules, and wiggle out of its troubles.

In the case of financial, legal, accounting, and management consulting sectors of the consulting industry, large advisory fees are generated by big events, such as initial public offerings, mergers, acquisitions, dispositions, and restructurings. In addition to the interests of the consulting industry being served by these events, executive compensation consultants often helped their clients get an income boost from them as well. Carly Fiorina, former CEO of Hewlett-Packard, and Compaq Computer Corp. CEO Michael Capellas withdrew from a bonus program that would have paid them $22.4 million for completing the merger of these companies.[7] When the media got wind of these payments, Fiorina and Capellas were embarrassed into forgoing their own bonuses, but they left a $33 million post-merger retention bonus pool in place that was divvied up by other executives.

Enron, as usual, takes the prize for gall. Fiorina and Capellas' decision not to take their merger-triggered bonus came as a result of increased media scrutiny of these payments. Just as the Hewlett-Packard and Compaq merger was being finalized, the press picked up a shareholder outcry when Ken Lay was set to take a $60 million bonus for negotiating a rescue by Dynergy as Enron was collapsing. Enron shareholder pressure prompted Lay to announce that he would not take the payment to which he pointed out he was contractually "entitled." Perhaps he was prescient; the Dynegy merger never happened. Record numbers of mergers and acquisitions generated a windfall of fees for consultants, and compensation consultants made sure company executives were in on the action.

Large financial services fees are also generated by transactions, such as those Andrew Fastow was executing for Enron in the course of robbing Peter to pay Paul book juggling within those more than 3,000 special-purpose entities he created. At the end of every quarter, Fastow was pulling off multiple multi-million-dollar financial transactions involving millions in fees to financial institutions. People in the financial industry soon got wise to Enron's pattern and quickly began squeezing the most out of Fastow when he came running to them in a panic. Bankers knew Enron was hooked on transactions, and their personal bonuses were riding on getting the most out of clients, plus it was their quarter end, too.[8]

Members of boards of directors, their families, and cronies were often on the receiving end of consulting fees in addition to their other compensation and perquisites. Accounts of Enron are rife with examples of this type of conflict of interest involving the board. Perhaps an even more toxic corruption to come out of the consulting boom was in academe, as we discuss in Chapter 9. Academics formed consulting companies on the side or associated themselves with consulting firms, leveraging their academic affiliations into consulting credentials.

The consulting boom tipped the scales in terms of the relationship between theory and practice. Some began to question the fad-driven nature of management, suggested calling a halt to mindless change, and plead for more common-sense management.[9] Yet new theories abounded, and executives wanting to appear on the cutting edge of the new economy and complying with the exhortation to change or die bought into new theories before they were tested as if they were gospel.

The proportion of consultants who actually have significant experience outside the consulting sector has always been small and shrunk as the industry boomed. College graduates aspired to become consultants right out of school, and, more than ever, did. Accounting schools marketed the degree as a quick road to consulting, knowing this increased enrollments. Students getting degrees from elite schools filled the ranks of prestigious consulting firms and could walk right into a vice presidency, especially in new economy companies. Their heads filled with the latest theories and little else, consultants assumed an increasingly ubiquitous and powerful place in enterprises that hired them.

Consultants don't have to be bothered with the hard detailed work of running a business, except their own, which is a special variant of enterprise. Consultants who successfully move out of the consulting industry have a notoriously poor track record. The consultant who makes an effective manager tends to be the exception, not the rule. Many consultants devise grand plans and then sell them as many times as possible in order to be profitable. Unique engagements are called "one-offs," and these come with a higher price tag. The consulting industry depends on "reusability" to increase profits.

Not surprisingly, failed companies, such as Enron, could boast of consulting with the most expensive hired guns on strategy and operations. How could Enron not have a winning strategy with firms such as McKinsey advising it? How could Enron not have the best, most honest accounting and finance practices when a premier firm like Andersen provided oversight and advice? How could Enron not be financially sound when the major investment houses and banks were providing millions of dollars worth of advice every year? When we look at the bigger picture, the other massive failures were using consulting in similar ways, often even the same consulting firms. Fees galore were pouring into the consulting industry, and the key to increasing profits on the widening revenue stream was to shoehorn basic theories into as many clients as possible. The key to follow-on fees was to sell change; the Big Enchilada was an outsourcing contract.

There is also the matter of the government's regulatory agency fees assessed on public corporations. Creating fee structures that make public corporations, rather than general taxpayers, pay for governmental services and regulatory needs, seems like a sensible idea. Assessing fees based on transactions seems fair because it causes corporations that generate more work to pay their own way. It seems like a good idea to fund regulatory entities, such as the *Security and Exchange Commission* (SEC), by dunning public corporations for its operating costs.

The SEC is a good example of how good intentions and seemingly sensible solutions to funding fairness issues can go awry. The SEC collects fees from three primary sources: about one-third from securities that are registered for sale, about two-thirds comes from securities that are traded, and one percent is reported as deriving from tender offer, merger, and other types of filings. The SEC also collects registration fees from accounting firms that want to qualify as auditors for publicly traded companies.

Soon after Enron declared bankruptcy in December 2001, it became glaringly obvious to the American public that the SEC had been severely under-funded for years. Arthur Levitt, Jr., was the SEC chairman

---

through most of the 1990s. Levitt wrote a post-Enron book detailing how he was threatened with de-funding if he didn't make sure the SEC backed off on reforms he was vigorously trying to push through against the wishes of corporations.[10] Conflicts of interest, primarily related to their consulting activities, had built up within the audit industry, causing public auditors to largely align themselves with corporate interests. Large audit firms spent their vast lobbying money fighting against the same reforms corporations vigorously opposed. Levitt remarked that Enron represented everything he feared happening all taking place in just one company. Powerful forces had prevented his reform attempts.

One of the first political responses to the scandalous state of SEC oversight revealed by media coverage of the collapsed corporations in 2002 was for the president to step to the podium and declare a doubling of the SEC's budget. President Bush did not, however, submit this amount to Congress; it was far less. The SEC's pre-Enron budget allocation for 2001 was $422 million; for 2002, $514 million. President Bush announced he would increase the budget to $776 million for 2003 and then actually submitted a request for $568 million. After considerable wrangling, Congress overrode the reduced amount, passing a measure for $716 million. SEC budget requests for 2004 and 2005 are $811.5 million and $913 million, respectively.

The real story about SEC funding is in the fee collections. In 2000, the SEC collected over $2.2 billion in fees—$1.89 billion *more* than its $377 million budget for that year. For years, the SEC had been a "profit center" taking in far more than it used. In 2001, when Enron's fraudulent accounting came to a head, the SEC collected nearly $2.5 billion in fees with a budget of $422 million. And what happened? In January 2002, a month after Enron declared bankruptcy, the Fee Relief Act went into effect, reducing SEC fees.[11] SEC fees directly reflect the level of activity in our capital markets. More activity should directly translate into more oversight, and as it turns out, we could have afforded it. Instead, the government was treating the SEC like a cash cow.

The recent pharmaceutical scandal involving Vioxx revealed a similar dynamic within the U.S. *Food and Drug Administration* (FDA). Corporations pay fees to fast-track their drugs through the FDA. This effectively makes them "clients" and gives them too much power to control the FDA, which provides the public's oversight of the pharmaceutical industry.

Fees are at the bottom of many of the conflicts of interest that crept into America's business system. The Sarbanes-Oxley Act of 2002 addressed some of the issues in the auditing profession by limiting and requiring disclosure of non-audit fees collected by a company's outside auditors. The larger issue of fees flowing out of corporations requires shareholder and researcher attention.

Questions to ask:

- How much does the complex "structured financing" of companies actually cost?

- Are executives misusing consultants to legitimate a questionable action, as rubber stamps, or as scapegoats?

- Have executives developed a knee-jerk reaction to hire consultants whenever they think there is a problem or an opportunity?

- Should departing executives receive guarantees of consulting fees as part of their "package?"

- Are there serious conflicts of interest created by fee arrangements?

- Are consulting expenses simply too much—this is, after all, real money leaving the corporate coffer.

11

HOW WE NEARLY LOST AMERICAN CAPITALISM

Some see private enterprise as a predatory target to be shot, others as a cow to be milked, but few are those who see it as a sturdy horse pulling the wagon.

—*Winston Churchill*

American capitalism has delivered on its promises. American standards of living are, by some measures, the highest in the world. The variety of goods and services readily available and the quickness with which companies adapt to sudden changes in consumer taste is impressive.

Look at cell phones. Motorola is credited with inventing today's cell phone in 1973. With increased built-in usefulness and availability, cell phones have become a major form of communication. Retail landline business is endangered as, in just a few years, cell phones have morphed into hand-held computers and cameras as well as communication devices. Most recently, the cell phone business is being threatened by Internet telephoning capabilities.

Cable systems are rapidly becoming multi-purpose tools for connecting homes to the outside world. Mother Bell and her "baby bell" offspring are adding services, merging and running as fast as they can to compete with cable and exploit new technologies. Constant change, new and improved and often cheaper goods and services are all what we expect from our economic system (along with the destruction of marketplace losers).

Our economy brings a surfeit of choice. The enormous variety of product variation and differentiation can even create decision-making paralysis as people dither over small, sometimes meaningless, differences. While some people find researching even the smallest purchase invigorating, others find it stressful and agitating.[1]

Our flexible, innovation-oriented capitalism allows individuals with new ideas, energy, drive, and persistence to start new business ventures. Many are self-financed initially with family savings and borrowings. Most of these "entrepreneurs" do not have illustrious family names, and their ethnicity might not be mainstream America. Only a very few of these hard scrabble beginnings will lead to enormous enterprises and great fortunes within the lifetime of their founders.

The demise of local small business is now often a painful cost of tough global competition. Europeans have been even more distressed than Americans with the injury suffered by small, local retailers. Entrepreneurial businesses are an important segment of the American economy. Only recently did the aggregate economic value of America's small businesses dip below that of large corporations. Many viewed this shift with alarm.

At its best, capitalism is a major structural support for an open society in which humble beginnings do not foretell the future. It accomplishes this in the process of fostering an open competition in what kinds of technologies and products will be most successful in the marketplace. A belief in social mobility, rags to riches, is essential for a thriving democracy. Capitalism is the mechanism by which this belief is made sustainable.

America has an implicit bargain with free enterprise capitalists. They deliver an ever-increasing supply of affordable goods and services, rising standards of living, and employment. America delivers a supportive legal and social environment. That usually translates to minimum government interference with business and a culture that tolerates significant disparities in income. Income and lifestyles can be very good for winners, but it is has not been a "winner takes all" society (so far).

WorldCom

This now infamous company was also a well-publicized example of the economic potency and motivational energies created by American capitalism.

WorldCom was founded in the mid 1980s (as LDDS, Long Distance Discount Service) by a former Canadian junior high-school basketball coach and, more recently, an owner of some Mississippi motels. Unquestionably, Bernard Ebbers was a man of modest means. Yet, he conceived of a new kind of telecom that would exploit the economic potential unleashed by the Bell system's breakup and industry deregulation.

Within a decade, reincarnated as WorldCom, and after large numbers of acquisitions, the upstart had grown to be the fourth-largest U.S. telecom. In the midst of its growth spurt, WorldCom was doubling revenues almost every year. In three years, revenues soared from $8 billion to $40 billion. Truly an incredible story. In addition to the CEO's not insubstantial earnings, shareholders, who had invested $10,000 in 1990, would have had stock worth $870,000 at the 1999 peak price.[2] As you know, this success story had an unhappy ending, suggesting some of the pitfalls of unrestrained capitalism... but that comes later.

Incredibly rapid growth can occur because many financial institutions and shareholders are willing to lend or give money to promising ventures, regardless of the religion, politics, or race of the management. Founders and CEOs sometimes go to great lengths to create Horatio Alger-like myths about themselves whatever their basis in fact. It's always better to be self-made in America, or it has been.

America's capital funding is flexible and mobile. As tastes change, as new technologies develop or innovative services are offered, resources shift to what appears to be more promising, that is, more likely to be more profitable, manufacturers or service providers. They, in turn, can grow, and the less-adaptive or less-needed goods and services will find it more difficult to get needed financing.

As the brilliant economist Joseph Schumpeter described, the shifts in capital resources ("creative destruction") get signaled by profit.[3] Profit is a gyroscope that keeps resources directed toward their most high-value use and shifts them away from lower returns. Thus, businesses that are very profitable attract new competition either from better-run organizations or newer, alternative products or services. Over time, new businesses that were once able to charge quite high prices for something new and attractive find that they have to lower their prices to meet competition, and eventually their high profits decline.

As you no doubt recognize, this is Adam Smith's theory of pure competition from Economics 101.[4] An "Invisible Hand" directs resources, capital, and people to where they are most valued by consumers. Self-correction, fully automated with no computers, is the marvelous hard core of capitalism. Poor quality or obsolete goods and high prices get zapped without some authority declaring them excessive. Society gains with more desirable goods and services. Shoddy merchandise stays on the shelves as the good stuff flies out the door. Everyone has a chance to grab the "brass ring."

No government regulators are needed to tell companies to manufacture more DVDs and fewer VCRs, to discount long-distance calling, or to adopt customer service stressing that "the customer is always right." The free movement of capital and the lure of profits do the trick. Decisions, for the most part, will be in favor of society. In America, the system has worked rather well overall according to a number of measures.

Those with a history bent will note that this is also a Newtonian world of mechanical perfection. But no one over the age of 16 should believe that life is quite as simple as that stuff from Economics 101 we have just regurgitated. There are barriers and interferences with this society-friendly automaton's decision making.

Accounting, a Backbone of Capitalism, Degrades

Students of accounting have learned that the "data" it provides can be even more subjective than statistics. The old auditing joke about profit being what you want it to be has been shown not to be funny by the hundreds of cases of corporate cooked books. The results in misdirected and squandered resources are often horrendous.

MCI WorldCom, seeking to please Wall Street, wildly exaggerated its profitability. This led competitors to engage in a frenzy of fiber-optic cable purchasing. Literally hundreds of thousands of miles of cable were laid that would go unused. Enormous quantities of telecom corporate resources were wasted. Recently, the cost to our society was increased when a large proportion of this embedded cable was sold to foreign telecoms, weakening our own international position in this vital industry. The price paid: 25 cents on the dollar!

Similarly, Enron executives dissembled on the profitability of its trading operation. They and others even dissembled on their actual, current sales prices for natural gas that they submitted to pricing services. What appeared to potential competitors as an extremely lucrative adjunct to the highly regulated utility business caused many other utility companies to pour huge amounts of borrowed money into trading operations. A side effect was the neglect of the upgrading America's utility infrastructure. Many of those utilities almost bankrupted themselves when trading failed to meet even minimal profit expectations. Again, financial resources were misdirected by phony data.

Investment banks directed enormous amounts of capital (principally by underwriting debt) into companies that were misstating their profits. Mutual and pension fund stock purchasers, misled by false earnings projections from investment bank research analysts, added to the social waste as they poured shareholder funds into scores of dubious Internet-related companies.

Was it shareholders own fault? Some say, yes. Individuals had lost their savings because they lost their common sense in their irrational exuberance. The system was fine, it just looked impaired because of greedy investors who had forgotten the old adage about staying bearish or bullish, but never being piggish.

Too clever "financial engineering" facilitated the conversion of corporate accounting into an art form. Techniques evolved, some legal and not a few fraudulent, to hide debt and "create" revenues and even earnings. Investors and stock analysts were deceived and bamboozled by what was anything but transparency.

The ability of savvy accountants and the inherent ambiguities in *Generally Accepted Accounting Practices* (GAAP) and *Generally Accepted Audit Standards* (GAAS) rules allowed companies to both hide debt (often parking it in off balance sheet accounts or "erasing" it with "finite reinsurance," which is a loan in everything but name) *and* exaggerate earnings and book value.

Is Government Regulation Really Necessary?

America's capitalism has worked so well that many executives and political conservatives have developed strong, emotionally charged convictions that government regulation is wrong. It can only hurt the operation of "free enterprise." According to these beliefs, our marketplace is a self-regulating system; miscreants will be punished by the market at some point. The purist free enterprisers, sometimes called free enterprise *fundamentalists*, believe that critics are either Cassandras or socialists or both.

Market Manipulations

In the past, threats to our capitalist system primarily were external. They grew out of the way companies dealt with their markets and their competition or potential competition. The bad guys fixed prices and colluded with competitors.

In reality, most markets were never quite that "free." For three-quarters of a century, America sought to deter restraint of trade and price fixing by its famous Sherman Act. The Sherman Act forbade unfair trade practices along with laws against price fixing and the kind of bid rigging we see in the insurance brokerage scandals engulfing companies such as Marsh and McLennan and Aon.

As our colleague, Professor James Kuhn, likes to say, corporate leaders spoke glowingly of our free enterprise system, but they were less enthusiastic about "free markets." Their preference was what they called "fair competition," a kind of gentlemanly competition in which no one would seek to land knock-out blows on a competitor. They competed with each other, but only up to a point. That game ended in this new era of unceasing, tough worldwide competitive pressure.

Even with our long-established laws forbidding price fixing, new revelations appear of major corporations who in theory compete with one another but are actually colluding to divide up markets and/or fix prices. Recently *Archer Daniels Midland*, Marsh & McLennan, and numerous others have been caught in these scandals. Companies usually pay stiff fines and get some bad publicity, but this doesn't seem to deter future schemes. As profit margins get squeezed by global competition, there may be more efforts to impair the functioning of free market (while touting belief in free enterprise).

Market dominance can also hurt free markets. A frequently cited example is Microsoft's dominance in PC operating systems. Microsoft has used its early control of desktop software to seek to exclude other companies from successfully developing complementary software. Both U.S. and European anti-monopoly governmental interventions have helped blunt Microsoft's effort to monopolize a significant portion of the global computer-application market by means of its successful operating system.

A Newer Threat to American Capitalism

The market "bubble" began as the last century was coming to its end and the Internet was bursting with its promise of almost infinite profits and the expected accompanying growth in public company share prices. The bubble's end was signaled by the sudden demise of the dotcoms in early 2000. Then it was accelerated by the implosion of Enron, by market capitalization, the seventh largest company in America. What followed was coupled with the effects of September 11, 2001—a well-documented stock market crash; the bursting bubble. We were used to dealing with bad guys who sought to fix prices, but not the new breed of executives who upset the functioning of markets by manipulating and publishing deceptive corporate accounting and hiding debt.

Investigative reporters, states' attorney generals, and the SEC (rather slowly and sluggishly) discovered that executives had developed a variety of personally self-serving practices. Unlike external aberrations, which unfairly raised product prices, the internal mischief bloated share prices and executive compensation and robbed shareholders. Many of these involved deceptive financial statements; others went so far as conspiracies to mislead investors and lenders and even outright fraud. Worse yet, all the oversight mechanisms considered critical to corporate governance failed. Gradually, we have learned that auditors, attorneys, bankers, regulators, and boards of directors had fallen down on the job.

Shareholders aided and abetted the scams in their own way and paid a heavy price for their willingness to believe that the "New Economy" was coming and that they could be part of the utopia that was just over the rainbow. From the point of view of pure free enterprisers, shareholders were complicit recipients. They should have known that you win some and you lose some.

As America's economic system's defects were being revealed and disseminated by the media, defenders of the faith sternly reminded the doubters and free market apostates that no one said that business was moral. It is amoral, and the necessary energizer of the capitalist system was the chance to gain lots of money and concomitant power. This was the driving force behind new businesses and ambitious CEOs.

People ignored a larger issue. Society can be a winner in a free market system (as well as the shareholders who make the right bets) *as long as the game isn't rigged*. It has to be the good guys and gals that win, not the cheats and those who would commit fraud and deception or purposefully inhibit the free workings of the market and the movements of the famous Invisible Hand.

The defenders of absolute free enterprise had a final retort. In most cases, everything defamed companies did was perfectly legal; their executives just took advantage of loopholes consistent with accounting rules and/or little known details of incredibly complex and arcane tax law. Indeed, many of the most egregious corporate "sins" had begun as an effort to "stretch the envelope," test the limits, to use aggressive, "creative" accounting and a wealth of complex debt instruments, euphemistically called "structured finance." Corporate accountants, auditors, the due diligence of bankers and the scrutiny of internal and external corporate lawyers had all certified this new financial legerdemain as legal.

Very likely, many of these innovative financial techniques just slipped over to the illegal side of the ledger, as we know, an intrinsically slippery slope. What is illegal versus legal might not always be an easy call. Some slippage is inevitable in companies with aggressive management, willing to "live on the edge." Everyone knows that both laws and accounting principles have inherent ambiguities, without which we could do with truckloads fewer attorneys and even shutter a few courts.

Financial reports that are deceptive, misleading, and often impenetrable by anyone without substantial time and expertise are wrong, just wrong. Even forensic auditors and government regulators have often had to spend months, in some cases years, to fully penetrate complex, corporate accounting and financial reporting. How could the Average Joe ever be expected to figure out the Rube Goldberg constructions financial engineers had cobbled together to produce "structured finance"?

In a letter to then secretary of the Treasury, Paul O'Neill, Alan Greenspan in early 2002 spoke openly about the severe limitations of generally accepted accounting practices:

> ...a disturbing amount of corporate accounting has come to rest on little more than conforming to...GAAP, without endeavoring to judge whether the companies' accounts in total do, in fact, represent a full and accurate portrayal of the current financial status of the corporation.[5]

O"Neill and Greenspan and Arthur Levitt, while he was head of the SEC, sought ways to force CEOs to portray a company's financial health in terms that helped any reasonably intelligent investor to judge whether it was a decent investment. Needless to say, they failed. CEOs could perform as the PR guys, touting their companys' great perform-ance; no need for honesty. One result was that many companies were so weakened by executive decisions intent on hiking share prices (and the value of their own options) that they went into bankruptcy or were crippled for several years.

The absence of what is called transparency became the major flaw in the operation of the U.S. economy as the 1990s drew to a close. Transparency refers to prices and company financials. It had been con-ventional wisdom that it was the "little guy" who was at risk of being conned by slick salespeople because he or she didn't know the legiti-mate price for a diamond or a fur coat or a new car. Now we have seen sophisticated investors and corporate buyers being tricked.

In several industries, presumed market-based choices were distorted by conflicts of interest; the buyer's impartial guide to the marketplace was receiving an "under the table" payment by the seller. The most flagrant occurred in the placement of large corporate pension funds and insur-ance policies. Brokers and consultants who supposedly sought the best investment or underwriter for a given client were selecting funds and underwriters on the basis of the hidden fees they received.

Edward Siedle, a former SEC lawyer, who investigates money manage-ment abuses for pension funds draws this startling conclusion: "Our investigations reveal that investment consultant pay-to-play schemes involving collusion with money managers have cost (pension) funds amounts ranging from 10 to 15 percent of assets."[6]

In a similar distortion of market pricing, American Express and Morgan Stanley have been accused of providing incentives to their stockbrokers to push their own mutual funds. Buyers were deceived into thinking the broker was recommending the "best" fund for them. As is only too well known, investment banker research analysts were writing recommendations that were little more than touts for stock their companies had underwritten.

The amount and persistence of deception disclosed an almost total failure of *all* the oversight and regulatory checks that most versions of a free market economy take for granted. It was total systems failure:

- The SEC or the New York Stock Exchange were not effectively performing minimal regulatory activity to check that security laws were not being violated.

- Boards of directors were shown to be passive, rubber stamps; simply creatures of the CEO, with exceptions being all too rare.

- Internal and external auditors were easily fooled or co-opted by management intent on cooking the books.

- Bankers were not intent on performing the due diligence that assures that borrowers are likely to be able to repay their loans so depositors benefit.

- Outside counsel, distinguished lawyers, could be paid large fees to write opinions that executive decisions were well within the law and accepted financial practice.

- Investment analysts did a poor job or no job of studying the financial statements of those companies intent on deception and/or fraud. Instead, they allowed themselves to be an adjunct marketing arm of their investment banker colleagues.

- Credit rating agencies discounted important financial realities when assigning ratings, which became the holy grail of companies like Enron. Getting the rating up or keeping it from sinking became a preoccupation and there was no hesitation on management's part to use deception.

Powerful motivations are released with the possibility of huge winnings not just in money, but also in status and power. When accompanied by a modest likelihood of painful punishments, the odds favor deceptive, if not illicit manipulation increase. Stock options and a soaring market removed any inhibition that might have been felt by many executives to avoid the temptation of doing "whatever it takes" in the way of financial manipulations to score.

The degree of ambiguity and the complexity of the issues are highlighted by the difficulties experienced by government regulators and injured shareholders and debt holders seeking punishment and redress. Successful prosecutions are taking years, enormous amounts of time and money. The general public has expressed an almost blood lust for revenge for having been taken to the cleaners. Further, there are big political stakes in being able to prove that white collar criminals get punished at least as severely as street crime. The party in power has no desire to be proven soft on crime, all kinds of crime, and there are an increasing number of executives who are now serving jail time for these financial crimes.

Is Self-Dealing a Likely Concomitant of Capitalism?

There is another flaw in the widely held belief that free markets self-correct for the benefit of all. The major players in the marketplace are large, hierarchical companies. By definition, their top management is given and requires great discretion in decision making.

Management decision powers include executive compensation, although there is an annual ritual of securing board of directors' and shareholder approval. A tacit assumption in a free market economy is that executives will not plunder their own companies. They will exercise responsible self-discipline, self-control, and will not run off with everything not tied down. The restraint was supposed to be their fiduciary responsibility to protect the interests of the shareholders.

Business economists typically worried about government, trade unions, and bureaucratic work rules creating business costs and inefficiencies. Increasingly, a company's own executives demanding and receiving astronomical compensation are injuring the treasured "bottom line"; taking as much as 10% of corporate earnings.

Distinguished economist and diplomat, John Kenneth Galbraith, described the current avarice issue succinctly in a prescient book many years ago:

Management does not go out ruthlessly to reward itself…a sound management is expected to exercise restraint…. With the power of decision goes opportunity for making money…. Were everyone to seek to do so…the corporation would be a chaos of competitive avarice.[7]

Here is just a small sample of well-known examples of how "competitive avarice" became a commonplace: A senior executive at Viacom, the media conglomerate, served only shortly more than a year and decided he was not happy with the situation. He then received a $30 million severance allowance for voluntarily quitting. As another example, in early 2005, the CEO of Gillette got an extra $185 million for selling the company to P&G.

Given the impenetrable deceptions of shareholder proxy statements, "it is next to impossible to know for sure how much executives make in total compensation."[8]

Free enterprise theory fails to take into account that executives have the power to take from shareholders via their compensation packages. A special committee of the board of directors at Hollinger International "investigated claims that Lord [Conrad M.] Black and top executives took 95% of the company's net income over seven years through payments and excessive fees."[9] The U.S. SEC filed suit against Canadian-based media magnet, Lord Black, Hollinger's former chairman and CEO, and F. David Radler, its former COO, accusing them of bilking the company of tens of millions of dollars and conspiring to conceal their dealings from shareholders and regulators.

Watered stock has been with us for a long time; both the cattle and the financial variety. Most shareholders had no idea how much their stock holdings were being watered down by executive stock option programs, employee option plans, and the use of stock to make acquisitions and mergers happen. Investors will find out how watered-down their holdings are when the new rule requiring stock option expenses to appear on the books goes into effect in mid-2005.

Many shareholders are unaware that the stock buy-back programs are simply using shareholder funds to minimize the dilution created when executives exercise options.

A basic premise of free enterprise capitalism is that senior executives will engage in no activities in conflict with their fiduciary responsibilities. Excessive compensation, of course, appears to be just that kind of conflict. One could argue that avaricious executives had become the real owners of their corporations, not the shareholders.

The bursting bubble revealed a number of blatant violations of what most would assume was a minimal rule of good behavior. Many CEOs accepted bribe-like "gifts" from investment bankers who sought to get or maintain their company's business. The financials were manipulated to yield enormous executive bonus payments. Too many executives have short-changed shareholders by demanding huge severance payments that complicate buyouts.

Enron again provides perhaps the most flagrant example of executive self-dealing. Enron's chief financial officer, Andrew Fastow, established a semi-private "company" whose business was investing in Enron projects. The small coterie of executives brought together in this entity were guaranteed returns many times their very modest investments.[10] In fact, Fastow alone skimmed off over $60 million from Enron shareholder equity through this blatant self dealing. This was in addition to his Enron compensation.

The Danger of a Backlash

A premise of the American way of doing business relates to its system of taxation. Americans have a worldwide reputation for being relatively good, that is, honest, taxpayers. The operation of our government and the public infrastructure is dependent on tax receipts.

Historically, business has provided a significant share of tax revenue. Not a majority of tax revenue, but still consequential. Increasingly, there are signs that some companies are going to excessive lengths to avoid taxes. Not just being tax conscious, but buying into tax shelters that may be legal but are considered abusive. Many were concocted and sold by a company's own auditors who also "serviced" the company's senior executives. Many believe that selling these conflicts with the role of outside auditor.

In most cases, what many executives did was all perfectly legal and above board. But they were playing the loopholes. Using fancy side shots, taking exploitative compensation, and tolerating conflicts of interest all have a corrosive effect on society at large, quite aside from distorting the market. When citizens start thinking that they have really been taken by a "junta" of bankers and rogue CEOs, confidence in the fairness of our free enterprise system begins to waver. The wavering becomes more extreme when people become aware that the rogues have taken the "riches of the kingdom" and that the bad guys do a great deal better than the good girls.

Ken Lay, the infamous Enron CEO, suffered no immediate penalty in the fall of 2001 when he confidently announced that the upcoming quarter looked great and the company's stock was a tremendous bargain. Just a few weeks later, the company announced a big loss and the public learned that the SEC was initiating a major investigation. By the close of 2001, Enron filed for bankruptcy. It took hard talking to get Lay to resign, and even then he wanted to collect over $60 million in severance pay.

Adding insult to injury, these beneficently rewarded executives at the top of the food chain appeared to be avoiding any of the responsibility associated with being at the pinnacle of the organization chart. A nice double play. Eisenhower and Truman's commitment to remembering "where the buck stops" was not in their rule book.

As self-serving corporate financial practices were being disclosed, these same executives practiced sophisticated "plausible deniability." Over and over again, investigators seeking the sources of malfeasance heard CEOs and CFOs repeat the following mantra:

> We were assured by our auditors and our attorneys that there were no wrong doings. As any good leader, I delegated responsibility. I hired competent people who I could trust knowing that they would inform me if there were problems I needed to address.

Executive Seductions; The Real Threats to American Capitalism

The corporations that contributed to America's many real economic miracles deserve our respect. They sought to build long-run shareholder value by building robust companies based on market-pleasing products and services. These are corporations that continuously improved and sought new products and services. Profits have been shared among shareholders in dividends and rising share prices, employees and executives and the investment capital requirements of a successful business. Risks have to be taken to develop new products and services for uncertain future markets, and managements borrow today with realistic confidence that funds will be available to repay those loans with higher future earnings. In addition, there are substantial contributions to social betterment programs.

Many of the well-publicized, costly, and shocking failures were companies that had little resemblance to the enduring earlier giants of American business. Some of the old giants didn't even resemble their earlier selves by the twenty-first century. In retrospect, the differences that proved calamitous were obvious "accidents waiting to happen." Most were companies in which personal integrity, fairness, and some sense of commitment to the larger society had lost their meaning. Secondarily, the effectiveness of monitoring and oversight institutions, which should play a critical role in determining how many will "go rogue," left out a great deal.

Rather than devoting themselves to creating and marketing products and services that would earn broad acceptance, executives converted product companies into financial companies. Enron, for example, had become an unregulated investment bank under Jeffrey Skilling. Finance was the preeminent corporate function; "financial engineering" became the name of their game. The focus was on the creation of good numbers for the investment community and the development of ever more abstruse financial instruments.

Free market capitalism was not supposed to do these things, which is why some Americans and many Europeans are now expressing doubts about the *capitalism Americane* proudly exported just a few decades ago. When a significant number of people questions the legitimacy and fairness of the economic system, you have problems, big social and political problems, as well as economic ones.

Business, at times, is its own worst enemy. In tune with our increasingly polarized political world, almost any suggestion that there is a need for change is bashed as an obvious effort of untutored populists to hamstring free enterprise. You are either for us or are against us. Government's role should steadily decline, and less is always better.

Looking Forward

Recent history tells us that capitalism without a supportive legal system can be a license to steal here, as well as in Russia. An under-funded SEC, among other things, meant reduced surveillance in the 1990s, and the number of deceptive accounting practices and tax abuses soared astronomically.

But constraints come only secondarily from the impersonal "rule of law." Much more critical as a control are the norms and values of culture. Contemporary American acquisitive culture has been undercutting the very premises of capitalism: honest reporting and executives who believe they should serve shareholders interests—not their own investment accounts, a half dozen homes connected by Gulfstream jets and enormous yachts, and their children and grandchildren's comforts. Many conservatives take pride in a social Darwinian culture, survival of the fittest. Losers are less fit and deserve less. But when "survival" is the result of gross deception and self-dealing, a "winner take all" philosophy, evolutionary platitudes are grossly deceptive. Winners may rapaciously suck up too much. Some will find it is easier to win by cheating than by the fierce competition that capitalist theory assumes. This is social Darwinism at its insidious worst.

Most students of business and well-read citizens have taken for granted that free enterprise always works as advertised. Capitalism flourishes in and supports democracy, and like democracy, it requires work to maintain its vitality. The major reason: capitalism and democracy both involve people, their passions, and their foolishness. Both institutions are always at risk and are more fragile than it is comfortable to admit. They can degrade into authoritarian regimes and stratified societies with an angry underclass.

A kind of fundamentalist capitalism insists that free enterprise's original conceptions represent perfection and therefore should never be touched. According to their beliefs, intervention only makes matters worse or is willful blindness. "If it ain't broke, don't fix it" makes good sense, but....

By way of contrast, we believe the real world has no self-maintaining systems (the solar system comes close to an exception), and some of the parts of our business system are "broke." The most distinguished defender of the free market faith, Milton Friedman, has written that free markets can insure individual freedom *only if* society provides justice and equity to all. He concludes that *respect for the rules and norms of society is a necessary bulwark of a free market system.*[11]

No one thought our free enterprise system was threatened by unscrupulous land peddlers, who sold naïve northerners underwater Florida real estate a half century ago. (Who knows; it might be worth millions today.) More worrisome are the deceptions and lack of transparency practiced by elite financial institutions.

Mutual funds were the capitalist stock market's answer to investment scams and the limited sophistication of the smaller investor. (But we learned that fund managements can deceive their shareholders by allowing large investors to "scam" the funds by late and excessive trading.) The first of June 2005, Citigroup agreed to pay the SEC $200 million to settle another deception.

Their Smith Barney funds had negotiated lower mutual fund administrative costs with transfer agents. Rather than reducing the administrative fees charged to fund shareholders, they kept the millions of savings for themselves. This was clearly unethical and their auditors, Deloitte, thought it was illegal. Fund shareholders, in effect, were paying phantom costs![12]

12

THE MYTHIC CEO: WHY REAL LEADERS BECAME AN ENDANGERED SPECIES

Traditionally, senior business executives were almost unknown to the public at large; they preferred anonymity. Their names appeared on major charity event programs and other public good works, but rarely in the business news. Rarely was CEO compensation a news item, and most corporate leaders received income commensurate with their positions. Lee Iaccoca, the CEO who rescued Chrysler in the 1980s, was a great exception; he savored PR and worked the media like a pro to benefit the company. His compensation made news when he cut his $360,000 salary to one dollar and said, "I intend to spend it very carefully."

Iaccoca may have spurred the trend toward CEOs reinventing themselves as mythic figures. Refinements in the field of public relations and more newspaper and TV business news helped. Hiring PR consultants paid for personally by the executive became common. It was their job to mythologize. Company-paid PR and marketing also focused on executives, and CEOs became stars in their companies' advertising. Meetings were staged for "production values" by Hollywood-trained specialists. CEOs appeared larger than life on the same giant screens used for rock concerts.

A hot stock market and big baskets of options moved many CEOs front and center, immodestly receiving public recognition, incredible pay, and celebrity status. They took more credit than was their due, given that we've always known the link between a CEO and his company's performance is tenuous at best.

While corporate greed is now widely scorned, it seems only yesterday that a relatively small cadre of CEOs were lionized by the media, the public, and, of course, the stock market. They were the modern equivalent of (and were actually termed) rainmakers, conjuring miraculous corporate growth: size, revenue, earnings, and most important, in share prices. The now-familiar pantheon of icons included such headliners as Enron's Ken Lay, Microsoft's Bill Gates, GE's Jack Welch, CitiGroup's Sandy Weill, IBM's Lou Gerstner, and WorldCom's Bernie Ebbers. A few really were excellent founders or "transformational" leaders.

CEOs' fame and apparent leadership gifts entitled them to compensation and lifestyles fit for kings; probably more opulent than that enjoyed by the declining population of real European royalty. Their status and recognition put these CEOs on a public recognition par with Hollywood stars and famous professional athletes. While their grandiose lifestyles and compensation might appear over the top, it was unquestioned at the time, given their leadership "gifts."

Executive star billing took place in those heady days of great public enthusiasm about stock market trading. The media fed and ginned up the public's interest in business news. Business stories were more arresting when complemented by pictures of a colorful CEO. Their eye-popping compensation and succession of "big deals" generated broad interest. Corporate and personally hired PR consultants sought to leverage the news value of the CEO's persona to further boost share prices, not to mention their ego gratification. It appeared as though some CEOs were becoming the equivalent of a marketing "brand."

When the glitter and paper profits suddenly faded for many of the high flyers, CEO adulation was replaced by angry criticism. Many of those who had appeared so responsible for the big wins were now at the center of devastating corporate scandals. For the first time, their total compensation came under scrutiny.

America's Royalty: Mythic CEOs

GE's CEO, Jack Welch, was arguably the most admired CEO in America. His books and books about him were enormously popular, and he is still a highly paid lecturer and consultant. Welch's strategic decisions helped make GE a highly profitable company and wiped away vestiges of a drifting bureaucracy. However, when his marriage dissolved in a much publicized divorce battle over the equitable division of assets, the details of his GE compensation became embarrassing public knowledge. Some of his future benefits, which were not required to be disclosed to investors, were exceedingly costly. Divorce proceedings made these part of the public record, and the media picked up on it.

Even after retirement, Welch was given the indefinite use of a company-paid, luxury apartment in New York City. Many of his personal bills for wine and laundry would be paid; as well as personal dinners at one of New York's costliest restaurants, prime sporting event season tickets, personal security, use of a corporate jet, and the like. All this was on top of large retirement payments. Although Welch's post-retirement benefits received broad media coverage, some of his peers received similar shareholder beneficence, minus the more personal items.

Other "royals," CEOs like Dennis Kozlowski, fared less well in the media. As their companies failed, their excesses were considered beyond the pale. A $6,000 shower curtain and lots of costly art for Kozlowski's company-paid furnished New York City apartment was part of the story. Later, during his trial, video of a sybaritic partially company-paid overseas birthday party costing $2 million was another embarrassing disclosure.

We suspect that there will gradually be more revelations of the extra, hidden benefits granted to top level, already wealthy and highly paid executives. In May 2005 the SEC sued Tyson Foods for failing to disclose perks received by its former Chairman, Donald Tyson (whose personal fortune is in the billion dollar class). Tyson paid $38,000 for his oriental rugs, $15,000 for a London vacation, an $8,000 horse, half a million for personal use of company houses in Mexico and England, $400,000 for friends and family to use company jets, $200,000 for housekeeping costs for five homes, over $100,000 for lawn care and telephone for those houses, lots to maintain nine cars, and so on.[1]

We detail the trivia of Tyson's billing to suggest again the analogy to royalty. The "people" (in this case the shareholders) pay for the equivalent of lifetime care regardless of the executive's actual fortune. Such ridiculous, petty perks are probably less costly to shareholders than the looting of Adelphia's John Rigas or Parmalat's Calisto Tanzi. They treated the company treasury as a perpetually full honey pot to buy things they wanted.

Compensation Excesses

After the stock market pummeled, the shares of the many of the "bubble's" most popular companies, shareholders, and the general public began to take serious notice of the extraordinary compensation packages of CEOs. Their magnitude and the implicit greed behind them tarnished the image of mythic CEOs who had been receiving full credit for investors' lush paper profits.

Stories of excesses have not ceased. In one example, a billion-dollar bonus was divvied up by the CEO, who got the lion's share, with two other Computer Associates' top executives. Recall that the profit numbers justifying this incredible bonus, as well as many others, had been inflated by accounting misdeeds. Even Franklin D. Raines, former CEO of Fannie Mae, the esteemed semi-public mortgage bank, is alleged to have improperly deferred expenses in the late 1990s to ensure his and other senior executives' bonuses.[2]

Compensation packages of $20 or $30 million were no longer a rarity. Only recently has the general public learned that many were inflated because CEOs hired their own personal compensation consultants. These consultants helped design the large array of tax-advantaged compensation far in excess of the published salary and locked in by meticulously worded contracts. As the spotlight was shown on gross excesses that had to be disclosed, compensation consultants helped create more "stealth compensation" that was not required to be disclosed to the SEC or investors.

Typically, the CEO's pay package included bonus payments. Some bonuses were guaranteed, which seems a bit of a contradiction, while others were dependent on various performance measures, some of which could and were manipulated. Additionally, CEOs demanded several kinds of stock options, unrestricted and restricted stock, insurance (that would build equity rapidly), large pension contributions, deferred compensation (some that paid compound interest significantly above market rates), hundreds of thousands of dollars to cover tax liabilities as well as tax consulting fees, huge severance payments, low-interest loans to facilitate the exercise of options (now outlawed), and a variety of so-called perquisites like promises of future consulting fees and extensive use of corporate jets for friends and family.

The corporation usually promises to pay legal bills (expecting insurance will cover most of these). There have been recent cases where hundreds of thousands of dollars have been expended to defend an executive who is presumed to have fraudulently obtained bonuses from his company. (That "benefit" will have to be repaid if and when the executive is convicted, unless, of course, he declares bankruptcy.) The HealthSouth CEO added to his package by getting an extra half-million dollars for himself to help pay for any needed legal defenses the day before the company declared bankruptcy.[3]

These "packages" were so complex and arcane that unenergetic boards could easily fail to grasp the total dollars the company was committing itself to pay. The furor over the roughly $187 million payout of deferred compensation and other remuneration that Richard Grasso demanded from the New York Stock Exchange was based on the allegation that his board never understood all the terms of his compensation package.[2] Less well-known is that Grasso had also had the Exchange pay $130,000 each for two personal drivers and $240,000 for his assistant. All befitting a mythic CEO.[4]

Severance Payments

"Golden parachutes" symbolize the excessive compensation expectations of some CEOs. Of course, they also spotlight the enormous gap between the typical employee "package" and the parachute. The company gets no benefit from the CEO after his departure, and these large payouts are on top of other carefully crafted compensation. Most are unknown to shareholders until they are about to be paid. Sometimes, these payments get made whenever there is a merger. It was alleged that former Florida Power and Light executives, including their then CEO, received such a payment for a merger that never took place. Even though that structure change had been abandoned, the executives apparently were reluctant to return the payment.

More than a decade ago, when Sandy Weill was acquiring the broad array of financial companies that would become CitiGroup, he set his sites on acquiring Primerica. While negotiating the purchasing price for this financial conglomerate, Weill discovered that the company's CEO had a confidential employment contract that guaranteed him and some close associates a $90 million severance payment. It took Weill's aides some time to tease out the details of this added cost of the acquisition that had not been disclosed and was buried in corporate documents. Yet, this was not an unfriendly acquisition. Gerry Tsai, the CEO, was eager to cash out his Primerica stock; severance appears to have been some "frosting" he wanted added to the deal.[5] Weill was tempted to retract his offer. Later, angry shareholders complained that these enormous severance payments were 6% of Primerica's total value.[6]

A similar incident occurred during the last-ditch effort of Ken Lay to merge Enron with Dynergy. When Dynergy's CEO discovered the generous severance Lay had buried in the deal, he was furious. The deal fell through and Enron went bankrupt.

The president of Gillette received a payment of $185 million. He had negotiated Gillette's sale to P&G, and this would compensate him for no longer being CEO. Big money even for a big deal.

Stock Options

Whether and how options should become a cost to the issuer has been vigorously debated for decades. Corporations and some of their audit firms spent vast sums fighting disclosure of options as expenses. In December 2004, the SEC finally announced that companies will be required to expense them starting in mid-2005. It was not unusual for three-fourths of the total compensation of the CEO to consist of profits made by exercising stock options. Typically, the CEO has been granted a vast majority of all employee options awarded in a given year. In recent years, in anticipation of the SEC change, many companies have issued fewer employee stock options, and CEOs have made up the difference in cash bonuses.

In Chapter 3, "The Stock Market and Executive Decision Making," we said these option plans created a new class of shareholders, "privileged shareholders," given their special ability to correlate insider knowledge with stock purchases and sales. As what we have termed the ultimate inside trader, astute CEOs sought to time the exercise of portions of their accumulated options. Options are usually exercised about the time the CEO is intending to sell shares. The CEO is in an excellent position to know when share prices have outrun the company's likely near-term performance.[7] It should be noted that these shares cannot be sold in the period shortly before the announcement of earnings, but that's of little consequence. Executives learn about significant events that are going to affect earnings before they are converted into "announced earnings."

Secretary of the Treasury, John Snow, provides an example. News stories a few years ago alleged that while CEO of a major railroad, CSX, he used a $25 million company loan, secured by $7 million of shares he already owned, to exercise a bundle of options. Apparently, to his chagrin, the newly purchased shares went down in price. As a "privileged shareowner" he returned the newly purchased shares to the company and had the loan cancelled.[8]

Investors in companies whose shares have tanked have been outraged to learn that the CEO (and other senior executives) often dumped big portions of their holdings shortly before bad financial news became public. CEO Ken Lay collected over a hundred million dollars the year before Enron declared bankruptcy.[9] Lay was not an exceptional case.

In 2005, senior executives of CheckPoint sold a bundle of shares before the public knew that the company had suffered a major embarrassment. Its data warehouse security was inadequate, and a hundred thousand people had personal data revealed to potential "identity theft" scam artists.[10]

Unlike run-of-the-mill shareholders, CEOs and other senior executives also sometimes get the price at which they would buy stock adjusted. Their boards were encouraged to recommend that new options with a lower strike price be issued as a substitute for those that were now "under water," that is, too expensive. These were likely CEOs being rewarded for poor performance.

But perhaps the most telling critique is provided by *The Economist* citing a study by the well known Boston Consulting Group. Their study of public companies recently convicted of fraud found that

"The value of stock options granted to the CEOs of those firms in the years before the frauds became public was 800% greater than those granted to the CEOs of comparable firms not found guilty of any wrong doing."[11]

Why Such Enormous Compensation?

Various surveys differ, but in the past 20 years, CEO pay in large companies has gone up from 40 times their average employee to from 500 to a 1,000 times the average corporate employee. Alarmingly, studies suggest that in 2004, average compensation for CEOs of large companies was still climbing.

There has been little exploration of why some (surely not all) CEOs demanded and got outrageous amounts. Some of the excess is a leapfrog-the-leader phenomenon. X gets more so Y wants still more and Z insists on the jackpot. Compensation experts advising the boards of directors abet the process. They do surveys enabling the board to put its CEO into the upper levels of the distribution, which further pumps up the averages. As in fabled Garrison Keiller's "Lake Woebegone," where all children are above average, so are most CEOs it seems.

Market forces do play some part in ratcheting up compensation. Executive Z has an outstanding reputation and a particular board is determined to get Z; cost is irrelevant. Perhaps the analogy to pop and movie stars and professional athletes is legitimate. At any one time, there are a small number of marquee CEOs, and their market value will bear no resemblance to the earnings of non "stars." However, unlike performers and athletes (at least those not on steroids), there is much more ambiguity surrounding what is star-quality performance. Recent research suggests that executive pay goes up with little relationship to performance.[12]

The real total compensation package can easily double the total that appears if proxy statements and annual reports are not read meticulously. And then there are other sources of income. Dick Strong, whose ownership stake in Strong Funds was once valued at a billion dollars, engaged in questionable market-timing trades in his own funds. Jeffrey Greenberg, former CEO of the giant insurance broker Marsh & McLennan invested in independent partnerships spawned by his company that could have had serious conflicts of interest with their parent.[13] This is the kind of thing that got Andrew Fastow, CFO of Enron, into deep trouble.

It would be negligent to place all the emphasis on compensation. There are "imperial CEO's," those with a sense of omnipotence and omniscience, who seek other satisfactions. Maurice Greenberg, the extraordinary CEO of the insurance powerhouse, American International Group, apparently was obsessed with his company's share price.

The revelations in the Spring of 2005 showed him stretching good accounting practice to maintain AIG's reputation for extraordinary continuous earnings growth. Of course, predictable earnings translates into high share prices. There were even suggestions that he pressured the specialists at the NYSE who handled AIG shares.

Greenberg built the company and has a superb reputation for managing its complex affairs. His personal fortune was enormous. But apparently the company's share price had great psychic importance for him. Given this obsession, he may have exceeded the bounds of responsible financial management, although there is no questions that the company's financial performance is and probably will continue to be superb. [14]

Greed and CEO Personality

The question of why this happens still begs an answer. After all, some of the executives described took home hundreds of millions of dollars in half a dozen years, what used to be called a princely fortune, enough to support future generations and then some. Perhaps these idolized captains of industry believed their own publicity.

Pay, of course, is part of a scorecard, a "marker;" it tells the world how successful and important you are (or at least how important your board considers you).

A psychological explanation is that over-the-top rewarding reflects a personality disorder: narcissism, symptoms of which include hubris, grandiosity, and enormous self-assurance. A narcissist is someone with such an overgrown sense of entitlement, of being so worthy, that nothing can be too much. There is never guilt or concern with what others may think. Failure is rationalized as someone or something else's fault. Even though the additional income that might be obtained by some questionable activity or a no interest corporate loan is a modest increment to what is already being taken home, a narcissist would presume that whatever can be obtained is part of his or her entitlement. They revel in profligate spending.

We interviewed two consultants whose assignments had brought them into close contact with a number of well-known CEOs of large corporations. Their explanations of why a number of CEOs sought such over the top compensation were very similar. One said that some believed, "I am like a god; I am worth it." They would talk of their accomplishments and conveniently forget any failures. Sometimes, they mention how a Hollywood star would get many millions for one picture.

The other consultant reflected on changes he had observed when an executive had been promoted to being the CEO. "His personality seemed to change from being a conscientious, very hard-working manager. Power was a narcotic. He would even say that he could now do anything and everything he wanted. The result was sometimes capricious decisions." In psychiatric parlance, this is called "blossoming." After constraints lift, a narcissist comes into full flower.

Arthur Levitt, Jr., the former head of the SEC provides his view of what he calls "imperial CEOs":

> Just about all post-Enron CEO firings involved talented, powerful individuals who conflated their positions with their personalities. Like modern-day sun kings, they thought the company was them. They thought themselves indispensable and demanded exorbitant compensation.[15]

HP's Fiorina

Carleton (Carly) Fiorina, the dismissed CEO of *Hewlett-Packard* (HP), is a "mythic" CEO. Many agree she is superb at marketing products and herself, a truly charismatic figure. At the same time, there are accounts describing her as arrogant, authoritarian, and insensitive.

She was controversial from the outset of her short tenure at HP. There was a huge signing bonus and payment to move her yacht from the East to the West Coast. She played for high stakes: pushing vigorously and effectively for the controversial $18.9 billion purchase of Compaq against the objection of powerful board members. Her victory then diluted existing HP shareholders' value (and is likely to require a big write off of its true acquisition costs). HP's stock price has floundered in this period.

According to reports, members of the HP board felt that her self-confidence caused her to be inflexible. She did not seem responsive to criticisms that she was ignoring problems surrounding the execution of her strategy. Unlike CitiGroup's rambunctious Sandy Weill, she did not appear to stress the importance of execution. She was acclaimed as a "visionary," but didn't develop effective operations and was alleged to have fired or scared away many who could fill such roles.

She blamed HP's corporate culture for their profitability problems. However, one employee pointed out that she had ruthlessly rid herself of HP management that didn't see things her way.

(She may still have a point; even when a new CEO dispenses with intractable managers, people in organizations can resist the impositions of a new CEO, especially if they threaten strongly held values.)

Fiorina made $159 million between 1999 and 2003, when she received a substantial bonus before being forced to resign in 2004 (but with a $21 million severance package).[16] Apparently, even when dissatisfied, boards are reluctant to cheap out on CEO bonuses.

Managers we interviewed who had worked under her at Lucent felt that one of her problems was an over-reliance on highly ambitious performance targets to achieve goals. They said that the targets were so unrealistic that they were forced to "fudge" numbers, even forge signatures, and forward false reports. She had no interest in exploring why targets might not be attainable in the business climate of the time or what strategy changes might be needed. Lucent's downfall has been attributed in part to booking new huge orders regardless of the credit worthiness of the purchasers increasingly financed by Lucent.

HP employees and the press speculate about whether HP would have hired Fiorina if they had waited six months. Six months after Fiorina went to HP, Lucent showed signs of deterioration. A senior Lucent executive addressing the graduating class of the first new manager training session to follow the explosive downfall of Lucent candidly expressed his explanation of her problems at Lucent...

According to this Lucent executive, Rich McGinn (then CEO) "took his eye off the ball." McGinn was distracted by his new celebrity, caught up in his new hobby, collecting and racing expensive antique boats. Presumably Fiorina had filled the power vacuum. After a period, Lucent employees began to read very negative news stories about Lucent and were seeing announcements of thousands of firings. (Most of the new managers he was lecturing would soon be gone as well.)

Just as many were predicting that Fiorina would never work again, her name was floated as a possible candidate to head the World Bank.[17] While this suggests the strength of her reputation, as we know, Mr. Wolfowitz got the job....but, after all, he had the advantage of being an insider.

The Rush to Pump Up Profits

The most fundamental goal of a real corporate leader is building the business, its vitality, its robustness, and its ability to grow well into the future. These long-term objectives may be less compelling when the CEO knows that his tenure is likely to be only half-a-dozen years. Chapter 3 describes the powerful bias in decision making flowing from short-run, stock market-related pressures. Investors' expectations of rapid price appreciation and the executive's own compensation and portfolio incentives combine to make near term earnings trump more long term goals. Impetuous investment decisions can be one of the fall outs.

Alluring New Markets

Lots of companies, such as AOL and Enron, signed deals that could pump up immediate revenue or earnings but not contribute to building their businesses. Many of the supposed benefits of the deals were illusory as well. Utilities plunged into the new market of energy trading because it seemed like a sure way of booking quick profits. Some began building costly new electricity generating plants without having any assured market. Telecoms, and those seeking to become telecoms, rushed to become broadband service providers. After all, the demand for Internet access was exploding, but ultimately, not as much as people were led to believe.

Just about all those broadband ventures failed. Companies buried thousands of miles of what became "dark" (i.e., unused) fiber-optic cable. The corporate losses here were huge. Enron wrote off about a billion dollars on their venture into this new territory. Internet usage was growing more slowly than the hype suggested (the Big Lie discussed in Chapter 4, "Black Boxes and Big Black Lies").

Some telecoms paid a high price. Excessive enthusiasm and lack of financial constraint led to more than 60 bankruptcies in 2001 and 2002, and 500,000 lost jobs. Now several years later, after all the fiber-optic cable fire sales, burdensome debt, and lost jobs, the industry is consolidating while investors lick their wounds.

Energy companies that followed Enron's lead and engaged in energy trading are still seeking to reduce the enormous liabilities created by impetuous contracts they signed guaranteeing future deliveries of gas at prices now way below the current market. The CEOs of most of these companies rushing to harvest huge profits had little understanding of the dynamics and uncertainties of these new markets. They ignored the great volatility inherent in energy markets and, in Enron's case, other commodities as well. A number of the new electricity generating plants being built "on spec" were left unfinished. Deregulation in the electricity market was partial, and the national grid wasn't really a national highway. So surplus or undervalued power could not readily be sold into more attractive markets.

There were also costly missteps in the rush to become service providers when outsourcing became all the rage. Locking in a steady stream of income for several years seemed like a no-brainer. Naturally, Enron was among the companies getting into the services market fast. Enron wrote contracts promising to do everything down to changing the light bulbs for clients, giving little thought to the realities, logistically and in terms of cost, of fulfilling those promises. In general, major outsourcing deals worked out so badly for clients that many of them are bringing these functions back in-house.

High-powered CEOs neglected some "principles" of Economics 101: high profits attract competition, which quickly reduces margins. Guaranteeing future prices is a game for speculators who are expert at dealing with high risk. CEOs also neglected the crippling burden created by the huge amount of borrowing or low-balling of outsourcing quotes required to quickly become major players.

Some were "go for broke" strategies based on what should have been an obvious fallacy: that markets (and profits) will grow in a steeply sloped straight line. CEOs were behaving like speculators, not responsible fiduciaries for their shareholders. Their quickly boost-revenue or earnings strategies failed, leaving companies close to or in bankruptcy, spending years focusing on asset sales to reduce onerous debt levels rather than building their businesses.

Many of these overconfident executives devoted themselves to managing profits, not managing their businesses. These may seem like the same thing; they're not. A rising stream of sustainable profits are the end product of a demanding process of doing a lot of things "right." In the 1990s, instead this became a matter of financial engineering more than building real business improvement. The strategy field often spoke of doing the "right" thing; it is doing the "right thing right" that counts.

Acquisitions and Cutbacks

Many CEOs developed reputations for "hollowing out" their companies, slashing payroll costs to the bone, as another quick way of pumping profitability. One of the early, well-publicized examples was a media favorite, "Chainsaw" Al Dunlap. His fame lay in jump-starting profits, and therefore, stock price, with just such moves. When the dust settled, the best examples of his "leadership" were shown to be unprofitable. Bad management had created a variety of product and service problems that far outweighed the immediate cost savings. Dunlap also resorted to accounting tricks and is now barred from serving as an officer or member of the board of a publicly held company.

Unquestionably, many companies were too fat to support current levels of output. In some cases, cutbacks were necessary. But over time, they exceeded real need, and on occasion did more for PR. The cuts put great strain on impacted departments and embittered the remaining employees.

Employees in many companies that have experienced severe cut backs report a sense of exploitation from overwork and live with the stress of economic insecurity.

Overseas outsourcing is frequently in the news. The immediate cost savings appear irresistible—payrolls cuts by half or two-thirds. Here, too, some of the efficiencies are illusory. Some CEOs shot their companies in the foot. Huge corporations like Dell and JP Morgan Chase are beginning to bring back critical functions, such as customer service. They have discovered that the knowledge, flexibility, and adaptability of their Asian centers cannot compare with the service offered by U.S.-based centers.

Structural Change

Some of these CEOs rushed to make major changes in their companies' structure. What had been centralized was now decentralized, and what had been decentralized was now centralized. Just the adjustments and confusion created by reorganization ought to have given some pause to these choices.

These are critical decisions and can have a profound impact on performance. They need to be made cautiously and not hastily. Usually, sound organization structures consist of a mixture of operations that are centralized and those that are decentralized; choices made after careful studies of operations.

Adding new businesses by means of acquisition, cutting staff, and outsourcing can bolster the "bottom line" quickly. Nortel, for example, acquired dozens of companies over a short span of years and then developed serious "indigestion" in its profits, and its stock price withered.

Some companies were burying real operations costs, even operating losses, in the write-offs associated with the typical acquisition. Excessive write-offs for an acquisition also might assure a big profit jump in the following year.

Managing profits for the short term, for pay and personal glory are the major sources of destructive executive decision making. Plus, published profit growth in companies run by storied CEOs made news, which grew their reputation and future job-hopping potential.

Investment Bankers Aided and Abetted High Risk Strategies

High-flying CEOs depended on investment bankers to fund their quest to inflate the bottom line, and they flattered CEOs' egos in many attentive ways. Bankers played a key role in what was often a reckless expansion of debt incurred chasing misunderstood markets or as a support for "financial "engineering." There was real synergy in their relationships. CEOs didn't look too closely at the accounting supporting reported earnings, and the bankers didn't question very vigorously the credit risks inherent in excessive leverage.

Investment bankers are highly paid professionals who receive enormous bonuses for successfully courting CEOs, as well they should considering their fees (see Chapter 10). Many CEOs basked in the attention of these astute, articulate, overconfident bankers, who also might get them into the best clubs.

Sophisticated financial professionals had developed a dazzling portfolio of new borrowing instruments, far more complex than old fashioned common and preferred stock, notes, and bonds. Many promised their CEO clients more debt without more pain or even shareholder scrutiny. As we have said before, companies began to use more so-called "off the books" financing. Unlike traditional kinds of financial transactions, the financial implications of these off the books creations cannot be interpreted consistently by accounting professionals. There is no way of telling shareholders or the SEC what is really going on in terms of debt, cash flow, or income.[18]

Leaders seeking to build their enterprises recognize they must balance many factors in making important decisions. Some will be mutually contradictory; others elusive. Betting on the future should be based on an in-depth understanding of all the economic and even political and social forces. Assumptions that great profits will come quickly and in large proportion to the amount of capital at risk always need challenging.

The traditional role of senior finance managers was to help CEOs assess risk to the financial viability of the firm and to prepare for uncertainties as they help fund a growing business. In the companies we have described, CFOs and vice presidents of Finance actively collaborated in high-risk, overheated strategies.

Leadership and Implementation

Many of the famous, and now infamous, CEOs of companies who appeared responsible for soaring profitability were not good leaders. They scored high on securing funding and obtaining stock market enthusiasm. Internally, they were scorekeepers, pressuring subordinates to score high on measures that the investment community would reward. They paid well for those who hit their targets and readily punished those who failed. How those results were attained was a matter of indifference.

In the early 1990s, a distinguished Harvard Business School professor, Michael Jensen, lamented the failure of CEO salaries to keep up with inflation. He reported that his research disclosed that CEOs needed big increases in salaries. Like others, Jensen was concerned that CEOs were unassertive, acting like agents and hired hands, not owners.[19] Shortly thereafter, companies began giving CEOs huge baskets full of options to energize them to be more entrepreneurial.

The unanticipated consequences of buying into Jensen's "agency theory" and the growing belief in "rain making," mythic CEOs were destructive, both to corporations and the reputation of American capitalism. Outsized compensation became acceptable. A nasty spiral began twisting in the 1990s, and bigger encouraged still bigger. Issuing all those options (value based on manipulable earnings) was not that different from putting a few dollars into the eager hands of a child. Those dollars just begged to be spent and as quickly as possible.

CEOs treasured their compensation packages and supported aggressive accounting, which too often morphed into the illicit. Their leadership focused on the bottom-line numbers. Conveniently, the CEO's personal bottom line converged with the corporation's reported quarterly and annual earnings per share. Managers up and down the line learned that they had to do whatever it takes to make the numbers, or better, exceed them. Many soon discovered creative ways to work "outside the box."

These CEOs devoted themselves to *managing share price, not managing the business*. Managing real profit often didn't even matter to some anymore as long as financial illusions could be created to propel share prices up. This satisfied boards, shareholders, and "The Street," plus got them bonuses and a great price for their exercised options.

The days of the mythic CEO for whom no amount of compensation was excessive hopefully are gone or disappearing. Part of American business's undoing has been the pleasure CEOs took in media attention as a corporate "rainmaker," of personifying a great money machine. As many of their companies' shares went south, no amount of PR could keep the press accounts from turning derisive. Compliant boards of directors, previously content to ignore their responsibilities to shareholders, were shocked (and legally pressured) into becoming more vigilant, more responsible…finally.

Important leadership lessons must be relearned. Huge payouts attract (or perhaps convert) CEOs for whom quickly accumulating a personal fortune is a major source of ego satisfaction.

Meeting and overcoming the challenges of building a robust, dynamic business, the ever-changing competitive and technical issues, and gaining the confidence and respect of the multiple constituencies of every business are what provide the satisfactions of real corporate leaders. This quarter's bottom line is only one of many measures of accomplishment and often a very transient one in our volatile economy.

The measure of a CEO's worth can only be ascertained over some period of time. Those who cannot defer gratification, who want huge financial returns now, are unlikely to be motivated to lead a complex business system in such a way that long-term investors benefit, in contrast to traders and hedge funds. Worse still, they and the public come to believe that business success is the product of the "right" CEO, finding the magical leader, the rain maker, who single-handedly transforms a laggard company.

Perhaps more troubling still, leaders devoted to self-serving decisions feed derisive and divisive anti-capitalism rhetoric. The system is flawed if so few have so much, is the rallying cry.

For the most part, mythic executives are not leaders in any sense of the word. They often produce "profits" based on questionable accounting; not real growth of the business. They refused to give back bonuses and their stock sales profits that had been based on financial scams even when the SEC or courts had assessed corporate penalties. Their self-serving interests obviously were their primary priority, not the business or its shareholders, sad to tell.

13

SEEKING AND VALUING REAL LEADERSHIP

You can trust Americans to do the right thing...after they have tried every other alternative.

—Winston Churchill

M ost of the CEOs of corporations accused of accounting fraud and related misdeeds defend themselves by claiming ignorance and lack of involvement. Their attorneys' arguments have a simple minded and, for some, persuasive logic. CEOs focus on making big decisions: strategy, acquisitions, and the like.

CEOs have delegated the running of the company to trustworthy subordinates, so the story goes. Thus, they have no knowledge of inappropriate or illegal activities that might have been taking place. No one told them, and they never asked. Overeager subordinates could have misinterpreted the CEO's drive to get better performance numbers and took it upon themselves to achieve these by illicit means. The Sarbanes-Oxley Act attempts to end what has become this boiler plated "cop out" from charges by requiring CEOs to sign company financials and face serious criminal charges if they have been fudged.

The Leadership Failures of Those Mythic Leaders

One obtains a consistent picture of the leadership styles of most "mythic" CEOs from reading the financial press. By building its "plausible deniability" defense, top management may have been destroying their ability to understand the businesses for which they are responsible, building a "Chinese wall" separating the executive suite from the real work of the organization. These self-protective and somewhat incredulous denials distort everything known about effective leadership. Aside from whether they can be convincing to juries, they are good examples of people failing to do the right things…or not even knowing what those might be.

Failed executives perceived leadership in simple-minded terms. They set the company on a course dictated by their absolute assurance that their strategy was correct. They sought to cut costs ruthlessly, layoffs galore, and jump start performance with large carrots and even larger sticks. They offered big financial incentives to those who would meet very demanding objectives.

When company financial performance failed to meet objectives, they blamed the world around them. It was the ingrained, dysfunctional corporate culture. Key subordinates had failed to do their jobs and should be fired. (They typically were dispatched in short order.)

They had no in-depth understanding of the underlying businesses, their technologies, and the intricacies of the market. These people could not develop wise responses to failure and would not rethink company strategy. Recall earlier examples of companies continuing to bury hundreds of miles of unused fiber optic cable and the construction of electricity generating plants that were going to be connected to a poorly functioning national grid.

Selection

How can the "right" people be selected? Highly paid headhunters don't have a consistently good record. They, and then corporate boards, are misled by candidates who have had important job titles and are articulate self promoters. Little was learned about how they managed, how previous organizations responded, and to what extent good past performance was related to exogenous factors or their effectiveness. They know precious little about the candidate's personality, behavior under pressure, flexibility…all the things that build trust and motivation in subordinates and customers. Headhunters and boards are tempted to rely too heavily on the PR these executives have been able to generate and the most recent reported profitability of the unit they managed.

One clue about a candidate's motivation could be the overall size of her compensation requirements.[1] Candidates attended by costly compensation consultants and seeking a small fortune in guaranteed bonuses, massive option grants, and an array of less-visible forms of payment should be suspect. These self-indulgent potential CEOs typically have very short-run time horizons; they want to make it "big" in the very short run and are likely to make managerial choices with this impatience.

Thus, boards need to improve their ability to select executives with sharply different character and motivation. We know that almost all successful top executives seek and take great satisfaction in proving to themselves that they can really manage and grow a business. More than anything else, they seek that top position for the personal challenge and excitement, not primarily the monetary rewards. They expect to work hard, very hard, to obtain the satisfaction associated with great accomplishment.

A good example is one of the most respected CEOs, Roberto Goizueta. He was Coca-Cola's transforming CEO in the 1980s. The company was bound by the past and floundering prior to his appointment. Goizueta had worked himself up through the organization and proceeded to create more wealth for shareholders than any CEO in history. He never sold a share of his Coke stock and devoted his full energies to building the company. He continued to live in the same house he bought when he emigrated from Cuba.[2]

Desirable candidates also will make it clear to the board that they need and expect to expend substantial effort getting to know the company, its people, and its operations. Those who presume that a good manager can manage anything and move easily from one situation to a very different one are likely to be executives whose managerial efforts run on automatic pilot. They never bother to learn what the real issues are or how to "customize" their initiatives to the new organization.

Boards often mistakenly rely too heavily on executive search firms eager to get their fees. Their primary criterion is often previous job titles. The boards themselves need to know how to probe character and how subordinates viewed their leadership skills. With more attention to this, there would be fewer examples of new, heavy-handed CEO bullies who run rough shod over people and practice slash and burn tactics to show quick results that validate their selection and gain board support.

There is little doubt that executives obsessed with the short term are quite content to neglect investing for long term performance, building the future and exploiting the full potential of the company.

Breaking the Close Tie to the Stock Market

Many of the issues that have slammed corporations are related to the stock market, to the price of company stock. Of course, the CEO must seek to deliver share price growth, and share price is important in making acquisitions and avoiding vultures. The rub comes in getting hooked on reporting quarterly profits to meet "The Street's" expectations and having these grow predictably and continuously.

As we, and many others, have said perhaps too often, only in very exceptional cases can this occur. There are just too many uncertainties, too many things that can derail good plans. Yet CEOs have been both excessively rewarded and punished for maintaining the fiction and doing whatever it takes to make the hurdle. As previous chapters have described, "what it takes" usually got translated into "reverse accounting"…facilitated by those "black boxes."

CEOs, obsessed with monitoring Wall Street and their companies' share price, are tempted to encourage "fine tuning" (translation: partially contrive) quarterly and annual reported earnings by hiding costs and exaggerating sales and income. Generations of statisticians have taught us that efforts to reduce the variability of a system that has significant inherent variability typically ends badly. Such damping efforts actually *increases volatility*. "Smoothing" and "window dressing" earnings is a fool's game, but the fooling continues. Those fooled, of course, are the consumers of those earnings numbers.

The paucity of leaders who seek to build their companies in the long run, not their reputations in the short run, is suggested by a recent academic study of senior corporate officers. The (perhaps obvious) conclusion was that short-term earnings are their most important goal. The authors found (less obvious) that the executives in their study might very well sacrifice a potentially highly fruitful longer-term commitment if it would cause the company to miss "The Street's expectations."[3]

CEOs of publicly traded companies have to accept the reality that even in the best run companies, earnings are neither totally predictable nor do they normally increase at a reassuring 10 or 15%. (Unless, that is, the CEO is heading a really well-entrenched monopoly…but that would raise some other questions.)

When a company has good leadership, one of the frequently stated reasons for taking a company private is to rid itself of these stock market-sourced pressures. The recent spate of moves to privatize suggests how difficult it is for conscientious executives to avoid succumbing to the dictates of the stock market.

When John Reed was co-CEO of the huge and powerful CitiGroup, he was quoted going against the crowd by asserting, "I just don't care about quarterly earnings. My concern is what the company is making five years from now—increasing market share, building the franchise."[4] In recent years, such strong words, breaking close ties with the stock market, have rarely been uttered.

In a like vein, when Google, the much heralded search engine, went public, it issued an "owners' manual." (Hopefully, they continue to read it and their deeds follow their words.) The following is an excerpt:

> As a private company, we have concentrated on the long term, and this has served us well. As a public company, we will do the same…Outside pressures too often tempt companies to sacrifice long-term opportunities to meet quarterly market expectations… We won't "smooth" quarterly or annual results: If earnings figures are lumpy when they reach headquarters, they will be lumpy when they reach you…(We) do not plan to give earnings guidance in the traditional sense. We are not able to predict our business within narrow range for each quarter….and we believe that artificially creating short-term target numbers serves our shareholders poorly.[5]

Regrettably, boards, reacting to charges of too often being "out to lunch" in recent years, pressured by the big funds, began to pummel CEOs who weren't consistently hitting an acceptable earnings (and thereby market price) target. They considered this was their only way to be responsible to shareholders.

In sharp contrast, to attract and sustain real leader, there should be some mutual agreement between the board and a new CEO that enshrining quarterly earnings is "against nature" and tempts harmful mischief. To obtain and sustain good leadership, the board needs the courage to tell the CEO that the company's goal is significant growth over several years. There may well be quarters in which earnings are flat or even down a little, but the company gets the reputation of being consistent in its ability to maintain fiscal responsibility and earnings that grow over time.

How Leaders Use Symbols and Their Own Behavior to Communicate Values

CEOs often appear at charity balls and on the letterhead of organizations engaged in public service to represent their and their company's social responsibility. Often, it is not clear whether it is the CEO's social standing or the company's image that is being served.

Demonstrating leadership primarily requires behavior that communicates directly to customers and employees. Effective CEOs, for example, make a point of visiting and learning from customers, not just when an account is in crisis. They respond themselves when consequential issues of service or cost arise which might influence the loss of an important customer. Many CEOs spend a good deal of time on the road building customer loyalty and seeking feedback on what may be going wrong.

Customers need to develop confidence in the integrity of the seller. Corporate and personal integrity facilitates the operation of the free market system. A broad range of buyer/seller transactions depends on trust where there cannot be complete information. It is the trust that the other party has integrity, speaks the truth, and that the transaction is "transparent." Trust is derived from other parties learning that the seller is providing them with what they need to know to assess the quality and price and deliverability…and whatever else is relevant to an exchange taking place between well-informed parties.

Imagine the reaction of clients of those insurance brokers previously discussed who were creating mock bids so their clients would accept the insurance underwriter they had already pre-selected for them. Or, predict the reactions of clients of brokerage firms who were being directed to those mutual funds who paid special bonus commissions to those brokers? Or the reactions of fund investors who learned their funds favored a handful of hedge funds that got special trading privileges that were costly to the fund's non-special investors? As we know, great numbers of people took their money and ran.

Some years ago, the then CEO of Johnson & Johnson (J&J) demonstrated his company's integrity and his personal commitment to customer safety over costs when he ordered the immediate withdrawal of all outstanding bottles of Tylenol from store shelves. A single bottle showed signs of tampering at one store, and that was enough for him to demonstrate that J&J would tolerate no risks to customer health. The decision became famous for its leadership implications.

Employees also need to see for themselves the character and values of people at the top of their company. They need to see a real person with whom to identify, not just emails, letters, or a disembodied amplified intercom voice or a televised talking head.

Most of the previous chapter's mythic CEOs are aloof and well insulated from all but their senior staff. They set tough goals and seek to blame those lower in the hierarchy when these are not attained. Consistently, such CEOs are perceived by those in the trenches as having their own compensation as their primary interest, not the welfare of the business and its employees.

By way of contrast, executive leaders get involved and even "get their hands dirty" to show that they expect to be a source of help, not just a judge of who are the winners and who the losers. Here is a striking example of an executive demonstrating his commitments:

> During the 2004 pre-Christmas rush, Michael Duke, president of Wal-Mart Stores, personally visited an Atlanta store in the early hours of the morning. He was personally going to help customers load newly purchased TVs into their cars (!). While there, he got a call reporting that other Wal-Mart stores were not doing as well as expected. He then proceeded to drive to the store of competitors in the area to check out their business to help formulate remedial measures. Prior to that final rush, just after Thanksgiving, Duke had concluded that Wal-Mart was behind in anticipated holiday sales. Engaging in rapid exchanges with store managers and buyers he developed a consensus on what new reductions should be taken on special items to boost buyer purchases and took measures to increase supplies of these.[6]

Real leaders conduct occasional unscripted meetings across the company. Then employees can ask tough, even embarrassing, questions and hear the top guy (or gal) explain. Seeing this person allowing and then constructively responding to tough criticism contributes a great deal to the employees' confidence in their executives.

CEOs with an appreciation of leadership requirements insist on cutting their compensation when their companies are confronting hard times.

They don't hog annual option grants. If the company is seeking to be leaner, they look for ways to demonstrate that savings need to start at the top. Use of company planes for personal jaunts, excessively fancy sales conferences with their professional entertainers, executive meetings at distant resorts, and even costly art collections in executive offices—may get abolished.

Employees are eager to assess a new boss. Therefore, observable decisions become critical evidence in developing a judgment whether this one is really worth respecting.

A new chief executive of a major financial institution spotted a line of limousines in front of the corporate offices. He personally dismissed them when he learned that these costly cars and drivers were simply waiting for senior executives who might want to go someplace in the city (by limousine instead of a readily available taxi). The whole organization learned that he had also fired off an order to the executives responsible for ordering a waiting car that this behavior was not to be repeated. The ranks cheered this symbol of a new era in which the "top guys" for a change would also be making some sacrifices.

Respected leaders go out of their way to show concern and compassionate support when a catastrophe strikes an employee's family. Here is another exceptional example that was personally witnessed going back to the worst days of the Cold War.[7]

Tom Watson, then CEO of IBM, developed a personal concern that IBM employees were at risk should the U.S. be attacked by the Russians. It seems far-fetched today, but back then, Watson thought that employees needed to have backyard bomb shelters to protect their families from atom bombs. He said that IBM would pay a significant portion of the cost of a family's shelter. Far-fetched or not, it was a powerful indicator that Watson and the company really cared about the welfare of employees.

IBM's remarkable employee benefit contrasts sharply with a well-publicized Tyco policy designed to help a small number of executives. Under the leadership of Dennis Kozlowski, Tyco paid relocation allowances because the company was shifting its executive offices from New Hampshire to New York City. The policy enabled its well-paid

General Counsel to purchase costly New York City and Park City, Utah, condos. (He already had a home just outside the city and the company had no operations near Park City.)

Working with the Board

As noted in Chapter 7, "Directors: Why the Weak Oversight," boards can perform useful functions beyond selecting (and firing) the CEO, certifying financials, and deciding on mergers and acquisitions. Not being subordinates with vested interests, board members should be able to offer wise, dispassionate counsel to the CEO.

There is an inherent dilemma here. The board is also judging the CEO's performance and has the power to remove the CEO it deems inadequate. It requires sensitive board selection to get members who will be worthwhile counselors of the CEO and be able to separate that role from being his or her evaluator. It requires CEOs with self-confidence that does not border on hubris or arrogance to seek out honest judgments and criticism from those who aren't on their consulting payroll or subordinates.

CEOs understandably can be reluctant to share their uncertainties, worrying that it will be seen as a sign of weakness or executive indecision. However, the CEO has to be willing to have a favorite option shot down. Of course, there will be times when the CEO, responsible for results, after taking this negative feedback into account, still goes ahead.

Taking risk is part of the job. Great CEOs have often allowed themselves to be way out on limbs where the potential returns were great. Openly sponsoring the funding of risky new products with long development cycles are a good example. But, and it is a big "but," the continued funding needs to be a well-reasoned decision, not willful, impetuous, or to save face.[8]

Involved Leaders: Internal Oversight

Real leaders know that evaluating people and rewarding them solely on the basis of a single numerical score is an invitation to many managers to stretch the limits. The greater the potential prize for hitting the target, the greater the likelihood that questionable techniques will be employed to win the jackpot. The founder of Merrill Lynch understood this. Remarkably, given today's world, he felt strongly that brokers should *not* work on commission because this would compromise their professional judgment and commitment to the client. As everyone knows, commission pay and bonuses were well entrenched in the brokerage industry by the 1990s.

Obviously, targets can play a useful role in motivation and identifying problems requiring attention. However, executives need a great deal more information about the ongoing business before making decisions about what actions to take along these lines then just the current "scores."

Why Operations Are So Important; Looking Inside; Not Just Out

Business is now confronting savage capitalism. No longer are there easy profits to be made by being first to market, controlling a resource or a product in short supply. Those profits won't last; new and ever-more responsive and global competitors are ready to eat that lunch.

Responding to those challenges requires that leaders must know how to create organizations that can cope with the shortest product lifecycles executives have ever known. Rather than years or even decades, products may have to change in months. Retaining and building profitability also requires ever-quicker responses to customer complaints, quality problems, and changing market preferences. In this speeded up, economically global world, new components or materials keep appearing and old standbys disappear. New technologies offering improved performance or lower cost are flooding already chaotic markets.

Meeting today's business demands requires finding and retaining managers who can cope successfully with challenges like this:

Division A discovers that its output is being rejected by a good customer because of some minor defect or a competitor's new offering. Retaining the customer requires the manager of A to get the manager of B to modify the components it is providing or the engineering specifications B has been using. But B can't or won't agree because that would increase her costs, bust her already tight schedule, or involve prolonged negotiations with Engineering. Usually Division's C, D, and E will eventually be involved if that good customer is going to be retained. They, too, all have legitimate constraints that could impede efforts to maintain that customer.

Without high-level leadership that encourages and rewards these kinds of behavior, organizations tend to degrade with time. They become less effective in everything they are supposed to do. Rather than introducing change to deal with inefficiencies or quality problems, these are hidden or pasted over (often by creative accounting). Differences between functions and divisions become high, impermeable walls, injuring cooperation. Observers talk about the "chimneys" or "silos" getting taller. These fiefdoms learn how to shift blame for problems to other departments. Internal conflicts, and the destructive politicking that accompanies them, sap energies that should be devoted to problem solving and innovation.

CEOs and senior executives who are real leaders take on the task of countering this gradual corrosion of coordination and integration. This means knowing how to identify and reinforce subordinate managers who are effective at managing change. These managers have learned to identify rigidities in the system, including subordinates who lack flexibility and the willingness to bend their routines to solve problems for which they won't get credit.[9]

A primary focus thus is motivating actions that lead to better coordination and company performance. Telling subordinates to just keep their eye on the bottom line doesn't help. It hurts. Divisions defend their own financials at the expense of the larger organization.

Toxic bonus systems easily become entrenched, counter-cooperative drags on overall company performance. Dr. David Kay, chief weapons inspector in Iraq before the war, gave a startling and telling response during his congressional testimony. When asked what was most frustrating during his inspections, he responded vigorously and angrily with an example. He had to sort out an employee bonus complaint. Chemical and biological weapons inspectors were upset about a discrepancy between their bonus pay and that of nuclear inspectors. The two types of inspectors cut across organizational boundaries, and Kay had no hand in determining the bonus of either group.

It is striking that HP's board recently chose Mark Hurd to replace Carly Fiorina. There is a sharp contrast in leadership styles, the successor CEO is almost the diametric opposite of his predecessor, Ms. Fiorina. Hurd is known as some who can execute, can build trust, and is low key.[10]

Freedom and Security on the Scales

Just how difficult coordination can be is illustrated well in the unsolved challenges confronting the Department of Homeland Security.

A well-publicized rationale for creating the Department of Homeland Security was the need to prevent another 9/11 catastrophe. A basic security requirement was developing the ability to carefully screen those seeking to enter the U.S. through our many and varied ports of entry. Remember, one of those Saudi terrorists was already on our terrorist lists when they came through JFK. As reported in December 2004, three years later, ninety-nine percent of foreign visitors do not have their fingerprints checked against an integrated database of potential or actual terrorists. A struggle among Homeland Security, the FBI, and the State Department on technical issues has continued unabated for three years.[11] To make matters worse, in early 2005, the FBI had to announce scrapping their $170 million effort to create a seamless information system that would handle case files from preliminary field investigations all the way through any court resolution of the case.

> Clearly, there are profound issues of leadership here that have not been addressed. From the top down, leaders were not intervening to keep the process of integrating systems moving forward and to resolve the in-fighting and turf battles among the agencies that controlled parts of the puzzle.
>
> Meanwhile, at a "trade fair" for the Chinese government, American vendors were among those demonstrating systems that integrate smart "identity" cards with fingerprint recognition technologies and other state of the art government surveillance and censorship systems. To be fair for Americans balancing freedom and security issues is a more complicated matter.

A recent laudatory article about Exxon Mobil's extraordinary consistent profitability credits this to Lee Raymond, their CEO, who has consistently focused attention on operations and not solely on deal making.[12]

Meeting goals, including profitability (as well as integrating software systems) is the *end result* of doing great numbers of things right. As in sports, the good leader doesn't just pressure the team to win. The CEO doesn't just demand high profits. A good CEO knows how to assess whether subordinate managers are really good leaders, finding and solving operations' problems instead of depending on exhortation and threat. Those senior executives have to know when to step in themselves to end a stalemate that is injuring the company's responsiveness to competition and to be willing to use their energies and prestige to do this.

It is easy to understand why executives who reach the stratospheric levels of top management are happy to wash their hands of this messy part of the job and focus on tractable numbers and word-filled plans. A typical excuse is, "I don't want to get involved in the politics of the business."

CitiGroup's CEO, Charles Prince, announced in late October 2004 that he was going to get involved in the messy part of the job. He openly admitted to the Japanese parliament that lax corporate governance and an "aggressive sales culture" caused the abuses the Japanese government had discovered. Prince was apologizing to the Japanese government for his company's infractions. (As we know, unlike the U.S., Japan has a culturally based tradition of heads of companies accepting personal responsibility.)[13]

Prince announced that he would begin checking on "how" results were achieved, not simply looking at the "what," that is, results: "Under my leadership, lack of compliance and inappropriate behavior simply will not be tolerated, and we will take direct action to ensure that proper standards are upheld and that these problems do not reoccur."[14] Note how this is central to what has been described as real leadership.

This leadership initiative was motivated by the extraordinary embarrassment associated with the repeated malfeasance of CitiGroup's private bankers in Japan. Several years earlier, CitiGroup had been warned by the Japanese government that their bankers were engaging in illegal practices. Then in 2004, they were accused of ignoring possible criminal ties and money laundering by their clients. Top management's intervention was clearly called for. The company had been self-destructing one of their most important markets for the future.

Strong, unambiguous statements from leaders are useful, but they have to be supported by observable steps, including swift reactions to questionable managerial actions.

Some years ago, an outside investigation had alerted a major New York bank that it was being used by criminals to launder money. Almost overnight, the CEO instituted drastically changed procedures. There were no efforts to understate or hide the problem. All existing accounts were checked for traces of suspicious deposits, and outside law enforcement agencies were called in voluntarily by the CEO. Strict standards for accepting any new account, even credit cards, were instituted. Many potential new retail customers were turned away if there was the slightest suspicion that they might be associated with criminal elements. The whole bank learned that the CEO was determined to root out any traces of questionable activity, and every possible effort would be employed to be sure this problem never recurred.

Energetic real leaders have a number of informal techniques to sample qualitatively the strength and responsiveness of their organizations. They seek assurance that a wide variety of legal and business standards are not being neglected or fudged. Some early warning signals get detected because the top-level leaders actually make the effort to talk directly and informally with people throughout the organization. (A management expert coined the corny term "walking around management" some years ago.)

We would suggest that board members get around in organizations more, too. Remember, Andy Grove of Intel credited more active engagement of the company's board members, including site visits with employees, as a factor in having a well-functioning board.

Quite recently, an alert high-level official happened to hear a conversation in the executive dining room that suggested that a director had a highly inappropriate conflict of interest. After some investigation, it became apparent that the director had to be pressured to resign to avoid an embarrassing public scandal.

In companies that eventually paid a high price for malfeasance, there sometimes were one or two brave informers who sought to alert senior management. They were providing shocking revelations well worth checking out. As we know, they weren't and disasters ensued. Unfortunately, the reality is that whistle blowers are ignored, even punished, almost without exception, and they usually quit within a short time.

The first thing Ken Lay, former Enron CEO, did after talking with Sherron Watkins, who was suggesting a much-needed investigation of Andrew Fastow's deals as CFO, was to call the company's outside attorney to see if he could fire her. The Sarbanes-Oxley Act of 2002 strengthened protections for whistle blowers. Whistle blowers who are motivated by genuine concerns for doing the right thing in spite of high risks should be rewarded, not viewed as pariahs.

Balancing Resource Allocation

Departments compete for resources, particularly capital, to support the company's major initiatives as well as what are considered less important or support activities. Of course, that's common sense. More interesting is the unintended top management communication that some products or services are no longer deemed important (and may eventually be candidates for closure).

Parts of an organization considered unimportant or neglected often lose their best people who seek jobs in the more favored parts of the business. The remaining staff often becomes demoralized, and management creates a self-confirming prophecy: the less promising areas of the business run downhill while the favored areas get a chance to run uphill.

Involved Leaders: External Oversight

Leaders don't "bet the farm." That's an old expression that means avoid risking everything on the assumption that you are going to win big. The telecom and merchant power cases in preceding chapters were examples of CEOs taking on strangling debt in the belief that high future returns were assured. Ebullient telecoms had raised a trillion dollars in the period 1998–2001 only to lose hundreds of billions after. Those CEOs were extrapolating the future based on current data and the assumption that future growth would follow an excitingly steep, upward straight line. As we have seen, these were self deceptions.

It is well known that efforts to predict the future almost always are flawed. America's international affairs provide examples similar to the experience of business. A complex, dynamic world dictates uncertainty. Energy and raw material prices, continuity in political regimes, governmental regulatory policies, financial stability of individual companies, the relative profitability of various industries, and stages of the business cycle—all are "wild cards." Each of these, as well as dozens of other factors, is going to affect returns on investment.[15]

An interesting example of failed predictions is NASA's shuttle program. The agency had predicted that this new technology would reduce the $1,000 per pound cost of lifting men or materials into space to as little as $50 a pound. Given a number of unforeseen technical problems in the new shuttle program, the actual cost approached $10,000 a pound![16]

An old but sound adage in managing large, complex systems is to always, absolutely always, expect the unexpected…and you won't be disappointed.

Good leaders avoid "go for broke strategies," as tempting as certain opportunities may appear. They also invest their energies in seeking a wide range of opinions and knowledge. Ideally, these can be found on the board. Real leaders continue to monitor the environment for evidence that unanticipated factors make earlier decisions more questionable or even incorrect. They are willing to admit mistakes and make mid-course corrections. Personal pride, saving face, are not factors in their decision making. Most mythic, imperial leaders easily fail this test.

Real Leadership Isn't Just Good Packaging

Some final words on leadership. Many believe that business leaders a generation ago were quite different in style and motivation. There is a suggestive study of Harvard Business School graduates of half a century ago who are now in senior management. The following is the author's striking conclusion:

> They grew up in the Depression, fought in World War II, went to the HBS on the GI bill, and many came from the working class. They went into business with low expectations. They did not have a strong sense of entitlement. Wealth would be created patiently over many years. They were thankful for what they had been given, and many believed in social equity…. The author believes that many of these men are angry over today's huge compensation packages believing there has been a loss of values.[17]

We would wager that most of these executives had quite different leadership styles, closer to some of the behavior described in this chapter, than those "mythic" executives we described earlier. Does it take a depression to provide more leaders who are not self-centered and whose goal is building the business? Are the combined pressures of global competition and current patterns of stock market investment opposed to good leadership?

From the previous chapters, we think the answers to both of those questions are NO.

For some executives, leadership is perceived as a luxury, put down as no more than old-fashioned "people management" skills. That is unfortunate. It is much, much more. Employees and clients welcome having someone at the top whose character and action speak integrity and not overbearing self-confidence. And who take responsibility for what goes on inside their organizations because they are involved in these matters.

They would like to be working for a firm in which top management works hard to build the business, not their retirement and severance packages and when necessary takes the blame rather than automatically blaming others.

Without high standards set by the CEO's example, not words, some employees will learn to look good by cutting corners, "pushing the envelope," skirting the rules or even the law. Inevitably cynicism and demoralization follows as a very small, elite minority rakes in high approval ratings and personal returns.

Customers have more loyalty to a company whose top echelon is credible and responsible and believes in transparency in all transactions. There will always be tests of how their supplier responds to an emergency request that is critical to the customer's business.

Organizations don't run on momentum or solely on generous reward systems. For lots of reasons, research tells us they tend to self destruct at worst or just gradually become less effective over time. That does not happen when the CEO shows that he is interested, understands, and knows how to intervene when there are persisting and costly turf battles, failures of coordination, and poor service or quality problems—all messy and frustrating.

Real leadership is much, much more than enjoying the power and esteem of being in the catbird seat. It is a composite of skills and understanding of organizational systems that produce business vitality and growth. Real leaders are morally grounded people who are willing to assume responsibility. They realize that with privilege and status comes duty, and that wealth has its limits. Real leaders have a sense of proportion and willingness to work hard, to get beyond superficial, facile, or faddish solutions. There are great challenges these days: rebuilding eviscerated companies, getting out from under crushing debt, a demoralized workforce, and tarnished reputations add considerably to already difficult jobs.

14

WE CAN DO BETTER

Devious financial manipulations have increased in number and diversity, as well as in costs incurred by shareholders, job holders, the reputation of business, and our free enterprise system. It has been an epidemic. Millions of Americans have been hurt, directly and indirectly, by malpractices in a broad range of companies. Executive greed reached extraordinary heights. Beggar, thy neighbor took on new meanings. There has been a meltdown of corporate ethics.

Executives are confronting some negative reinforcement. Public scorn and humiliation provide a learning experience. Some executives have been jailed; great numbers are facing trial and an incredible number of personal lawsuits.

Back To Basics

Investors and the general public also should have learned a great deal more about contemporary American capitalism in the past decade than they ever expected. Some are old lessons that needed relearning.

Enron was such an incredible scam that most of us assumed that such significant corporate misbehavior has to be an isolated incident. Additional revelations still left the press and the public talking about a few "bad apples." As the decade progressed, distinguished corporate names began appearing in news stories associated with one or another financial deceptions. These include outstanding organizations like

CitiGroup, JPMorgan Chase, Goldman Sachs, Merrill Lynch, American International Group, Marsh & McLennan, Royal Dutch Shell, Fannie Mae, and Berkshire Hathaway's major subsidiary General Re, among many, many others. In 2005, the list appears to still be growing.

What had investors and the American public not understood or too easily forgotten?

Basic free enterprise 101 is the first answer. Corporate profits and associated share prices do not grow in straight lines. Free markets are inherently volatile and even well managed companies will have down quarters (and years) intermixed with good. Investors and brokers still feign ignorance of the realities of free markets They are dynamic; surprises are likely. But the market pummels the share prices of even excellent corporations like IBM when their actual quarterly earnings differ negatively from those predicted by "The Street".[1]

Finance 801 is the second. (Notice, this is an advanced course.) Financial engineering has become much more sophisticated in this period; some would just say devious and deceptive. Off-balance sheet entities, finite insurance, various kinds of derivatives, part of "structured finance"—all help to give corporate earnings the appearance of predictability. They can also hide losses and even create paper profits. The appearance, remember, not the reality. A distinguished journalist recently coined a phrase for this: "financial statement beautification."[2]

America's major investment banks and insurance companies have become the facilitators. In the process, they help to make company financial reports, used by market analysts and even trained auditors and government regulators, more murky; misleading and, in some cases, unintelligible.

At the core of the needed public reeducation is good old accounting. As everyone should know, it is not your grandmother's bookkeeping. But there is more to advanced Accounting 901 than its complexity.

It is comforting to think of accounting, a company's basic measurement tool in conducting its business, as totally objective and inflexible. We presume that there are no "fielders' choices." Of course, even within the rules of GAAP, there is substantial room for maneuver; subjective choice that can be pushing the limits, the "envelope." Better managed companies with nothing to hide are conservative; others much less so. The more pressure and executive inducements to hit earnings targets (and boost share prices) the greater the likelihood of "push the limits" accounting. (Witness the recent revelations concerning the presumably very solid, superbly managed AIG insurance company.)

While Dick Cheney was CEO of Halliburton, the company was seeking to acquire Dresser Industries. Unfortunately, Halliburton's stock had been falling, making any acquisition more costly. As luck would have it, a subsidiary was confronting major cost overruns on a huge Middle Eastern refinery construction project. So, Halliburton changed its accounting practices. It reported income for the subsidiary assuming the client would eventually pay for the cost overrun. (The new accounting was technically permissible under generally accepted accounting practice.) The subsidiary could now report a 40% increase in quarterly profits instead of a loss.[3]

One of the most surprising accounting deceptions was provided by that huge, prestigious, blue chip international oil company, Royal Dutch Shell. Apparently fearing that it would be downgraded by the market, aside from being embarrassed with their peers, executives disguised the true level of their petroleum reserves. This would also be an admission of an ineffective exploration program and poor management. Top management failed to disclose to the public for several years that they had reasons to believe that estimates of reserves were overstated by as much as 20%. They even concocted what was called an "external story line" or an "investors' relations script" when it became necessary to level with its shareholders.[4]

Psychology 101 is also worthy of review, particularly learning theory. What happens if people are placed in positions in which there are enormous rewards for achieving certain goals or targets and punished if they don't? We have described how many of the most troubled corporations had management decision making driven by their compensation plans. This turned management around by 180 degrees.

Rational corporate strategy took a back seat to that powerful motivational energy: the executive compensation plan. Instead of representing the owners, the shareholders, top management in many of the companies we have discussed, ran the business as though it were *theirs*. The *real* owners profited only if they moved fast when share prices bumped up.

Culture or Character

We have learned sadly that executive behavior is the wild card in business performance. Too many executives are prone to temptation and self-serving that punishes the shareholders whom they are expected to represent and serve.

Anthropologists would point out that a large, diverse nation with substantial mobility decreases the influence of social norms, such as treating the customer (employee, investor, et al.) as you would a friend, or neighbor. In earlier times, we believed that you should be ashamed of yourself if you didn't treat people well. Most transactions now are largely impersonal, and friendships are transitory. Americans move more than other people, often sensing that they are starting over. Divorces from vendors and brokers are almost as frequent as among married couples.

In the 1990's implicit constraints got even looser in our society. Excess became more socially approved. The term increasingly used was "social Darwinism," winner take all…or as much as they can.[5] Business schools teach a simple view of free enterprise: pursuing one's self-interest, over time gives everyone more. But there is evidence that this encourages the "players" to expect the worst from others who may be clients, peers or even bosses. Presuming that these others may use "foul" means as well as fair, brings out the worst in you.[6]

Below are just a few examples from our files illustrating some executives' fall from grace.

There have been many recent stories about major retail chains claiming excessive deductions from vendor bills for alleged shortages in shipments, late deliveries, and mismarkings. Store profits have been under pressure and one reaction is to exploit vendors with limited bargaining power. Saks Fifth Avenue, the luxury retail chain, is being investigated by the SEC for deducting millions of dollars without authorization from their vendors. They have admitted more than $20 million of such deductions and fired three executives. They are also being sued by one of their vendors for driving them out of business.[7]

HealthSouth is a fine example of insensitivity to traditional social constraints. According to *The Wall Street Journal*, Richard Scrushy, the CEO, shortly after the company went public in 1987, instructed his executives to do whatever was necessary with the accounting to make sure their reported earnings matched Wall Street's expectations.[8] Scrushy apparently cleared $77 million for himself between 1999 and 2001, the period during which HealthSouth's reported earnings were 100 times greater than what the SEC estimates they should have been with legitimate accounting.[9] By some estimates, the total accounting fraud at HealthSouth reached $3.5 billion.[10] (If the accounting scams started a decade earlier, it is interesting to note that they were not discovered by the firm's auditor over that lengthy period.)

Florida Power and Light's management is another fine example. They had a compensation contract that paid them substantial funds when there was a "change in control." FPL planned to merge with Entergy. But the merger was never consummated. Nevertheless, their senior executives collected a total of $62 million for the phantom "change." The CEO alone got almost $23 million. Initially, those executives refused to pay back the money that clearly was not theirs. Four years later in 2004, about $10 million was returned.[11]

A current lawsuit against the CEO and top management of Global Crossing asserts that its founder and CEO, Gary Winnick, sold about $800 million of his company's stock in the period 1999–2001 "…when serious problems at the company were not being disclosed."[12]

The former chief financial officer of Capital One Financial sold tens of thousands of shares when he learned the company faced regulatory penalties. Interestingly, he neglected to tell his colleagues the bad news.[13] Perhaps he wished to limit the amount of insider trading.

In 2005, the top two executives of CheckPoint made over $16 million selling company shares. What they knew and outsiders did not is that their data warehouse had been penetrated, and great numbers of people had personal information stolen. The company's inadequate security created a great deal of corporate criticism and caused the stock to drop when the news became public.[14]

Customers and Investors Are Fair Game

All management textbooks emphasize the obvious: Loyal customers are very important. Surely one of the saddest revelations of the decade is the incidence of flagrant cheating of customers. Earlier Marsh & McLennan's bid rigging was discussed. Even more shocking is what was learned about mutual fund management; their incredible dereliction of fiduciary responsibility to shareholders.

It has been estimated that market timing cost longer term investors at least $5 billion by destabilizing the funds.[15] What could the executives have been thinking? In a sense, they were killing the fabled golden goose or fouling their own nest if one prefers that homily.

Reviewing the various news stories that revealed these illicit raids on mutual funds, it appears that there may have been less than a hundred "players," largely hedge funds, scamming the system. Just one example, in 2003, the big fund distributor, Alliance Capital, had $600 million worth of market timing arrangements, but there were just ten privileged investors involved.[16] The revelations caused many funds to lose billions of dollars as angry investors sought more honest places to put their money.

In April of 2005, the financial press highlighted the indictment of 15 former New York Stock Exchange traders. They had been exploiting their own customers to the tune of millions of dollars by trading for their own acccounts based on the buy-sell orders they had on their books.[17] But they were also hurting their futures. As sophisticated, large clients learn they are being scammed they begin to use electronic trading more frequently; putting the New York Stock Exchange at risk.

As noted in Chapter 11, pension consultants appear to resemble third-world organizations who demand bribes to facilitate obtaining a contract in their country. (We righteously forbid and punish American companies who pay such bribes.) The SEC is finally investigating major pension consultants who demand huge payments from money managers who wish to be recommended to pension funds. Bribes take diverse forms: For example, paying thousands of dollars to attend the consultant's educational seminars or to buy the consultant's special software to track a fund's market performance. Remember the consultant is already being paid by the client to find the "best" money manager for its particular pension fund.[17]

Pure greed appears more common. Looting the business is the dark side of capitalism. It can favor those who will deceive, exploit, and do almost whatever is necessary to gain greater personal wealth and the sense of winning, of "beating the system."[18]

As this is being written, the financial press reveals that the top three Viacom executives paid themselves an incredible total of $160 million in compensation.[19] With all the publicity given to executive greed, the trend has not abated even in company like Viacom whose stock declined last year.

We almost all have read about John Rigas who looted Adelphia, the large cable company he had founded, by a billion dollars or more. There was an almost identical story this past year involving Calisto Tanzi, head of the founding family of the huge Italian food company, Parmalat.

What is more distressing are examples of executives gaining control of efficient successful companies they had not built, draining them of cash and injuring their ability to continue to be profitable organizations, supplying valued goods and services.

Two former investment bankers took control of the largest utility in Kansas. They began to add non-utility businesses. They then concocted a devious scheme to spin off the utility portion in a manner that would personally net them $100 million. According to federal prosecutors, this was a scheme to loot the company that had pushed it close to bankruptcy.[20] A similar scheme was uncovered at *Dayton Power & Light* (DPL), an Ohio-based utility.

A twist on this scenario eviscerated Montana Power. This was a venerated, profitable utility that had served its customers well for years, and it had accumulated a variety of resources that generated power. News stories assert that Goldman Sachs pressured the CEO, also a large shareholder anxious to garner profits, to sell off the company's assets and get the value out of the power-generating dams, plants, and energy sources.[21]

Step two for Montana Power was investing the proceeds of asset sales in a tiny telecom subsidiary, Air Touch, by adding lots of fiber-optic cable. In a relatively short time, Air Touch was close to worthless, almost all the utility employees had lost their jobs, and power rates soared for Montana consumers. Yet the top four executives who destroyed the company received over $5 million.[22]

Smaller companies have become prey to executives who gain control. AK Steel had been a proud success story. The company was created from the failing large steel company, Aramco, about 15 years ago. It led the industry in efficiency and relative profitability in its early years of a recovery. Then new management took control and began paying itself very high salaries and bonuses as the company moved to greater losses. The CEO was being rewarded for lack of success. On his watch, the company that had been an industry leader came close to total collapse in part because of its executives' compensation drain on the company's resources.

What Doing Better Means

New rules and new laws by themselves will never stop all malfeasance. There are always loopholes to be exploited by motivated, ingenious people seeking a "killing."

Deterrence has to come from the larger business system…and the recognition that our free market capitalism is analogous to a big software program. There are countless ways for hackers to gain unfair advantage or to degrade the basic functioning of the system. And part of the system is the public. It also requires a culture change—revulsion toward those who cheat and exploit and seek wildly excessive personal gain at the expense of investors or clients.

From America's founding, individualism has been a proud attribute, a reaction to the feudal, class-bound societies of Europe. When individualism is carried to extremes, the "commons," social responsibility, ethical values…all get short shrift. Gradually, many of the good things about our society wither in the dominance of raw selfishness. Public anger cannot be far behind.

American business is being pressed like never before by "savage competition," a good deal from Asia. Maintaining reasonable growth in these times requires excellence in management devoted to building the business, not its personal financial legacy. Future investment returns, already expected to be modest, largely depend on the ability of corporations to be effective in the world marketplace. This is a tough goal that has to be supported by eliminating incentives to cheat and dissemble. Also worthy of elimination are those executives for whom personal greed is a prime motivator. Quarterly earnings surely are not the best measure of a company's ability to meet the tough tests of survival and growth in the twenty-first century.

The current emphasis on holding CEOs to tough performance standards may backfire. Unfortunately, performance is too likely to mean short term profitability and concomitant share price growth. This deceptively simple measurement can deter executives from taking on the tough challenges of remaining competitive in this global economic world. Doing better requires a longer run perspective.

A recent full-page PR advertisement sponsored by Tyco, a company much in the news for its self-serving previous top management, contains some wise counsel: "[Tyco employees seek] to build and work within a *culture* of passion, performance, integrity and accountability across the company."[23] Let's hope that deeds follow words.

Not surprisingly, a more eloquent and powerful leadership statement comes from the business sage, Warren Buffet. This was in response to the recent revelations concerning his company, General Re's involvement in some questionable uses of finite insurance to hide losses and beef up company reserves. He is speaking to his management:

Berkshire can afford to lose money, even lots of money; it can't afford to lose reputation, even a shred of reputation. You and I are the guardians of that reputation. And in the long run we will have whatever reputation we deserve…There is plenty of money to be made in the center of the court. There is no need to play around the edges…I trust you to make these calls yourself. But if any time you want to check your thinking against mine, just pick up the phone.[24]

American private enterprise has a fine history. It has served the public well by innovation and an incredibly diverse quantity of well-priced goods and services. Its performance was outstanding in helping to win World War II by an almost overnight outpouring of critically needed munitions, ships, planes, and supplies.

In feudal times, business was considered dirty business. "Gentlemen" who had estates, were in government, the church, or the military. They weren't in trade or commerce. Over the centuries, the status of business and businessmen soared.

We don't use the term gentlemen much; it's dated and sexist. But it's worth thinking about how business can regain prestige in our society, aside from the income of its executives. The world-famous British philosopher, Alfred North Whitehead had an idealistic answer, but one worthy of attention. He was asked to speak at the opening of the Harvard Business School back in 1929. (Two surprises.) His counsel to the new faculty, think "greatly" of yourself…and your profession.[25]

With such self respect there could be less need for enormous compensation packages to confirm the worth and importance of the executive. Self-respecting leaders take satisfaction in giving highest priority to serving the business and protecting the interest of employees, vendors, shareowners, and the communities that house them. That is the only kind of leadership that generates loyalty and motivates high performance.

As many executives would say to me in my earlier research, "I would pay somebody to let me do this job, to be able to demonstrate what I can accomplish, my way and fulfilling my strategies." It is winning the game that counts to real leaders, not the payoffs.

Executives and those specialists that support them, the bankers, lawyers, and accountants, should have some sense of real professionalism. Professionals take pride in high levels of competence, internalize standards of ethical behavior and the need to place the interests of the clients and shareholders they serve above their own.

Management is an extraordinarily challenging profession; planning strategy in an increasingly uncertain world and leading diverse and competitive groups and individuals to come together with a common purpose. When our business schools and boards of directors seek candidates who primarily seek challenge and the sense of accomplishment there will be a sharp decline in malfeasance and cheating and exploitation.

For the most part, Americans forgive and forget, a byproduct of our optimistic culture. It's not surprising that shareholders want to believe that corporate financial scams are now over. But this view neglects the embedded dynamic favoring cheating on corporate financials. Short-term investor pressures to meet quarterly goals are reinforced by Board CEO evaluation criteria and executive bonus formulas. Even the best U.S. companies like Coca-Cola and AIG have not been able to resist tampering with the numbers.[26] Prestigious Bristol-Myers Squibb paid over $800 million in penalties for misleading investors on previous years' earnings, and two of their former executives were indicted on securities fraud in June 2005.[27]

A more distressing example of executives succumbing to reported earnings pressures is provided by recent disclosures concerning Citigroup's Smith Barney brokerage division. An SEC investigation disclosed that they had cheated their mutual fund investors. Smith Barney renegotiated its outsourced fund administration costs but continued to charge the old, higher costs to shareholders! (The Directors slept through this one.)[28]

But there is increasing retribution for companies with ethically challenged executives. Citigroup and JPMorgan Chase together have paid over 8 billion in fines in the past year for underwriting securities that had undisclosed risks for investors. (A salutary sum.)

Over the past decade there has been an increasing risk that real leaders with a long run perspective who seek to build robust businesses often get displaced by self-centered CEOs seeking to make a bundle in the few years allowed. As every business economist knows, staying competitive in a tough global economy requires leaders willing to look to the future and stay the course. Hopefully, boards and investors will learn to tell the difference, and America will be the beneficiary. And then, America will continue to be a beacon to the world, guiding many nations to choose free enterprise.

ENDNOTES

Chapter 1

1. Arthur Levitt. *Take On the Street: What Wall Street and Corporate America Don't Want You to Know* (New York: Pantheon Books, 2002).

2. A recent study by two law professors concludes that in the period 2001–2003, the pay of the top five corporate officers in major corporations took over 10% of earnings, double the mid 1990's rate. Cited by Alan Abelson. "Up and Down Wall Street." *Barrons*, April 4, 2005.

3. Lucien Bebchuk and Jesse Fried. *Pay Without Performance: The Unfulfilled Promise of Executive Compensation* (New York: Penguin, 2004).

4. Eric Dash. "The New Executive Bonanza: Retirement." *New York Times*, April 3, 2005.

Chapter 2

1. The uplifting of society's view of business is a product of industrialization. In more traditional societies, landowners, military officers, men of the cloth (no women then), and public officials (and trust babies, some of whom were women) all played top dog. Business was best left to those unfortunate enough to come from lesser families or immigrants. They did society's "dirty" work: commerce and banking.

2. Paul Krugman. "For Richer; How the Permissive Capitalism of the Boom Destroyed American Equality." *New York Times Magazine*, October 18, 2002.

3. David Cay Johnston. "Oregon Hearing to Look at Utility's Charging for Taxes It Didn't Pay." *The New York Times*, June 10, 2004.

4. Lynnley Browning. "Tax Ruling Casts a Long Shadow." *The New York Times*, August 30, 2004. A federal District Court Job ruled that Long Term Capital had acted in bad faith when they took over $100 million in tax deductions to shelter $40 million in taxes due.

5. Roger Lowenstein. *Origins of the Crash* (New York: Penguin Press, 2004).

6. Samuel L. Popkin. *The Rational Peasant: The Political Economy of Rural Society in Vietnam* (Berkeley and Los Angeles: University of California Press, 1979), 91.

7. Ibid.

8. Hobbes was a distinguished British philosopher who argued that man's natural state was jungle-like, that is the inhabitants would seek to survive by beating on one another.

9. Adam Smith. *The Wealth of Nations* (New York: Modern Library, 1993).

Chapter 3

1. Speculative trading performs a critical function in maintaining a healthy, responsive stock market. That is not a problem; it is a virtue.

2. Douglas Hunter. *The Bubble and the Bear: How Nortel Burst the Canadian Dream* (Toronto: Doubleday Canada, 2002).

3. Alec Klein. *Stealing Time* (New York: Simon and Schuster, 2003).

4. Michael Jensen and Kevin Murphy. "CEO Incentives—It's Not How Much You Pay, But How." *Harvard Business Review*, May-June 1990. This highly influential article strongly argued that executives needed to think like owners, and options were proposed as a method of accomplishing this. In addition to favoring much higher executive shareholdings, these Harvard Business School professors argued that CEOs were significantly underpaid. Their conclusion seems quite ironical in the light of data collected in the past five years. In a very recent interview, now retired Professor Jensen admits that his option proposals had been a mistake. Cf. Claudia Deutsch. "An Early Advocate of Stock Options Debunks Himself." *New York Times,* April 3, 2003.

5. Floyd Norris. "Smooth Earnings Growth was Reassuring, but It Was Often Fictional." *The New York Times*, May 6, 2005.

6. The Sarbanes-Oxley Act reined in these executive loans.

7. Bethany McLean and Peter Elkind. *The Smartest Guys in the Room* (New York: Portfolio, 2003).

8. Daniel Gross. *Slate*, December 10, 2002. It is reported that he borrowed 25 million in 1996 and had the loan from his company forgiven in 2000 when he returned the shares. Also reported in *The Financial Post*, January 8, 2003.

9. Paul MacAvoy and Ira Millstein. *The Recurrent Crisis in Corporate Governance* (New York: Palgrave Macmillan, 2003), 82.

10. Cf., William F. Whyte, et al. *Money and Motivation* (New York: Harper, 1955). Eliot Chapple and Leonard Sayles. *The Measure of Management* (New York: Macmillan, 1961).

11. Tracie Rozhon. "Saks Fires Three Executives Over Problems Found in Audit." *The New York Times*, May 10, 2005. Markdown money is paid by vendors to share the cost of store price cuts on unsold merchandise. Stores threaten vendors who don't "pony up" with loss of future business.

Chapter 4

1. In evolutionary terms, these are periods of adaptive radiation—new species are rapidly spawned, and then just as quickly become extinct.

2. David Faber (host). *The Big Lie: Inside the Rise and Fraud of WorldCom* (CNBC, Burrelle's Information Services transcript, September 9, 2003).

3. Ibid.

4. "Dark fiber" is the term used for fiber-optic cabling that has been laid but is not being used.

5. David Faber (host). *The Big Lie: Inside the Rise and Fraud of WorldCom* (CNBC, Burrelle's Information Services transcript, September 9, 2003).

6. Ibid.

7. Bethany McLean and Peter Elkind. *The Smartest Guys in the Room* (New York: Portfolio, 2003).

8. Ibid.

9. $60.6 million in ill-gotten gains is reported just for Fastow alone. Others in Enron were also involved.

10. Finally, in June 2005, KPMG acknowledged it had engaged in "unlawful conduct" in its creation of the abusive tax shelters detected by the IRS. Lynnley Browning. "KPMG Tax Shelters Involved Wrongdoing." *The New York Times,* June 17, 2005.

11. Ibid.

12. Ibid.

Chapter 5

1. There is a wealth of information available on the Internet about the Persepolis Tablets, including pictures and translations of some of them. The tablets date between 511 and 492 B.C.

2. Technically, the firm had changed its name to "Andersen." However, the new name did not have time to take hold and the firm is still generally referred to as "Arthur Andersen." Subsequent references to the firm in this chapter will use "Andersen."

3. Arthur Andersen had been the auditor for John Keating's Lincoln Federal Savings and Loan, and dropped this client. But because of the reach in time of the charges against Lincoln Federal, the firm did have a relatively small fine levied against it.

4. "Self-Regulation in the Accounting Profession Panel Discussion." *Challenge and Achievement in Accounting During the Twentieth Century: A Conference Celebrating the Fiftieth Anniversary of the Accounting Hall of Fame.* Daniel L. Jensen, Editor, (Columbus, OH: The Ohio State University, Fisher College of Business Publications, 2002).

5. David Duncan, the Enron engagement partner, pled guilty in a separate case.

6. "Capturing regulators" is a topic taught in some business schools. Students are given strategies for effectively controlling the regulatory and legislative processes of government.

7. The number of worldwide partners in the firm at the end was reported as being over 4,000 by a former partner. Just before the firm's demise, it had dramatically increased the size of the worldwide partnership. The nearly 3,000 figure is used in reporting on the firm, so it is used here.

8. Mary Ashby Morrison. "Rush to judgment: the lynching of Arthur Andersen & Co." *Critical Perspectives on Accounting*, Elsevier Ltd., 2004). The article is very heavily biased in the firm's favor and makes a questionable case for the "lynching" having been unjust. The author of the article was a former member of the firm, but that may have been before the 1990s, so the author's memory of the firm is potentially the source of serious flaws. However, some good facts are given and some interesting points are made.

9. Non-partner retirees are covered under a pension plan made secure for them by ERISA laws. Partner's survivors were also protected under provisions made for them in the retirement plan.

10. Loren Fox. *Enron: The Rise and Fall* (Hoboken, NJ: John Wiley & Sons, Inc., 2003), 211.

11. Ibid.

12. "Self-Regulation in the Accounting Profession Panel Discussion." *Challenge and Achievement in Accounting During the Twentieth Century: A Conference Celebrating the Fiftieth Anniversary of the Accounting Hall of Fame*. Daniel L. Jensen, Editor (Columbus, OH: The Ohio State University, Fisher College of Business Publications, 2002).

13. These comments were directed toward a scandalous affair at PriceWaterhouse-Coopers. "Self-Regulation in the Accounting Profession Panel Discussion." *Challenge and Achievement in Accounting During the Twentieth Century: A Conference Celebrating the Fiftieth Anniversary of the Accounting Hall of Fame*. Daniel L. Jensen, Editor (Columbus, OH: The Ohio State University, Fisher College of Business Publications, 2002).

14. Flynn McRoberts. "Repeat Offender Gets Stiff Justice." *The Chicago Tribune*, September 4, 2002.

15. Arthur Levitt. *Take On the Street* (New York: Pantheon Books, 2002).

16. Ibid.

17. Mark A. Covaleski. "The calculated and the avowed: techniques of discipline and struggles over identity in Big Six public account firms." *Administrative Science Quarterly* (Special Issued: Critical Perspectives on Organizational Control), June 1998.

18. Susan E. Squires, Cynthia J. Smith, Lorna McDougall, and William R. Yeack. *Inside Arthur Andersen: Shifting Values, Unexpected Consequences* (Upper Saddle River, New Jersey: Financial Times Prentice Hall, 2003), 97–100.

19. Flynn McRoberts. "A Revolution Sweeps Andersen, Pitting Auditors Against Consultants in a Race for Higher Profit." *The Chicago Tribune*, September 2, 2002.

20. Among themselves, former Andersen partners talk of "never loving that way again."

21. Flynn McRoberts. "A Revolution Sweeps Andersen, Pitting Auditors Against Consultants in a Race for Higher Profit." *The Chicago Tribune*, September 2, 2002.

Chapter 6

1. Flynn McRoberts. "Greed Tarnished Golden Reputation." *Chicago Tribune*, September 1, 2002.

2. Flynn McRoberts. "Civil War Splits Andersen." *Chicago Tribune*, September 2, 2002.

3. Ibid.

4. Robert Kutsenda had also been lead partner in an early 1990s audit scandal involving Supercuts, a chain of low-cost hair salons.

5. David Faber, host. "The Big Lie: Inside the Rise and Fraud of WorldCom." September 9, 2003, CNBC, Burrelle's Information Services transcript.

6. Flynn McRoberts. "Ties to Enron Blinded Andersen." *Chicago Tribune*, September 3, 2002.

7. Robert Bryce. *Pipe Dreams: Greed, Ego and the Death of Enron* (New York: Public Affairs, 2002).

8. Ibid, 232.

9. Flynn McRoberts. "Ties to Enron Blinded Andersen." *Chicago Tribune*, September 3, 2002.

10. William Webster was first suggested to be chairman of the PCAOB by Harvey Pitt, then head of the SEC. When it was revealed that Webster was associated with an accounting scandal, this proved the straw that broke the camel's back and Harvey Pitt resigned his position.

11. CFO Staff. "The Enforcer." *CFO Magazine*, August 2004.

12. Ibid.

13. "Vanderbilt Study Shows Audit Firms Will Continue to Put Own Interests First." *AScribe Newswire*, October 6, 2003.

14. Susan E. Squires, Cynthia J. Smith, Loran McDougall, and William R. Yeack. *Insider Arthur Andersen: Shifting Values, Unexpected Consequences* (New Jersey: Financial Times Prentice Hall, 2003) back cover.

15. Barbara Ley Toffler with Jennifer Reingold. *Final Accounting* (New York: Broadway Books, 2003), 113.

16. The report released by OFHEO in September 2004 is available online. Another report released in February 2003, "Systemic Risk: Fannie Mae, Freddie Mac and The Role of OFHEO," is also available online.

17. Editorial. "Bush's Medicare Deceit." *San Francisco Chronicle*, March 16, 2004, B8.

18. Gwen Ifill, host. "Cost of the Medicare prescription drug benefit." *Washington Week*, report by Ceci Connolly of *The Washington Post*, March 19, 2004, Burelle's Information Services transcript.

19. Associated Press. "Update 3: Fannie Mae Agrees to Boost Reserve Capital." September 27, 2004.

20. "FASB" is the Financial Accounting Standards Board; "GASB" is the Government Accounting Standards Board. These boards have a major role in setting the auditing standards and accounting principles used in our financial systems, and making the rules and sanctions that support them.

Chapter 7

1. Geoffrey Colvin. "CEO Pay Meets Its Match." *Fortune*, July 26, 2004.

2. Patrick McGeehan. "Despite Fight, Chief's Pay Wasn't Cut by MBNA." *New York Times*, March 16, 2004.

3. *Forbes*, January 12, 2004.

4. The classic exposition of this structural clash is by Adolph Berle and Gardiner Means. *The Modern Corporation and Private Property* (New York, Macmillan, 1932).

5. Brent Schindler. Inside Andy Grove's Latest Crusade." *Fortune*, August 23, 2004.

6. Landon Thomas, Jr. "Regulators Said to be Focusing on Board's Vote for Grasso." *New York Times*, March 26, 2004.

7. Patrick McGeehan and Landon Thomas, Jr. "Next for the Big Board; to Sue or Not to Sue." *New York Times*, December 2, 2003

8. *Report of the Senate Government Affairs Committee, Permanent Subcommittee on Investigation*, July 2002.

9. Robert Bryce. *Pipe Dreams; Greed and Ego and the Death of Enron* (New York: Public Affairs Press, 2002).

10. Bethany McLean and Peter Elkind. *The Smartest Guys in the Room* (New York: Portfolio Penguin Group, 2003).

11. Alec Klein. *Stealing Time: Steve Case, Jerry Levin, and the Collapse of AOL Time Warner* (New York: Simon & Schuster, 2003).

12. Nina Munk. *Fools Rush In* (New York: Harper Business, 2004), 170.

13. Patrick McGeehan. "Uncertified Results Filed by Publisher." *The New York Times*, November 22, 2003.

14. Robert Frank and Elena Cherney. "Lord Black Board: A-List Cast Played Acquiescent Role." *Wall Street Journal*, September 27, 2004. The A list included the likes of Henry Kissinger.

15. CF John Emshwiller. "Many Companies Report Transactions with Top Officers." *Wall Street Journal*, December 29, 2003.

16. A federal indictment of the CEO of Westar Energy accuses him of forcing out board members who objected to his executive compensation plans. *The New York Times*, December 5, 2003.

17. *The New York Times*. March 4, 2004.

18. *Business Review*. Albany, New York, November 14, 2003.

19. *Barrons* (Section T), August 2, 2004.

20. Robin Sidel. "J.P. Morgan to Pay 2 Billion." *The Wall Street Journal*, March 18, 2005. Previously, other investment banks involved in underwriting those bonds had been forced to pay 4 billion. In total, the banks who received 84 million in fees, paid 6 billion in penalties. Investors had paid 17 billion for the bonds.

21. "Special Report, Non-Executive Directors." *The Economist*, March 20–26, 2004.

22. Jonathan Glater. "*A Big New Worry for Corporate Directors*." *The New York Times*, January 6, 2005.

23. Karen Donovan. "Legal Reform Turns a Steward into an Activist." *The New York Times*, April 16, 2005. The activist is the sole fiduciary of NY State's Common Retirement Fund.

24. Mark Lewis. "Pitt to Webster; Mum's the Word." *Forbes.com*, October 31, 2002. (Author comment: Pitt is presumably the former head of the SEC.)

25. *The New York Times*, August 8, 2004.

26. Gretchen Morgenson. "Charity Begins at the Board, Just Ask AIG." *The New York Times*, April 10, 2005.

27. James Surowiecki. "Board Stiffs." *The New Yorker*, March 8, 2004.

28. Rita Farrell. "PeopleSoft Chief's Remarks Cited as Cause of Dismissal." *The New York Times*, October 5, 2004.

29. For a scholarly analysis of needed board reforms, see Paul MacAvoy and Ira Millstein. *The Recurrent Crises in Corporate Governance* (New York: Macmillan, 2004).

Chapter 8

1. Bill Kovach, Tom Rosenstiel, and Amy Mitchell. "Commentary on the Survey Findings: Specific Areas of Concern." *The State of the News Media 2004: An Annual Report on American Journalism*, conducted by the Pew Research Center for the People and the Press in collaboration with the Project for Excellence in Journalism and the Committee of Concerned Journalists. The report is available on the Internet at http://www.stateofthenewsmedia.org/journalist_survey.html.

2. Ibid.

3. David D. Kirpatrick. "TV Host Says U.S. Paid Him To Back Policy." *The New York Times*, January 8, 2005.

4. David Wallis. *Killed: Great Journalism Too Hot to Print* (New York: Nation Books, 2004).

5. For example, *Stealing Time* (covers the AOL and Time Warner merger) by Alec Klein, New York, Simon & Schuster, 2003, *The Bubble and the Bear* (gives an account of the rise and fall of Nortel) by Douglas Hunter, Doubleday Canada, 2002, and many books on Enron by journalists.

6. Bill Kovach, Tom Rosenstiel, and Amy Mitchell. "Commentary on the Survey Findings." *The State of the News Media 2004: An Annual Report on American Journalism*, conducted by the Pew Research Center for the People and the Press in collaboration with the Project for Excellence in Journalism and the Committee of Concerned Journalists. The report is available on the Internet at http://www.stateofthenewsmedia.org/journalist_survey.html.

7. Ibid.

8. Ibid.

9. Ibid.

10. Timothy L. O'Brien. "Mayday? Payday? Hit the Silk!" *The New York Times*, January 9, 2005.

11. Louis Columbus is an IT industry researcher who writes a column on industry issues.

Chapter 9

1. Benjamin Pimentel. "Jailhouse seminars." *The San Francisco Chronicle*, September 17, 2002.

2. Bethany McLean and Peter Elkind. *The Smartest Guys in the Room: The Amazing Rise and Scandalous Fall of Enron* (New York: Portfolio, 2003).

3. Ibid, 31.

4. Ibid.

5. Ibid.

6. Ibid.

7. Kathleen M. Eisenhardt and Donald N. Sull. "Strategy as Simple Rules." *Harvard Business Review*, January 2001, Vol. 79, Issue 1, 106.

8. Bloomberg News. *The New York Times*, December 9, 2004, C7.

9. "New Twist on Corporate Governance." *The New York Times*, January 11, 2005.

10. Kathleen M. Eisenhardt and Donald N. Sull. "Strategy as Simple Rules." *Harvard Business Review*, January 2001, Vol. 79, Issue 1, 106.

11. Bethany McLean and Peter Elkind. *The Smartest Guys in the Room: The Amazing Rise and Scandalous Fall of Enron* (New York: Portfolio, 2003).

12. George Stalk and Rob Lachenauer. "Hardball Manifesto." *Harvard Business Review*, April 2004, Vol. 82, Issue 4, 62.

13. Robert Shiller. "How Wall Street Learns to Look the Other Way." *The New York Times, February 8, 2005.*

Chapter 10

1. These days, companies are more scrupulous about not hiring their outside audi-tors to perform any non-audit–related work. As we see in the cases of Enron and others, conflicts of interest related to generating large fees are also problematic in legal, investment banking, and other types of consulting. Boards of directors and shareholders need to be alert to real costs of services commissioned by manage-ment as well as to the value these services might or might not add to the compa-ny. Asurix represented Enron's entry into global water markets.

2. Bethany McLean and Peter Elkind. *The Smartest Guys in the Room* (New York: Penguin Group, 2003) 233.

3. Alec Klein. *Stealing Time: Steve Case, Jerry Levin, and the Collapse of AOL Time Warner* (New York: Simon and Schuster, 2003).

4. Kathy M. Ripin and Leonard R. Sayles. *Insider Strategies for Outsourcing Information Systems: Building Productive Partnerships, Avoiding Seductive Traps* (New York: Oxford University Press, 2002).

5. Bethany McLean and Peter Elkind. *The Smartest Guys in the Room* (New York: Penguin Group, 2003).

6. Robert Bryce. *Pipe Dreams: Greed, Ego, and the Death of Enron* (New York: Public Affairs, 2002) 232–233.

7. Scott Morrison, "HP and Compaq chiefs to forego Dollars 22m: Revelation comes amid shareholder concern over Dollars 24bn acquisition." *The Financial Times,* November 16, 2001, 21.

8. See, for example, Bethany McLean and Peter Elkind. *The Smartest Guys in the Room* (New York: Penguin Group, 2003).

9. See, for example, John Macdonald. *Calling a Halt to Mindless Change* (New York: American Management Association International, 1998).

10. Arthur Levitt, Jr. *Take On the Street: What Wall Street and Corporate America Don't What You to Know; What You Can Do to Fight Back* (New York: Pantheon Books, 2002). This book contains a letter from Kenneth Lay, former CEO of Enron, urging Levitt to see things Enron's way, along with several letters from Congress applying pressure on behalf of corporate interests, including threats.

11. In 2003, some SEC fees were increased, but there is still a considerable gap between fees collected and the SEC's budget.

Chapter 11

1. Barry Schwartz. *The Paradox of Choice: Why More Is Less* (New York Ecco, 2004).

2. S. Romero and S, Schiesel. "Hubris the Fall of a Telecommunications Empire." *The New York Times*, March 3, 2004.

3. Joseph Schumpeter's works include *Business Cycles*, 2 vols. (London: Porcupine Pr,1989); *Capitalism, Socialism and Democracy* (New York: Perennial HarperCollins, 1962); *History of Economic Analysis*, edited by E. Boody (Oxford: Oxford University Press, 1996).

4. Adam Smith. *The Wealth of Nations*. Published in 1776.

5. Ron Suskind. *The Price of Loyalty* (New York: Simon and Schuster, 2004). The book is a detailed, candid account of what life was like for Paul O'Niell, a cabinet officer in the first Bush administration.

6. Gretchen Morgenson. "Unmasking that Pension Consultant." *The New York Times*, February 20, 2005. "Pay-to-play" refers to the practice of consultants requiring that money managers pay them one or another kind of fee in order to be considered as a "suitable" money manager for a pension fund.

7. Jesse Eisinger. "Follow the CEO's Money." *Wall Street Journal*, February 16, 2005.

8. John Kenneth Galbraith. *The New Industrial State*. Houghton Mifflin, 1967.

9. Bloomberg News. "Black Plans to Sue Hollinger for Libel." *The New York Times*, October 2, 2004, C13.

10. These ultimately fraudulent dealings also involved friends and family along with a few co-conspiratorial bankers in the U.K. who were convicted of fraud there.

11. Milton Friedman. *Capitalism and Freedom* (Chicago: University of Chicago Press, 1962). (Brought to our attention by Professor James Kuhn.)

12. Gretchen Morgenson. "What's Good for Business, If No One Else." *The New York Times*. June 5, 2005. Some of our "best and brightest" financial institutions are apparently still willing and able to "play the angles" and push "good accounting" limits through convenient loopholes. As we have seen, the enemies of free-market capitalism are inside the system.

Chapter 12

1. Gretchen Morgenson. "Only the Little People Pay for Lawn Care." *The New York Times*, March 2005.

2. James Hagerty. "Regulator Pressure Fannie Officers." *Wall Street Journal*, October 6, 2004.

3. Greg Ip, et al. "How Grasso's Rule Kept the New York Stock Exchange on Top But Hid Deep Trouble." *Wall Street Journal*, December 30, 2003. In 2001, his pay was roughly equal to the net income of the Exchange and exceeded the pay of CEOs of many of America's biggest companies.

4. Floyd Norris. "Unfettered Authority that Led to Overreaching at the Big Board." *The New York Times,* February 3, 2005.

5. Monica Langley. *Tearing Down the Walls* (New York: Simon and Schuster, 2003), 169.

6. Ibid, 178.

7. Increasingly, as a reaction to insider trading like opportunities for senior executives, companies are issuing restricted stock options. These can only be exercised after several years or until the executive leaves, and sometimes they require that certain performance objectives be realized.

8. Charles Stein. "Economic Life; Broken Promises." *Boston Globe,* December 17, 2002.

9. *Wall Street Journal,* July 9, 2004.

10. *Naples Daily News,* February 26, 2005.

11. "Fat Cats Turn to Low Fat." *The Economist.* March 5, 2005.

12. Lucian Bebchuk and Jesse Fried. *Pay Without Performance* (Cambridge, Mass.: Harvard University Press, 2004).

13. Alex Bernson. "Partnerhip Deals at Insurance Broker for Private Profit." *The New York Times,* October 21, 2004.

14. Cf. Jenny Anderson. "Insurer Admits Bad Accounting in Several Deals." *The New York Times,* March 31, 2005. This was just one of dozens of financial reports concerning AIG's convoluted accounting that appeared over a 2 month period in the spring of 2005.

15. Arthur Levitt, Jr. "The Imperial CEO is No More." *Wall Street Journal,* March 17, 2005.

16. John Markoff. "When + Adds up to Minus." *The New York Times,* February 10, 2005, and Ben Elgen. "Can Anyone Save HP?" *Business Week,* February 21, 2005.

17. "Fiorina in Line for World Bank—Report." *MarketWatch.com,* March 2, 2005.

18. C.Low and C. Mollenkamp. "Off-the-books, clean-up isn't a snap." *Wall Sreet Journal,* January 13, 2003.

19. Michael Jensen and Kevin Murphy. "CEO Incentives—It's Not How Much You Pay, But How." *Harvard Business Review,* May–June 1990

Chapter 13

1. There can be special compensation considerations when the candidate being sought is already a CEO of a substantial business and is comfortably ensconced in a community. He or she may have to sacrifice a large number of existing options and pension benefits and family location preferences. Outside pay packages may be required.

2. Interview with former senior Coca-Cola executive.

3. Justin Lahart. " Corner Office Thinks Short term." *Wall Street Journal,* April 14, 2004.

4. Monica Langley. *Tearing Down the Walls* (New York, Simon and Schuster, 329).

5. From what was called an "Owners' Manual" for new Google shareholders. *The New York Times*, April 30, 2004.

6. Tracie Rozhun. "Before Christmas Wal-Mart was Stirring." *The New York Times,* January 5, 2005.

7. I (Sayles) was then engaged in a major research project at IBM.

8. Cf. Alec Klein. *Stealing Time.* (New York: Simon and Schuster, 2003). This is an excellent recounting of Time's almost unbelievable overpayment for AOL. Time CEO, Gerald Levin, failed to consider any of his board's misgivings and warnings.

9. Cf. Leonard Sayles. *The Working Leader; The Triumph of High Performance over Conventional Management Principles.* (New York: The Free Press, 1993).

10. Laurie Flynn. "New Leader is Called a Trust Builder." *The New York Times,* March 30, 2005.

11. Elisabeth Bumiller. "Fingerprint System Bogged Down, Report Finds." *The New York Times*, December 30, 2004.

12. Jeffrey Ball. "Mighty Profit Maker." *Wall Street Journal,* April 8, 2005.

13. *The New York Times*, photo, October 26, 2004.

14. Todd Zaun. "Citigroup Tries to Repair Its Image in Japan." *The New York Times,* October 26, 2004.

15. Cf. Nassim Taleb. *Fooled by Randomness* (New York: Texere, 2001). The author argues persuasively that unexpected, unpredicted, major factors, not random events, move markets.

16. *The New York Times,* January 8, 2004.

17. David Callahan. *Kindred Spirits; Harvard Business School's Extraordinary Class of 1949 and How They Transformed America* (New York: John Wiley, 2002). As quoted in the *The New York Times,* June 15, 2004.

Chapter 14

1. On April 14, 2005, IBM's earnings disappointed the market, and its share price took a steep dip.

2. Floyd Norris. "Smooth Earnings Growth Was Reassuring But It Was Often Fictional." *The New York Times*, May 6, 2005.

3. Peter Elking and Joan Levenstein. "The Truth About Halliburton." *Fortune*, April 18, 2005. Also Joshua Marshall. "Vice Grip." *Washington Monthly.com*, January–February, 2003.

4. S. Labaton. "Justice Department Opens Inquiry into Shell Oil." *The New York Times*, March 17, 2004.

5. Cf. Robert Frank. *The Winner Take All Society* (New York: The Free Press, 2003).

6. Robert Frank. "The Theory That Self-Interest Is the Sole Motivation Is Self Fulfilling." *The Economist*, February 17, 2005.

7. Tracie Rozhon. "Clothier Sues Saks, Saying Excessive Markdowns Ruined It." *The New York Times*, May 18, 2005.

8. Jonathan Weil. "Unscrambling the Accounting." *Wall Street Journal*, March 20, 2003.

9. Ibid.

10. *The New York Times*. January 21, 2004.

11. Rebecca Smith. "FPL to Get Return of 9.75 Million from Executives." *Wall Street Journal*, August 17, 2004.

12. Timothy O'Brien. "A New Legal Chapter for a 90s Flameout." *The New York Times*, August 15, 2004.

13. *The New York Times*. July 27, 2004.

14. Harry Weber (Associated Press). "CheckPoint Pair Sold Stock Before Disclosure." *Naples Daily News*, February 26, 2005.

15. Randall Smith. "Prof. Zitzewitz Has Good Timing and Bad Timing." *Wall Street Journal*, December 9, 2003.

16. Rivas Atlas. "Alliance Settles Fund Trading Complaints." *The New York Times*, December 19, 2003.

17. Mary Williams Walsh. "S.E.C. Looking at Pension Consultants." *The New York Times*, May 17, 2005.

18. Jenny Anderson. "15 Specialists from Big Board are Indicted." *The New York Times*, April 13, 2005. Since specialists know how many shares are being offered for sale at what price and being offered to buy at what price, it is easy for them to ignore their responsibility not to use this information for personal gain.

19. Geraldine Fabrikant. "While Shares Fell, Viacom Paid Three 160 Million." *The New York Times*, April 16, 2005.

20. *The New York Times*. December 5, 2003.

21. CBS News.com. August 10, 2003. Referencing the original *60 Minutes* segment broadcast the previous February, 2003.

22. Transcript of *60 Minutes*. August 10, 2003.

23. *The New York Times, The Wall Street Journal*. October 2, 2004.

24. Timothy O'Brien. "The Oracle of Omaha's Latest Riddle." *The New York Times*, April 10, 2004.

25. As quoted in Alfred North Whitehead. The *Adventure of Ideas* (New York: Macmillan, 1933).

26. Melanie Warner. "Coca-Cola Settles Inquiry Over Practices in Japan." *The New York Times*, April 19, 2005.

27. Stephanie Saul. "Fraud Case Filed Against Ex-Officers of Bristol." *The New York Times*, June 16, 2005.

28. Gretchen Morgenson. "What's Good for Business If No One Else." *The New York Times*, June 5, 2005.

FROM THE AUTHORS

American business and its leadership have been the focus of my research and publishing for half a century. As both a researcher and consultant, I have been "inside" perhaps 40 or 50 companies, and I have a reasonable familiarity with the dynamics of management and organizations. Being a professor at Columbia University's Graduate School of Business also gave me some familiarty with New York's powerful banking institutions.

I never viewed America's enterprise system as representing perfection, but I respected the energy and intelligence with which most executives conscientiously sought to contribute to the growth of their companies.

I was unprepared for Enron, the scope of the malfeasance and the number of well-trained executives, board members, bankers, accountants, and legal talent who were accomplices to this huge, costly scam. How and why could one of America's largest companies become so fraudulent and no one, or almost no one, take notice?

As the months and the years passed, we all saw that Enron had been an early warning. More financial shocks and corporate revelations disclosed an array of well-embedded pressures, incentives, and institutions that were having a corrosive impact on our free market capitalism.

For the first time in my career, I was intensively studying and writing about unfolding current business events in real time; trying to "connect the dots," as we now say. I began to see the interconnections among changes in wildly generous executive bonus plans and their incredible option grants, growing public stock market participation and unrealistic share appreciation expectations on the part of large investors. I was learning a good deal about how "financial engineering" was transforming reporting to shareholders.

I soon discovered that doing research in real time is extraordinarily frustrating and consuming. I was seeking to read and collate everything being published regarding this unfolding destructive drama involving an ever-broader array of American business. (Perhaps greyhounds at the track have similar psychic frustrations—chasing but never being able to catch the target.)

I asked Cynthia Smith, someone with whom I had worked on several other projects, to share this project. She had expertise in auditing and accounting and had first-hand experience in high tech and the use of computers to facilitate financial manipulations. All these were areas in which I had no expertise. Further, she had just finished co-authoring *Inside Arthur Andersen: Shifting Values, Unexpected Consequences*, an important book on the demise of Arthur Andersen and its destructive relations with Enron. Smith had worked for Andersen and intimately knew auditing practice and its problems. Her Chapters 4, 5, 6, 8, 9, and 10 reflect this experience and expertise.

Her computer literacy enabled us to "mine" government and professional association Web sites and powerful university database collections. We also both interviewed many knowledgeable, experienced professionals and executives.

I wrote Chapters 1, 2, 3, 7, 11, 12, 13, and 14, and also contributed to Chapter 9.

Leonard Sayles
Dobbs Ferry, New York
May 20, 2005

Leonard and I came together on this project just as I finished co-authoring, *Inside Arthur Andersen: Shifting Values, Unexpected Consequences* (2003). This book focused on the destruction of one of the oldest, largest audit firms in the world as a result of its association with Enron. It was a difficult project because I, and my co-authors, had worked at the firm.

Leonard had been collecting data on the bigger picture for two years. We were able to pool my research for the earlier book with his and go forward together. We were driven to get at the deeper issues underlying this period of scandal. We were committed to providing constructive ideas throughout our discussion that would help mend a clearly still broken system.

It has been a privilege to work with Leonard Sayles, whose considerable and fine body of work stands the test of time. His analytical powers are prodigious. His energy and clarity of thought and writing are inspirational.

As we began writing, we assumed that our business scandals were large-ly behind us. They fact that they weren't confirms our premise that there are deep, systemic problems that we need to address. I hope our effort makes it clear that Americans should not slip into "denial" and must wake up to the fact that ultimately, Americans decide how America does business. Fifty percent of Americans have a direct stake in the integrity of our market systems. They can mobilize investor power. The other fifty percent also have a real stake; jobs, pensions, and quali-ty of life. They, too, can use their political power.

Cynthia Smith
April 5, 2005

SUPREME COURT OVERTURNS ARTHUR ANDERSEN CONVICTION

O n a narrow technicality, in a unanimous decision, the U.S. Supreme Court overturned Arthur Andersen's felony conviction of obstruction of justice, which had been upheld by the lower appeals court. The firm's appeal hinged on the instructions given by the judge to the jury as they deliberated their verdict. The Supreme Court found that the judge's instructions set the hurdle for a guilty verdict too low by failing to require proof that Andersen acted with the knowledge and intent to commit a crime. During the trial, the prosecution had presented evidence of intent, most notably David Duncan's guilty plea to obstruction of justice. The judge's instructions, however, were weakly worded on this point.

The Court said nothing about the quality of evidence presented, leaving the door open for the Department of Justice (DOJ) to retry the Andersen case, which some think unlikely because the firm is effectively out of business. Others believe the firm should be retried because not to retry could weaken the government's position on other appeals and future cases, giving credence to the charge that the DOJ was overzealous and abused its power in its prosecution of Andersen. In addition, other charges might have been developed against the firm, such as being in violation of the cease and desist order stemming from the Waste Management, Inc., case.

The same day the decision was announced and cheered by corporate interests, defense attorneys began motions in appeals courts and adjustments in strategies for upcoming cases. There was also immediate speculation that the decision would help Andersen's case in the myriad outstanding investor lawsuits brought against the firm, and might strengthen recovery of investor losses by triggering liability for payment from Andersen's insurer, which was off the hook because of the criminal conviction. Andersen could well have been bankrupted by these lawsuits even if a felony criminal charge had not been brought against the firm. The Sarbanes-Oxley Act of 2002 changed the rules on how documents should be handled, with the Andersen case in mind, strengthening and clarifying document retention requirements.

INDEX

Moral Intelligence
Enhancing Business Performance and Leadership Success

BY DOUG LENNICK AND FRED KIEL

Through a combination of research, and original thought leadership, th[e] authors demonstrate how the best performing companies have lead[ers who actively apply moral values to achieve enduring personal an[d] organizational success. These individuals exhibit moral intelligence: [a] strong moral compass and the ability to follow it, even in a world tha[t] may reward bad behavior in the short run. Lennick and Kiel reveal ho[w] dozens of companies benefit from the moral intelligence of their lead[ers. The authors help you build the specific moral competencies lead[ers need: integrity, responsibility, compassion, forgiveness, and more[.]

"The authors offer a timely, important, and practical personal guidanc[e] system that anyone in the business world would do well to adopt. Th[e] world of business would be vastly improved if *Moral Intelligence* be[came required reading."
— Daniel Goleman, Author of *Emotional Intelligence*

ISBN 0131490508, © 2005, 304 pp., $25.95

Winners Never Cheat
Everyday Values We Learned as Children (But May Have Forgotten)

BY JON M. HUNTSMAN

Next time someone tells you business can't be done ethically—corners must be cut, negotiations can't be honest—hand them Jon Huntsman's new book. Who's Jon Huntsman? Just someone who started with practically nothing, and made it to Forbes' list of America's Top 100 richest people. Huntsman's generous about sharing the credit, but in the 21st century, he's the nearest thing to a self-made multi-billionaire. Now, he presents the lessons of a lifetime: a passionate, inspirational manifesto for returning to the days when your word was your bond, a handshake was sacred, and swarms of lawyers weren't needed to back it up. This is no mere exhortation: it's as practical as a business book can get. It's about how you listen to your moral compass, even as others ignore theirs. It's about how you build teams with the highest values...share success...take responsibility...earn the rewards that only come with giving back. Huntsman's built his career and fortune on these principles—from his youth, refusing the Nixon administration's corrupt demands, to his lifelong commitment to charity, to the way he approaches his biggest deals. You don't live these principles just to 'succeed': you live them because they're right. But in an age of non-stop business scandal, Huntsman's life proves honesty is more than right: it's your biggest competitive differentiator. So, consider what kind of person you want to do business with. Then, be that person—and use this book to get you there.

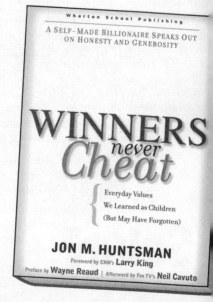

ISBN 0131863665, © 2005, 224 pp., $19.95